Canadian Living's
COUNTRY COOKING

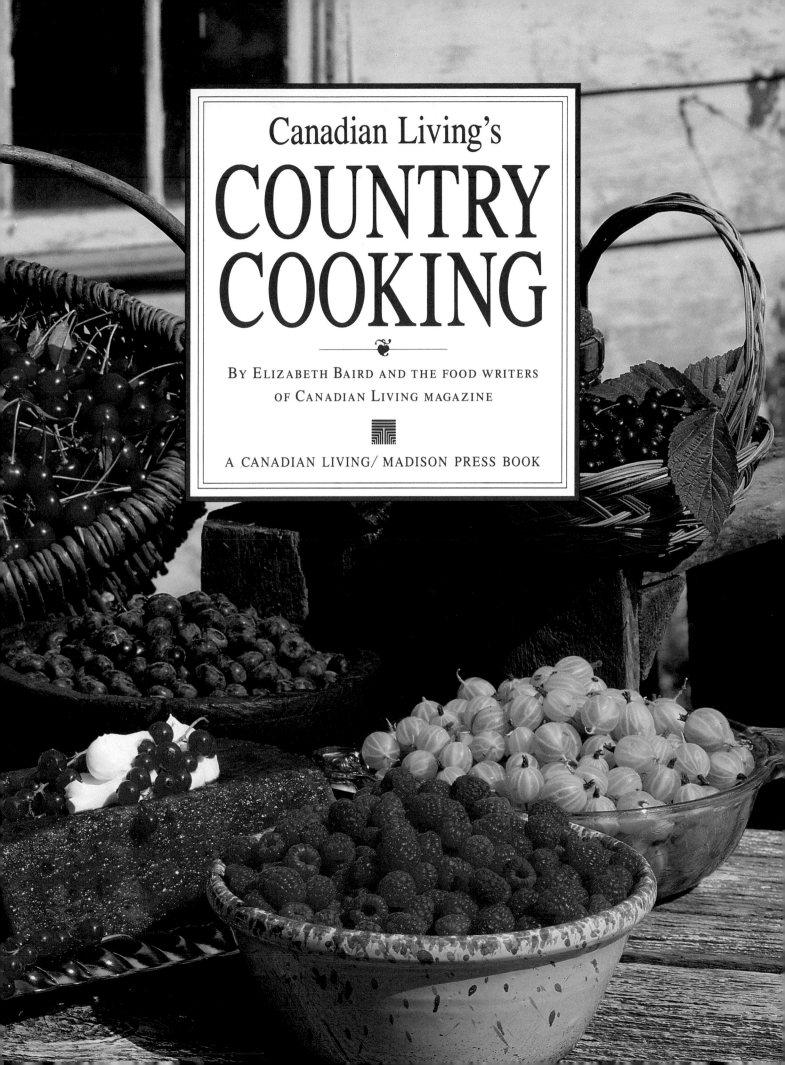

Canadian Living's
COUNTRY COOKING

By Elizabeth Baird and the food writers
of Canadian Living magazine

A Canadian Living/ Madison Press Book

Telemedia Publishing Inc.
50 Holly Street
Toronto, Ontario
Canada
M4S 3B3

Canadian Cataloguing in Publication Data

Baird, Elizabeth
Canadian living's country cooking

Includes index.
ISBN 0-394-22215-6

1. Cookery. I. Title. II. Title: Canadian living.

TX715.6.B34 1991   641.5   C91-093971-3

On our cover: (clockwise from left) Raspberry Pie (p. 164); Granary Buns (p. 101);
Lamb and Vegetable Broil (p. 71); Marinated Vegetable Salad (p. 88)

**Produced by
Madison Press Books
40 Madison Avenue
Toronto, Ontario
Canada
M5R 2S1**

Printed in Canada

CONTENTS

INTRODUCTION

What exactly *is* country cooking? And why is this kind of homestyle food so appealing in the '90s, even to the busiest cooks?

❧ To begin with, country cooking is about deliciousness. And that begins with quality ingredients — whether it's the finest plump chicken roasting to slow, golden perfection or a tumble of juicy berries in a summer cheesecake. Then, there's the right seasoning, the perfect doneness — all the skill and knowledge that make any dish that much better.

❧ And country cooking is simplicity. Not a lot of recipes with complicated sauces and hard-to-find ingredients but honest, good food, made from scratch so we know what's in it.

❧ Let's face it, though. For most of us, the country is far away, and our daily lives are closer to stop-and-go traffic than to the song of bobolinks on a rail fence. But when it comes to cooking, country is as close as your kitchen. That's because country cooking is all about hospitality and homeyness, the fun and warmth of getting together at the table. It's cooking that harkens back to simpler times and tastes, with delicious new updates for today's cooks and kitchens.

❧ With this special cookbook, it's easy to rediscover the tastes and pleasures of country cooking. So why not try your hand at gathering fiddleheads or putting up preserves, baking a classic apple pie or setting your table outdoors to enjoy supper under the grapevines?

❧ Our arbor supper sums up what country cooking is all about — a menu starring seasonal fruits and vegetables, dishes that are robust with flavor yet easy to make. Like all the recipes you'll find here, it's comforting, comfortable food that will please family and friends alike. Welcome to country cooking!

Elizabeth Baird

You're Invited To A Late-summer Arbor Supper

Beet and Buttermilk Soup

Chicken and Wine Vinegar Fricassée

Glazed Onions and Carrots

Rosemary Baked Potatoes and
Red Pepper Slices

Endive and Red Lettuce Salad with
Apple Wedges and Walnuts

Sweet Endings

Welcome to the arbor and to a sampling of the great country dishes that you'll find throughout this cookbook. Beets star in a cool make-ahead soup, rosemary-herbed potatoes pair up with chicken, and crunchy red apples blend with the tang of vinegar in the salad. As for dessert — the suggestions in our Sweet Endings sidebar will help you round out this special seasonal menu.

BEET AND BUTTERMILK SOUP

This most gloriously pink soup is delicious with traditional dill, or zippy with fresh coriander and a touch of hot pepper.

5	beets (1-1/4 lb/625 g total)	5
3 cups	buttermilk	750 mL
3/4 cup	chopped green onions	175 mL
2/3 cup	light sour cream	150 mL
2 tbsp	chopped dill or fresh coriander (or 2 tsp/10 mL dried dillweed)	25 mL
1-1/2 tsp	granulated sugar	7 mL
1-1/2 tsp	white vinegar	7 mL
1/4 tsp	salt	1 mL
1 cup	diced unpeeled cucumber	250 mL
	Dill sprigs	
	Chopped hot pepper and coriander sprigs	

In saucepan of boiling salted water, cover and cook beets until tender and skins slip off easily, about 25 minutes. Drain and let cool; slip off skins and cut into 1/4-inch (5 mm) dice. Cover and refrigerate until chilled. *(Beets can be refrigerated for up to 3 days.)*

❦ In large bowl, whisk together buttermilk, 1/2 cup (125 mL) of the onions, sour cream, dill, sugar, vinegar and salt. Cover and refrigerate until chilled or for up to 6 hours. Taste and adjust seasoning.

❦ Ladle buttermilk mixture into serving bowls. Swirl in beets and cucumber. Garnish with remaining green onions and dill sprigs or hot pepper and coriander. Makes 6 servings.

ROSEMARY BAKED POTATOES AND RED PEPPER SLICES

Potato slices soak up the robust flavors of sweet red pepper and rosemary as they bake.

6	baking potatoes (3 lb/1.5 kg total)	6
1	sweet red pepper	1
1/4 cup	olive oil	50 mL
1 tsp	chopped fresh rosemary (or 1/2 tsp/2 mL dried)	5 mL
1/2 tsp	salt	2 mL
1/4 tsp	pepper	1 mL
1/4 cup	water	50 mL

Peel potatoes if desired; cut into 1/4-inch (5 mm) thick slices. Halve pepper lengthwise; seed and slice into 1/4-inch (5 mm) thick slices.

❦ In large bowl, toss together potatoes, red pepper, oil, rosemary, salt and pepper; transfer to 13- × 9-inch (3 L) baking dish. Sprinkle with water.

❦ Cover and bake in 375°F (190°C) oven for 45 minutes. Uncover and bake for about 10 minutes longer or until potatoes are tender. Broil, if desired, for browner top. Makes 6 servings.

ENDIVE AND RED LETTUCE SALAD WITH APPLE WEDGES AND WALNUTS

This salad is a late-summer celebration of color, texture and taste — reds and greens, crunch and crisp,
the sweetness of apple in a tangy cider vinegar dressing.

1	small head red-tipped leaf lettuce	1
2	Belgian endives or heart of romaine lettuce	2
1	apple	1
1 cup	thinly sliced red onion	250 mL
1/2 cup	walnut halves, toasted	125 mL
	DRESSING:	
2 tbsp	apple cider vinegar	25 mL
1/2 tsp	salt	2 mL
1/4 tsp	black pepper	1 mL
Pinch	each cayenne pepper and granulated sugar	Pinch
2 tbsp	vegetable oil	25 mL
2 tbsp	walnut oil or more vegetable oil	25 mL

DRESSING: In bowl, whisk together vinegar, salt, black and cayenne peppers and sugar; gradually whisk in vegetable and walnut oils. Refrigerate, covered, for up to 6 hours.

❧ Separate lettuce leaves, discarding coarse or bruised parts. Cut endives vertically into quarters and apple into thin wedges, removing core.

❧ In large salad bowl, combine lettuce, endives, apple, onion and walnuts; sprinkle with dressing and toss. Makes 6 servings.

CHICKEN AND WINE VINEGAR FRICASSÉE

Easy but pleasing, this oven-braised chicken is wonderful with glazed baby carrots and tiny pearl onions.

5 lb	chicken parts	2.25 kg
1/2 tsp	each salt and pepper	2 mL
2 tbsp	vegetable oil	25 mL
2 tbsp	butter	25 mL
1 cup	chopped shallots or onion	250 mL
1-1/2 cups	chicken stock	375 mL
3/4 cup	white wine vinegar or cider vinegar	175 mL
1 tbsp	cornstarch	15 mL

Sprinkle chicken with salt and pepper. In large heavy or nonstick skillet, heat half of the oil and half of the butter over medium-high heat; cook chicken, in batches and adding more oil as necessary, for 4 to 6 minutes or until well browned on all sides. Transfer to large shallow baking dish.

❧ Drain off all but 1 tsp (5 mL) fat; add shallots and cook over medium-low heat until softened, about 4 minutes. Pour in stock and vinegar; bring to boil over high heat, scraping up brown bits from bottom of pan. Boil for about 5 minutes or until reduced by about a third.

❧ Pour over chicken. Cover and bake in 375°F (190°C) oven, turning pieces twice, for 25 to 30 minutes or until juices run clear when chicken is pierced and breasts are no longer pink inside.

❧ Transfer chicken to heated platter; strain pan juices into saucepan set over medium heat. Combine remaining butter with cornstarch; whisk into pan juices and cook for 3 to 5 minutes or until thickened and glossy. Taste and adjust seasoning; pour over chicken. Makes 6 servings.

SWEET ENDINGS

Every season has its sweet endings, and autumn's are among the most delicious. Make the most of just-picked apples, plums or pears to create a luscious dessert for this late-summer supper in the garden.

❧ Our Plum Tart (p. 162) is deceptively easy to make and is equally good warm or chilled. Or serve up thick slices of Pecan-Whisky Cake (p. 149) and add a dollop of fresh cream to each plate as you pass it.

❧ Whatever your fancy, you'll find over 50 sensational desserts in our Sweet Endings chapter from which to choose. The rest is up to you!

SAVORY STARTERS

*Whether it's a slice of country pâté on pumpernickel or a biteful of crab in a crispy shell,
savory appetizers are a superlative way to say "come on over!" Our delicious, no-fuss nibbles
are perfect for any gathering — arrange them attractively on trays for an open house, tote them
to a potluck supper, or simply let them set the mood for a splendid dinner party. And because
most of our recipes are make-ahead, having family and friends over is easy for
everyone — including you!*

GRILLED ANTIPASTO

*This make-ahead antipasto platter—vibrant with basil, piquant with balsamic vinegar and rich with the robust, smoky
flavors of grilled vegetables—is the ultimate summer appetizer.*

2	eggplants	2
2 tsp	salt	10 mL
1	each sweet red and yellow pepper	1
2	zucchini	2
1	large red onion	1
12	mushrooms	12
	Olive oil	
6 oz	thinly sliced mozzarella or provolone cheese	175 g
6 oz	thinly sliced assorted Italian cold cuts (salami, mortadella, prosciutto, cooked ham)	175 g
1	tomato, cut in wedges	1
1/2 cup	black olives	125 mL
	DRESSING:	
1/2 cup	olive oil	125 mL
1/3 cup	chopped fresh basil (or 1-1/2 tsp/7 mL dried)	75 mL
1 tbsp	balsamic vinegar (or 2 tbsp/25 mL red wine vinegar)	15 mL
1 tbsp	Dijon mustard	15 mL
3	cloves garlic, minced	3
1/2 tsp	each salt and pepper	2 mL

Cut eggplant into 1/2-inch (1 cm) thick slices. In colander, sprinkle eggplant with salt; toss to coat and let drain for 30 minutes.

❧ Meanwhile, place peppers on greased grill 4 to 6 inches (10 to 15 cm) from medium-hot coals or on medium-high setting. Grill, turning often, for 15 to 20 minutes or until charred. Let cool slightly. Peel, seed and cut peppers into 1-inch (2.5 cm) wide strips. Set aside.

❧ Diagonally cut zucchini into 1/2-inch (1 cm) thick slices. Cut onion into 1/2-inch (1 cm) thick slices. Trim stems from mushroom caps. Rinse eggplant under cold running water; pat dry.

❧ Lightly brush vegetables with oil. Grill, turning occasionally, mushrooms and onions for 8 to 10 minutes, then eggplant and zucchini for 10 to 15 minutes, or until vegetables are tender but not charred. Set aside separately.

❧ DRESSING: In bowl, whisk together oil, basil, vinegar, mustard, garlic, salt and pepper. Add mushrooms and turn to coat; transfer mushrooms to large shallow baking dish. Repeat with onion, then zucchini, peppers and eggplant, arranging vegetables separately in dish. Refrigerate and marinate for at least 8 or up to 24 hours; bring to room temperature before serving.

❧ To serve, attractively arrange vegetables and cheese on large platter. If using salami, fold into cornets by overlapping 2 or 3 slices, then folding in half lengthwise before forming into cone shape. Nestle among vegetables along with other cold cuts. Garnish with tomatoes and olives. Makes 6 to 8 servings.

VARIATION

You can easily change the flavor and presentation of the antipasto platter by substituting 3/4 lb (375 g) grilled seafood, such as shrimp, scallops or squid, for the cold cuts and cheese. For easy grilling, thread the seafood onto skewers.

SHRIMP MOUSSE

This delicate mousse, which can be made ahead and refrigerated for up to 1 day, is delicious served with thin triangles of black bread. Spoon it into the loaf pan or individual moulds that have the equivalent total volume.

1-1/2	pkg unflavored gelatin	1-1/2
1/2 cup	cold water	125 mL
1/2 cup	boiling water	125 mL
2 tbsp	lemon juice	25 mL
1 tbsp	minced onion	15 mL
2 tsp	chopped fresh dill (or 1 tsp/5 mL dried dillweed)	10 mL
Dash	hot pepper sauce	Dash
Pinch	salt	Pinch
10 oz	fresh or frozen cooked shrimp*	300 g
3/4 cup	mayonnaise	175 mL
1/4 cup	finely diced celery	50 mL
1/4 cup	finely chopped pimiento-stuffed green olives	50 mL
1/2 cup	whipping cream	125 mL
	Lettuce leaves	

In bowl, sprinkle gelatin over cold water; let stand for 1 minute to soften. Add boiling water, stirring until gelatin dissolves. Stir in lemon juice, onion, dill, hot pepper sauce and salt. Let stand until slightly thickened, 5 to 10 minutes.

❦ Reserve 3 whole shrimp for garnish. Chop remaining shrimp finely. Combine with mayonnaise; stir into gelatin mixture. Add celery and olives.

❦ Whip cream; fold into shrimp mixture. Spoon into oiled 8- × 4-inch (1.5 L) loaf pan; cover with plastic wrap and chill until set, about 4 hours. Line chilled serving plate with lettuce; unmould mousse onto lettuce and garnish with remaining whole shrimp. Makes about 4 cups (1 L).

*If using frozen shrimp, be sure to thaw first.

MUSHROOM PÂTÉ

This nutty mushroom pâté is delicious served on cucumber slices, melba toast, thinly sliced pumpernickel or French Baguette (recipe, p. 104).

1/3 cup	coarsely chopped pecans	75 mL
1/4 cup	butter	50 mL
3/4 cup	finely chopped onion	175 mL
2	cloves garlic, minced	2
1 lb	mushrooms, finely chopped	500 g
2 tbsp	dry vermouth	25 mL
1/4 tsp	salt	1 mL
	Pepper	
2 tbsp	freshly grated Parmesan cheese	25 mL
2 tbsp	sour cream	25 mL
1 tbsp	finely chopped fresh parsley	15 mL

On baking sheet, toast pecans in 350°F (180°C) oven for about 5 minutes or until fragrant; set aside.

❦ In large heavy skillet, melt butter over medium heat; cook onion and garlic, stirring occasionally, until softened, about 4 minutes.

❦ Add mushrooms; cook for 6 minutes over medium-high heat, stirring often. Add vermouth, salt, and pepper to taste; cook for 2 minutes or until most of the moisture has evaporated. Remove from heat; stir in cheese. Let cool.

❦ Mix in sour cream and parsley. Taste and adjust seasonings if necessary. Transfer to serving bowl. Cover and refrigerate until chilled or for up to 2 days. Just before serving, sprinkle with pecans. Makes about 1-1/2 cups (375 mL).

TWO-SALMON PÂTÉ

For sit-down events, serve a small slice of this easy and elegant pâté on leafy green lettuce and garnish with cucumber. For stand-up, pass-around affairs, serve squares of sliced pâté on toasted whole wheat bread or in endive spears with a sprig of watercress.

1	pkg unflavored gelatin	1
1/4 cup	water	50 mL
1	can (7-1/2 oz/213 g) sockeye salmon	1
1 cup	finely chopped smoked salmon (6 oz/175 g)	250 mL
4 oz	cream cheese	125 g
1/4 cup	light mayonnaise	50 mL
2 tbsp	lemon juice	25 mL
1/4 tsp	hot pepper sauce	1 mL
2 tbsp	minced green onion	25 mL
2 tbsp	chopped fresh dill	25 mL
3/4 cup	whipping cream	175 mL
	GARNISH:	
	Cucumber	
3 oz	thinly sliced smoked salmon	75 g
	Dill sprigs	

In small saucepan, sprinkle gelatin over water; let stand for 1 minute to soften. Warm over low heat, stirring, until dissolved. Remove from heat; set aside.

❦ Drain sockeye salmon, discarding juice. In food processor or blender, combine sockeye salmon, half of the smoked salmon, cream cheese, mayonnaise, lemon juice and hot pepper sauce; purée until smooth. Add gelatin mixture and process to blend.

❦ Transfer to bowl; stir in remaining chopped smoked salmon, onion and dill. Whip cream; stir about one-quarter into salmon mixture. Fold in remaining cream. Line 8-1/2- × 4-1/2-inch (1.5 L) loaf pan with plastic wrap; pour in salmon mixture and smooth top. Cover with wrap and refrigerate for at least 4 hours or until firm, or for up to 2 days.

❦ To unmould, unwrap top and invert serving platter over pan. Grasp platter and pan; quickly turn over and lift off pan. Remove plastic wrap.

❦ GARNISH: For cucumber twist, peel cucumber lengthwise at 1/2-inch (1 cm) intervals; cut about 12 to 16 very thin slices. Make cut in each slice from center to outside edge; twist in opposite directions to form "S" shape. Arrange around pâté.

❦ For each rose, cut smoked salmon into strip 1 inch (2.5 cm) wide and 5 inches (12 cm) long. Tightly roll up 1 inch (2.5 cm) to form cone. Pinch cone at base, letting free end dangle. Gather up strip, a little at a time, around cone, bending out upper edges to resemble petals. Garnish pâté with salmon roses and dill sprigs. Makes 12 to 16 servings.

VARIATION

CAPER AND CHIVE: Omit green onion and dill. Substitute 2 tbsp (25 mL) each chopped drained capers and chopped fresh chives.

> You can use any decorative mould as long as it has a 4-cup (1 L) capacity. Lining the pan or mould with plastic wrap makes unmoulding easier. Warm a knife under steaming hot water and use it to smooth away any crease lines left by wrap.

COUNTRY PÂTÉ

Country pâté—a classic blend of rustic flavors and textures—is especially appealing during the holiday season. For a quick lunch or a cosy fireside feast, accompany the pâté with crusty French bread, gherkins, chutney and red or white wine. As easy to make as meat loaf, and as satisfying, too, this humble pâté is hearty, welcome fare.

1/4 cup	butter	50 mL
1 cup	finely chopped onion	250 mL
4	cloves garlic, minced	4
1/4 lb	(approx) chicken livers, halved and trimmed	125 g
1 lb	ground pork*	500 g
1 lb	ground veal	500 g
1/4 lb	smoked ham, diced	125 g
1/4 cup	pistachios	50 mL
1/4 cup	brandy	50 mL
2	eggs, beaten	2
1-1/2 tsp	salt	7 mL
1-1/4 tsp	coarsely ground black pepper	6 mL
1 tsp	crushed juniper berries	5 mL
1 tsp	ground allspice	5 mL
3/4 tsp	dried thyme	4 mL
3/4 lb	(approx) thinly sliced fatback or fresh side pork**	375 g
3	whole bay leaves	3

In skillet, melt 3 tbsp (45 mL) of the butter over medium-high heat; cook onion and garlic for 3 minutes or until softened. Using slotted spoon, transfer to large bowl.

❦ Melt remaining butter in skillet; cook chicken livers over medium-high heat for 3 minutes or just until still slightly pink inside.

❦ Chop livers coarsely; add to onion mixture along with pork, veal, ham, pistachios, brandy, eggs, salt, pepper, juniper berries, allspice and thyme. Mix well.

❦ To test for seasoning, form 1 small patty from meat mixture. In small skillet, cook patty over medium-high heat for 1 to 1-1/2 minutes per side or until no longer pink inside; let cool and taste for seasoning. Adjust seasoning in meat mixture, if necessary.

❦ Line 9- × 5-inch (2 L) loaf pan or terrine with strips of pork fat, completely covering bottom and sides of pan and leaving slight overhang all around the pan. Reserve a few strips for top.

❦ Pack meat mixture evenly into pan; tap pan lightly on counter to release air pockets. Arrange bay leaves on top and cover with remaining strips of fat. Cover pan tightly with foil or lid.

❦ Place pan in large baking pan; pour in enough boiling water to come halfway up sides of loaf pan. Bake in 350°F (180°C) oven for 1-1/2 to 2 hours or until metal skewer inserted in center for 30 seconds feels hot and juices have no trace of pink. Remove foil and pour off melted fat. Let cool and re-cover.

❦ Place another loaf pan, containing brick or heavy cans, on top of pâté; refrigerate for 12 hours to allow flavors to mellow. To serve, scrape off fat and cut into 1/2-inch (1 cm) thick slices; cut each slice in half. *(Pâté can be stored in the refrigerator for up to 4 days.)* Makes 1 loaf, about 32 slices.

* For a moist pâté, use coarsely ground pork with at least 50 per cent pork fat.

** Fresh pork fatback is available at most butcher shops. Ask the butcher to slice it thinly. If unavailable, you can substitute fatty side bacon, which must first be soaked in cold water for 1 hour to reduce saltiness.

VARIATION

GAME PÂTÉ: Substitute ground duck, rabbit or pheasant meat for the ground veal. Substitute orange brandy for brandy.

Correct seasoning in a pâté is very important. Foods that are served cold must be seasoned more than foods that are served hot. To ensure that the pâté is seasoned to your taste, cook a small patty and let it cool before tasting. Adjust seasoning in meat mixture, if necessary.

CHICKEN WINGS WITH SOUTHWESTERN SAUCE

These succulent wings can be prepared ahead and either baked at the last minute or simply reheated.

4 lb	chicken wings	2 kg
1-1/4 cups	all-purpose flour	300 mL
1-1/4 cups	cornmeal	300 mL
2 tbsp	cumin	25 mL
2 tsp	salt	10 mL
2 tsp	black pepper	10 mL
1 tsp	cayenne pepper	5 mL
4	eggs	4
1/2 cup	olive or vegetable oil	125 mL
	CORIANDER DIP:	
1-1/2 cups	sour cream	375 mL
1/2 cup	mayonnaise	125 mL
1 cup	chopped fresh coriander or parsley	250 mL
1/2 cup	chopped fresh chives or green onions	125 mL
1	can (4 oz/125 g) chopped mild green chilies	1
2	jalapeño peppers, seeded and minced	2
1 tsp	salt	5 mL

Remove tips from chicken wings; separate wings at joints. Set aside.

❦ In shallow dish, combine flour, cornmeal, cumin, salt, black and cayenne peppers. In another shallow dish, beat eggs. Dip wings into flour mixture, shaking off excess; dip into eggs, allowing excess to drain off. Dip again into flour mixture and press mixture in firmly. *(Wings can be prepared to this point and placed on rack, covered and refrigerated for up to 8 hours.)*

❦ Brush baking sheets with oil; arrange wings on sheets and drizzle with remaining oil. Bake in 375°F (190°C) oven for 20 minutes; turn wings over and bake for 20 to 25 minutes longer or until crisp, brown and meat is no longer pink inside.

❦ CORIANDER DIP: In bowl, combine sour cream with mayonnaise; stir in coriander, chives, green chilies, jalapeño peppers and salt. Serve with wings on large platter. Makes 40 hors d'oeuvres.

❦

GET-TOGETHER FONDUE

A fondue pot, family, friends and a fireplace — what a lovely way to spend an evening! For a new twist to an old favorite, add blanched broccoli and cauliflower florets, sweet red pepper chunks, cubes of ham and cooked shrimp to the French bread dippers.

1-1/2 cups	dry white wine	375 mL
1 tbsp	lemon juice	15 mL
1	clove garlic	1
4 cups	shredded Swiss cheese	1 L
2 cups	shredded caraway Edam cheese	500 mL
1 tbsp	cornstarch	15 mL

In saucepan over medium heat, bring wine, lemon juice and garlic almost to boil. Reduce heat to medium-low; remove garlic. In bowl, toss together Swiss and Edam cheeses and cornstarch; gradually add to saucepan, a handful at a time, whisking constantly until cheese melts before adding more cheese. Cook until thickened and starting to bubble; transfer to fondue pot set over heat. Makes 6 servings.

VARIATIONS

TOMATOEY FONDUE: Substitute vegetable cocktail for wine. Substitute half small onion for garlic. Add 1/4 tsp (1 mL) hot pepper flakes if desired. Substitute 3 cups (750 mL) each shredded old Cheddar and Monterey Jack cheeses for Swiss and Edam cheeses.

CHEDDAR-BEER FONDUE: Substitute beer or ale for wine. Substitute 6 cups (1.5 L) shredded Cheddar cheese for Swiss and Edam cheeses.

EASY CHEESY TOMATO PIE

This tomato pie makes waiting for homegrown tomatoes worthwhile. Colorful rows of tomato slices blend with two different cheeses in a savory phyllo pastry tart.

3	sheets phyllo pastry	3
1/4 cup	butter, melted	50 mL
1/3 cup	Dijon mustard	75 mL
3 oz	mozzarella cheese, thinly sliced	90 g
3 oz	Fontina cheese, thinly sliced	90 g
2	tomatoes, thinly sliced	2
1	large clove garlic, minced	1
2 tbsp	chopped fresh oregano (or 2 tsp/10 mL dried)	25 mL
2 tbsp	olive oil	25 mL
	Salt and pepper	

Cut each sheet of phyllo in half crosswise; lay 1 half on tea towel, keeping remaining halves covered with damp towel. Brush sheet with some of the butter; place another sheet on top, making sure edges are not perfectly aligned. Brush with 1 tbsp (15 mL) of the mustard. Keeping edges uneven, layer remaining sheets, alternating butter and mustard, and ending with mustard. Gently lift into 14-3/4- × 4-1/2-inch (37.5 × 11.5 cm) rectangular flan form with removable bottom. Spread remaining mustard on top.

❧ Fold phyllo edges under to create ruffled effect. Cover with layer of mozzarella and Fontina cheese. Top with long rows of overlapping tomato slices. Sprinkle with garlic, oregano and olive oil. Season with salt and pepper to taste.

❧ Place form on baking sheet and bake in 375°F (190°C) oven for 35 to 40 minutes or until phyllo is golden. Makes 8 appetizer servings.

ASPARAGUS STRUDEL

This elegant spring appetizer can be served on its own or as a warm salad surrounded with green and red lettuce that has been lightly drizzled with a little orange vinaigrette. For larger crowds, the recipe doubles and triples very successfully.

1-1/2 cups	julienned leeks	375 mL
1/4 cup	creamy goat cheese (chèvre) or cream cheese, softened	50 mL
1 tbsp	grated orange rind	15 mL
1 tbsp	orange juice	15 mL
1 tsp	dried tarragon (or 1 tbsp/15 mL chopped fresh)	5 mL
1/2 tsp	pepper	2 mL
	Salt	
4	sheets phyllo pastry	4
1/3 cup	butter, melted	75 mL
12	cooked asparagus spears, cut in half (approx 1/2 lb/250 g)	12

In saucepan of boiling salted water, cook leeks for 1 minute. Drain and cool under cold water; drain again.

❦ Combine goat cheese, orange rind and juice, tarragon, pepper, and salt to taste; set aside.

❦ Lay 1 sheet of the phyllo pastry on work surface, keeping remaining phyllo covered with damp towel to prevent drying out. Brush lightly with some of the butter.

❦ Center 2 tbsp (25 mL) of the leeks about 1 inch (2.5 cm) from short edge of phyllo. Lay 3 pieces of asparagus on top. Spread 1 tbsp (15 mL) cheese mixture over asparagus. Top with 3 more asparagus pieces, then 2 tbsp (25 mL) of the leeks.

❦ Fold long sides of phyllo over mixture; brush phyllo with butter and roll up into cylinder. Place, seam side down, on greased baking sheet; brush with butter. Repeat with remaining ingredients to make 3 more rolls. *(Strudels can be prepared to this point, covered and refrigerated for up to 1 day.)*

❦ Bake rolls in 450°F (230°C) oven for about 12 minutes or until golden brown. Cut each roll into thirds just before serving hot. Makes about 4 servings.

CRAB-STUFFED CROUSTADES

Use mini croustades (tiny tart shells) or toast cups for this easy appetizer. Mini croustades are available in European delis and some supermarkets.

1 tbsp	butter	15 mL
1 tbsp	all-purpose flour	15 mL
1/2 cup	light cream	125 mL
1/3 cup	shredded Cheddar cheese	75 mL
4 tsp	lemon juice	20 mL
1 tbsp	mayonnaise	15 mL
6 oz	frozen crab, thawed and shredded	175 g
1 tbsp	finely chopped green onion	15 mL
Pinch	each salt and pepper	Pinch
24	mini croustades	24
	Chopped chives	

In small heavy saucepan, melt butter over medium heat; stir in flour and cook, stirring for 1 minute, being careful not to brown. Whisk in cream; cook until boiling and thickened, about 30 seconds. Stir in cheese, lemon juice and mayonnaise; simmer until blended. Stir in crab, onion, salt and pepper. *(Recipe can be prepared to this point, cooled, covered and refrigerated for up to 2 days.)*

❦ Fill each mini croustade with heaping teaspoonful (5 mL) of crab mixture. Bake on baking sheet in 400°F (200°C) oven for 8 to 10 minutes or until heated through and bubbling. Garnish with chives. Makes 24 appetizers.

Mulled Red Wine (recipe, p. 30) and Crab-Stuffed Croustades

SPECIAL OCCASIONS

Company's coming! Time to pull out all the stops, tuck a luscious make-ahead dessert into the fridge and mull over the menu. You'll find each of our recipes deliciously worthy of the occasion and the welcome. Choose a veal scallopini with brandy and mushroom sauce for an elegant dinner party, or dazzle a crowd with new-wave pastitsio or a four-star roast turkey with stuffing and all the trimmings.

ROAST TURKEY

Plump, golden and succulent, a perfect roast turkey turns any gathering into a festive occasion, especially when you pair slices of the moist meat with a herbed stuffing and rich glossy gravy. You can make the stuffing a day ahead, but don't stuff the bird until just before roasting.

15 lb	turkey	6.75 kg
1/4 cup	butter, softened	50 mL
1/2 tsp	each dried sage and thyme	2 mL
	Salt and pepper	
	OLD-FASHIONED STUFFING:	
3/4 cup	butter	175 mL
2-1/2 cups	chopped onions	625 mL
1 cup	each chopped celery and fennel (or 2 cups/500 mL celery)	250 mL
4 tsp	dried sage	20 mL
1 tsp	each salt, dried savory, marjoram and pepper	5 mL
1/2 tsp	dried thyme	2 mL
14 cups	cubed white bread	3.5 L
1 cup	chopped fresh parsley	250 mL
	STOCK:	
4-1/2 cups	chicken stock	1.125 L
1-1/2 cups	(approx) dry white wine or water	375 mL
1	onion, chopped	1
1/2 cup	each sliced carrot and celery	125 mL
	GRAVY:	
1/4 cup	all-purpose flour	50 mL
2 tbsp	butter	25 mL
	Salt and pepper	

OLD-FASHIONED STUFFING: In large skillet, melt butter over medium heat; cook onions, celery, fennel, sage, salt, savory, marjoram, pepper and thyme, stirring often, for 10 to 15 minutes or until vegetables are tender. Transfer to large bowl and toss with bread and parsley. Set aside.

Remove giblets and neck from turkey; place in large saucepan and set aside. Rinse turkey inside and out; dry skin and cavity well. Loosely stuff neck opening; fold neck skin over stuffing and skewer to back. Lift wings and twist under back. Stuff body cavity. Tuck legs under band of skin or tie together with string.

Place turkey on rack in roasting pan. Combine butter, sage and thyme; rub over turkey. Sprinkle with salt and pepper. Tent with foil, dull side out, leaving sides open. Roast in 325°F (160°C) oven, basting every 30 minutes, for 4 hours. Remove foil; roast for 1 hour longer or until thermometer inserted in thigh reads 185°F (85°C) and stuffing 165°F (75°C). Let stand on platter, lightly covered, for 20 minutes.

STOCK: Meanwhile, to saucepan with turkey parts, add stock, wine, onion, carrot and celery; bring to boil. Reduce heat to low and skim off fat; simmer for 3 hours. Strain into measuring cup, adding enough wine to make 3 cups (750 mL). Set aside.

GRAVY: Skim off fat in roasting pan. Stir flour into pan; cook over medium heat, stirring for 1 minute. Whisk in stock and bring to boil, stirring to scrape up brown bits. Reduce heat and simmer for 5 minutes. Whisk in butter; season with salt and pepper to taste. Strain if desired.

With carving knife and fork, cut legs from turkey, twisting loose if necessary. Cut thigh from drumstick at joint; carve dark meat from each piece. Cut off wings. With tip of knife toward body cavity, carve breast thinly, gradually angling knife to slice thick part of breast. Makes 8 to 10 servings.

SCALLOPINI WITH BRANDY AND MUSHROOM CREAM SAUCE

Veal scallopini are most impressive, even more so with a splurge of dried wild mushrooms like porcini and a splash of cognac. Serve with parsleyed noodles and a salad of mixed greens.

1	pkg (10 g) dried wild mushrooms	1
1/2 cup	warm water	125 mL
1-1/2 lb	veal scallopini	750 g
1/2 cup	all-purpose flour	125 mL
	Salt and pepper	
3 tbsp	vegetable oil	50 mL
3 tbsp	butter	50 mL
6 cups	sliced fresh mushrooms (about 1 lb/500 g)	1.5 L
2 tbsp	cognac	25 mL
3/4 cup	whipping cream	175 mL
2 tbsp	chopped fresh parsley	25 mL

Soak wild mushrooms in warm water for 20 to 30 minutes or until softened. Drain through cheesecloth- or paper towel-lined sieve; reserve liquid. Rinse mushrooms; chop finely and set aside.

❧ Dredge scallopini lightly in flour. Season with salt and pepper to taste.

❧ In large skillet, heat oil with 1 tbsp (15 mL) of the butter over medium-high heat; cook scallopini, in batches, for 2 minutes per side or until lightly browned, adding another tablespoon (15 mL) of the butter as needed. Transfer scallopini to warmed serving platter; cover and keep warm.

❧ Discard fat from skillet. Melt remaining butter over medium-high heat; add dried and fresh mushrooms. Cook, stirring occasionally, for about 5 minutes or until just tender.

❧ Add reserved mushroom soaking liquid along with cognac. Cook for 1 to 2 minutes or until liquid has almost evaporated. Pour in cream; cook for 3 to 4 minutes or until sauce is thick enough to coat spoon. Season with salt and pepper to taste. Reduce heat to low and return scallopini to skillet; cook for 2 to 3 minutes or until heated through. Sprinkle with parsley. Makes about 6 servings.

WILD RICE AND MUSHROOM PILAF

Stir in up to 2 cups (500 mL) cooked white or brown rice for a two-rice pilaf. Wild rice is a special-occasion accompaniment to any of the roasts in Sunday Dinners, *especially Roast Pork Loin with Sage (recipe, p. 48).*

2 tbsp	butter	25 mL
2 cups	sliced mushrooms (about 6 oz/175 g)	500 mL
1	onion, chopped	1
1 cup	wild rice, rinsed	250 mL
1-1/2 cups	chicken stock	375 mL
1/4 cup	chopped fresh parsley	50 mL
1/4 cup	toasted hazelnuts, chopped*	50 mL
2	chopped green onions	2
	Salt and pepper	

In large heavy saucepan, melt butter over medium-high heat; cook mushrooms and onion, stirring often, for 5 minutes or until tender. Add rice, stirring to coat grains.

❧ Stir in stock; cover and bring to boil. Reduce heat to medium-low and simmer, partially covered, for 45 to 55 minutes or until rice is tender and liquid is absorbed.

❧ Stir in parsley, hazelnuts, green onions, and salt and pepper to taste. Makes 6 to 8 servings.

*Toast hazelnuts on baking sheet in 350°F (180°C) oven for 6 to 8 minutes or until golden brown. Wrap in clean tea towels and rub off skins.

CHICKEN IN CREAM AND ONIONS

The touch of curry in this rich and saucy chicken dish makes it a delicious partner for steamed asparagus and Wild
Rice and Mushroom Pilaf (see previous page for recipe).

4 lb	chicken thighs	2 kg
2 tbsp	butter	25 mL
1 tbsp	vegetable oil	15 mL
2 cups	sliced onions	500 mL
3/4 tsp	salt	4 mL
1/2 tsp	curry powder	2 mL
1/4 tsp	pepper	1 mL
3/4 cup	dry white vermouth	175 mL
2 cups	whipping cream	500 mL
1/4 tsp	grated lemon rind	1 mL
1 tbsp	all-purpose flour	15 mL
1 tbsp	butter, softened	15 mL
1/2 cup	chopped fresh parsley	125 mL

Wipe chicken dry. In large skillet, heat 2 tbsp (25 mL) butter and oil over medium heat until butter foams; cook chicken until light golden, about 2 minutes per side. Remove and set aside.

❦ Add onions to skillet; cook until softened, about 5 minutes. Return chicken to pan; sprinkle with salt, curry powder and pepper. Pour in vermouth; cook, stirring, until almost all liquid has evaporated.

❦ Meanwhile, heat cream to steaming; pour over chicken. Simmer, covered, for about 20 minutes or until juices run clear when chicken is pierced, basting and turning chicken occasionally. Using slotted spoon, transfer chicken to platter and keep warm.

❦ Add lemon rind to skillet; boil, uncovered and stirring, for about 5 minutes or until thickened enough to coat spoon. Stir together flour and softened butter; whisk into skillet and cook, stirring, for 1 minute or until thickened. Taste and adjust seasoning. Pour over chicken; garnish with parsley. Makes 8 servings.

SPINACH RICOTTA-STUFFED CHICKEN BREASTS

Succulent and cheesy, this chicken dish is perfect for entertaining. Since the stuffing is inserted between the chicken and the skin, be sure to choose chicken breasts that are well covered with skin.

6	chicken breasts (about 2-1/2 lb/1.25 kg total)	6
1 tbsp	butter, melted	15 mL
	STUFFING:	
1 tbsp	butter	15 mL
1	small onion, finely chopped	1
1	small clove garlic, minced	1
1-1/2 cups	chopped fresh spinach	375 mL
2 tbsp	chopped fresh parsley	25 mL
1 tbsp	chopped fresh basil (or 1/2 tsp/2 mL dried)	15 mL
1/2 cup	ricotta cheese	125 mL
1/2 cup	shredded mozzarella cheese	125 mL
2 tbsp	freshly grated Parmesan cheese	25 mL
1	egg yolk	1
1/4 tsp	salt	1 mL
Pinch	each nutmeg and pepper	Pinch

STUFFING: In large skillet, heat butter over medium heat; cook onion and garlic, stirring often, for 3 to 5 minutes or until softened. Add spinach, parsley and basil; cook, stirring, for about 2 minutes or until spinach wilts and moisture evaporates. Remove from heat and let cool completely.

❦ In bowl, combine spinach mixture, ricotta, mozzarella and Parmesan cheeses, egg yolk, salt, nutmeg and pepper, mixing well.

❦ Using sharp knife, debone chicken, leaving skin attached. Gently loosen skin from one long side of each breast, leaving skin attached at curved side. Stuff about 1/4 cup (50 mL) stuffing under skin, pressing to spread stuffing evenly. Tuck ends of skin and meat underneath.

❦ Place on greased rack in foil-lined pan. Brush with butter. Bake in 375°F (190°C) oven, basting occasionally, for about 35 minutes or until golden brown and chicken is no longer pink inside. Makes 6 servings.

CHILI BAKED CHICKEN

These tender chicken pieces with their golden crispy coating are good hot or cold.

12	chicken breasts or legs (about 6-1/2 lb/3 kg)	12
1 cup	sour cream	250 mL
1/2 cup	minced green onion	125 mL
2	cloves garlic, minced	2
2 tsp	finely grated lemon rind	10 mL
3 tbsp	lemon juice	50 mL
1 tbsp	Worcestershire sauce	15 mL
1/2 tsp	dried thyme	2 mL
1/2 tsp	black pepper	2 mL
Pinch	cayenne pepper	Pinch
2-1/2 cups	fine cracker crumbs	625 mL

4 tsp	chili powder	20 mL
1/3 cup	butter, melted	75 mL

Wipe chicken; trim off excess fat and loose skin. In large glass bowl, stir together sour cream, green onion, garlic, lemon rind and juice, Worcestershire sauce, thyme, and black and cayenne peppers. Add chicken, turning to coat well; cover and refrigerate for 8 hours.

In shallow dish, combine cracker crumbs with chili powder. Roll chicken in crumb mixture, coating pieces thoroughly. Arrange pieces, without touching, on large lightly greased baking sheets. Drizzle with butter. Bake in 350°F (180°F) oven for 45 to 55 minutes or until coating is crisp and breasts are no longer pink inside or juices run clear when thighs are pierced. Makes 12 servings.

SEAFOOD CASSEROLE

A rich tumble of scallops, shrimp, lobster and crab napped in a cheesy cream sauce is an Acadian favorite.
Poach fresh scallops and shrimp but use frozen lobster and crab.

2 cups	water	500 mL
1 cup	chopped celery	250 mL
3/4 cup	chopped onions	175 mL
1/2 lb	scallops	250 g
1/2 lb	shrimp	250 g
1-1/2 cups	cooked lobster meat	375 mL
1-1/2 cups	crab meat (1/2 lb/250 g)	375 mL
3 tbsp	butter	50 mL
3 tbsp	all-purpose flour	50 mL
1 cup	light cream	250 mL
1-1/2 cups	shredded Cheddar cheese	375 mL
1/4 tsp	salt	1 mL
1/4 tsp	pepper	1 mL
	TOPPING:	
1 cup	shredded Cheddar cheese	250 mL
1/2 cup	fresh bread crumbs	125 mL
2 tbsp	butter, melted	25 mL

In saucepan, bring water to boil; cook celery and onions until tender, about 6 minutes. Using slotted spoon, transfer vegetables to large bowl.

In same saucepan, poach scallops over low heat just until firm and opaque, about 3 minutes. Using slotted spoon, transfer scallops to same bowl. In same saucepan, simmer shrimp until firm and pink, about 4 minutes. Drain, reserving cooking liquid; add water if necessary to make 3/4 cup (175 mL) liquid and set aside. Peel and devein shrimp; add to bowl. Chop lobster and crab meat into bite-size chunks, if necessary; add to bowl.

In large heavy saucepan, melt butter over medium heat; add flour and cook, stirring, for 2 minutes without browning. Gradually whisk in reserved cooking liquid and cream; cook, stirring, until thickened. Stir in cheese until melted. Add seafood mixture; season with salt and pepper. Transfer to 13- × 9-inch (3.5 L) baking dish.

TOPPING: Toss together cheese, bread crumbs and butter; sprinkle evenly over seafood mixture. *(Casserole can be made to this point, cooled, covered and refrigerated for up to 8 hours.)*

Bake, uncovered, in 325°F (160°C) oven for 35 to 45 minutes or until bubbling around edges and crisp and golden on top. Let stand for 5 minutes before serving. Makes 8 servings.

GRILLED HALIBUT WITH GARDEN VEGETABLES

Grilled halibut looks spectacular surrounded by an array of colorful vegetables and is a superlative almost-all-make-ahead dinner or lunch. The same recipe works very well with salmon and it's also great with chicken breasts, veal chops and lamb chops. If any of the suggested vegetables are unavailable, omit them or use others like green beans, asparagus, fennel, celery and turnips. Use fresh halibut because frozen halibut doesn't have as nice a texture.

	MARINADE:	
6 cups	chicken stock or water	1.5 L
1/2 cup	dry white wine	125 mL
1/2 cup	lemon juice	125 mL
1/2 cup	extra-virgin olive oil	125 mL
1 tbsp	black peppercorns	15 mL
1 tsp	coriander seeds	5 mL
1/2 tsp	salt	2 mL
1/4 tsp	dried thyme	1 mL
1/4 tsp	fennel seeds or aniseeds (optional)	1 mL
5	sprigs fresh parsley	5
1	clove garlic, crushed	1
1	small bay leaf	1
	VEGETABLES:	
1 cup	pearl onions, peeled	250 mL
1 lb	carrots, cut in 2-inch (5 cm) julienne strips	500 g
1	small head cauliflower, cut in small florets	1
1	small head broccoli, cut in small florets*	1
4	green and/or yellow zucchini, halved lengthwise and cut in 1/2-inch (1 cm) slices	4
1/2 lb	small button mushrooms, stems removed (about 2 cups/500 mL)	250 g
	HALIBUT:	
6	halibut steaks, 1-inch (2.5 cm) thick (each 6 to 8 oz/175 to 250 g)	6
1 tbsp	lemon juice	15 mL
3 tbsp	extra-virgin olive oil	50 mL
	Salt and pepper	
1	lemon, cut in wedges	1

MARINADE: In large saucepan, combine stock, wine, lemon juice, oil, peppercorns, coriander seeds, salt, thyme, fennel seeds (if using), parsley, garlic and bay leaf; bring to boil. Reduce heat and simmer gently for 15 minutes. Strain and return liquid to saucepan; bring to boil.

VEGETABLES: Add pearl onions to boiling liquid in saucepan; cook for 10 to 15 minutes or until tender when pierced with knife. With slotted spoon, remove onions and place in shallow dish.

Add carrots to boiling liquid; cook for 4 to 5 minutes or just until barely tender. Remove with slotted spoon and add to onions in dish. Add cauliflower to liquid and cook for 2 to 3 minutes or until barely tender; add to dish. Add broccoli to liquid and cook for 2 to 3 minutes or until barely tender; add to dish. Add green and yellow zucchini separately to liquid and cook each for 2 to 3 minutes or until barely tender; add to dish. Add mushrooms to liquid and cook for 1 to 2 minutes or until barely tender; add to dish.

Boil cooking liquid until reduced to about 1 cup (250 mL); pour over vegetables. Cover and marinate in refrigerator for at least 2 hours or overnight.

HALIBUT: About 10 minutes before cooking, place halibut in shallow dish. Combine lemon juice and olive oil; pour over fish. Cover and marinate at room temperature. Remove vegetables from refrigerator and bring to room temperature.

Brush grilling rack with olive oil. Season fish with salt and pepper to taste. Grill fish on medium-high setting for 10 minutes per inch (2.5 cm) of thickness, turning once, or until fish is opaque.

Place fish steaks on dinner plates. Spoon vegetables around fish. Spoon some of the marinade over fish. Garnish with lemon wedges. Makes 6 servings.

*Broccoli may discolor when cooked as above. If you prefer, steam broccoli separately and store in paper towel-lined plastic bag until ready to serve. Add to vegetables in marinade just before spooning onto plates.

ARCTIC CHAR WITH SHRIMP

If you can't get Arctic char, use salmon. Serve with boiled potatoes tossed with butter and parsley.

5 lb	Arctic char or salmon, deboned	2.2 kg
	Salt and pepper	
1/3 cup	butter	75 mL
1	onion, chopped	1
2	stalks celery, chopped	2
4 cups	fresh bread crumbs	1 L
2 tbsp	chopped fresh parsley	25 mL
2 tbsp	chopped fresh dill	25 mL
2	green onions, chopped	2
1 tsp	salt	5 mL
1/2 tsp	pepper	2 mL
1 lb	frozen cooked baby shrimp, thawed	500 g

Pat fish cavity dry; sprinkle with salt and pepper. In saucepan, melt butter over medium heat; cook onion and celery until tender, 5 to 8 minutes. Remove from heat. Stir in bread crumbs, parsley, dill, green onions, salt and pepper; mix well. Stir in shrimp.

Fill cavity with stuffing; sew or skewer closed. Bake on greased foil-lined baking sheet in 425°F (220°C) oven for 45 to 55 minutes or until flesh is opaque and flakes easily when tested with fork. Makes 8 servings.

SPARERIBS WITH MAPLE CHILI GLAZE

Pork spareribs are popular for casual entertaining. More expensive back ribs contain more meat and less fat, but side ribs have a lot of flavor, too, and make for a very economical meal. For side dishes, Refrigerator Slaw (recipe, p. 92) and New Potato Salad with Buttermilk Dressing (recipe, p. 86) suit the relaxed mood.

4 lb	pork back ribs, each strip cut in half	2 kg
2 tbsp	vegetable oil	25 mL
1	onion, finely chopped	1
2	cloves garlic, minced	2
3/4 cup	drained canned plum tomatoes	175 mL
1 cup	chili sauce	250 mL
1/2 cup	maple syrup	125 mL
1/4 cup	Dijon mustard	50 mL
2 tbsp	red wine vinegar	25 mL
2 tbsp	Worcestershire sauce	25 mL
1 tsp	salt	5 mL
1/2 tsp	pepper	2 mL
1/4 tsp	hot pepper flakes	1 mL

Place ribs in large pot; add enough cold water to cover. Simmer, covered, for 30 minutes or until just tender; drain well and place in large plastic bag.

Meanwhile, in saucepan, heat oil over medium heat; cook onion and garlic for 3 to 4 minutes or until tender. Press tomatoes through sieve to purée and remove seeds. Stir purée, chili sauce, maple syrup, mustard, vinegar, Worcestershire sauce, salt, pepper and hot pepper flakes into onion mixture. Simmer, uncovered, for 15 minutes. Cool. Pour over ribs in bag and turn to coat. *(Recipe can be prepared to this point, covered and refrigerated overnight.)*

Arrange ribs in single layer on foil-lined baking sheets. Brush with any remaining glaze. Bake in 350°F (180°C) oven for 20 minutes. Turn ribs; bake for 15 to 20 minutes longer or until tender and glazed, basting twice. Makes 6 servings.

PASTITSIO

A savory meat sauce is sandwiched between layers of creamy, cheesy pasta custard in this delicious variation on lasagna. Pastitsio *can be made up to one day ahead and baked before serving — so it's perfect for a buffet supper or family reunion.*

2 tbsp	vegetable oil	25 mL
3	onions, finely chopped	3
3	large cloves garlic, minced	3
3 lb	ground beef	1.5 kg
2 tsp	each dried oregano and basil	10 mL
1-1/2 tsp	cinnamon	7 mL
1 tsp	each salt, pepper, granulated sugar and dried thyme	5 mL
1 cup	dry white wine or chicken stock	250 mL
1	can (5-1/2 oz/156 mL) tomato paste	1
1	can (28 oz/796 mL) tomatoes	1
1/2 cup	minced fresh parsley	125 mL

PASTA CUSTARD LAYERS:

5 cups	medium pasta shells	1.25 L
3/4 cup	butter	175 mL
2/3 cup	all-purpose flour	150 mL
7 cups	milk	1.75 L
1 tsp	salt	5 mL
1/2 tsp	nutmeg	2 mL
1/4 tsp	pepper	1 mL
4	eggs	4
2 cups	creamed cottage cheese	500 mL
2 cups	shredded mozzarella or Swiss cheese	500 mL
1/2 cup	freshly grated Parmesan cheese	125 mL

In large heavy saucepan or Dutch oven, heat oil over medium heat; cook onions and garlic until softened, about 5 minutes. Increase heat to high; add beef. Cook, stirring to break up, for about 3 minutes or until meat is no longer pink. Stir in oregano, basil, cinnamon, salt, pepper, sugar and thyme; cook for 3 minutes.

❧ Pour in wine, tomato paste and tomatoes, mashing tomatoes with fork. Bring to boil; reduce heat and simmer, uncovered, for 20 minutes. Taste and adjust seasoning. Add parsley.

❧ PASTA CUSTARD LAYERS: In large pot of boiling salted water, cook pasta until tender but firm, about 8 minutes. Drain; transfer to large bowl. Toss with 2 tbsp (25 mL) of the butter. Set aside.

❧ In large heavy saucepan, melt remaining butter over medium heat; stir in flour and cook, without browning, for 3 minutes, stirring constantly. Gradually add milk, whisking until smooth; cook for about 5 minutes or until thickened. Season with salt, nutmeg and pepper.

❧ In large bowl, whisk eggs; whisk in about 1 cup (250 mL) of the hot sauce. Return mixture to saucepan; cook for 2 minutes, stirring. Remove from heat; blend in cottage cheese and mozzarella. Blend into pasta.

❧ In each of two 13- × 9-inch (3.5 L) baking dishes, spread one-quarter of the pasta mixture. Spread meat filling over each. Spread remaining pasta mixture evenly over meat. Sprinkle with Parmesan. Bake in 375°F (190°C) oven for 1 hour or until bubbly and heated through and top is lightly browned. Let stand for 10 minutes. Makes about 12 servings.

ENTERTAINING WITH EASE

A buffet supper is an ideal way to entertain when there are more friends and family than places at the table. Start with an easy help-yourself appetizer like Two-Salmon Pâté (p. 13) or Country Pâté (p. 15), set out with crackers and fresh crunchy vegetables. Or, top cream cheese with Tomato-Pepper Salsa (p. 176) and surround with corn chips.

❧ For the main course, choose a satisfying make-ahead casserole like the Pastitsio above, or try Fiesta Chicken and Sausage Stew (p. 30), Hearty Chicken Pot Pie (p. 35) or Seafood Casserole (p. 25). Toss up a great salad — Romaine, Boston and Bibb lettuces interspersed with radicchio or red-tipped leaf lettuce for color, watercress and arugula for bite and sliced fennel, radishes and cucumber for substance — and set out baskets of crusty warm-from-the-oven bread.

❧ For a sweet ending, let the season dictate which scrumptious desserts to tempt your guests with — whether it's a cool Rhubarb and Strawberry Trifle (p. 138) in the spring, Layered Berry Cheesecake (p. 136) in summer, spicy Dutch Apple Pie (p. 166) made with the first apples of autumn, or warming Pecan-Whisky Cake (p. 149) served in front of a cosy fire.

SIMMERING POTS

There's no more wonderful way to say ''welcome to my kitchen'' than to fill it with the appetizing aromas of simmering pots. Their ingredients release a rich store of flavors with the magic of time — chicken, chunky beef, spicy hot sausages, meatballs, lentils and beans plumping in chili and herb-rich tomato mixtures. These are simmered suppers worth waiting for, a cure-all for cold-weather-weary appetites.

FIESTA CHICKEN AND SAUSAGE STEW

There's nothing like crisp wintry air and a day spent cross-country skiing to whet appetites. This satisfying stew will be a hit with everyone, including the cook, since it's even better made a day ahead and reheated. And while the buffet table is being set, warm up by the fire with mugs of steaming mulled wine (see sidebar, this page).

4 lb	chicken pieces	2 kg
1 tsp	each dried oregano, marjoram and dry mustard	5 mL
1/2 tsp	each salt and pepper	2 mL
1/4 tsp	cayenne pepper	1 mL
2 tbsp	olive oil	25 mL
1 lb	chorizo, Italian or other spicy sausage, sliced	500 g
1	head garlic, separated into cloves	1
4	carrots, cut in chunks	4
1	each sweet yellow and red pepper, cut in thin strips	1
1	can (28 oz/796 mL) plum tomatoes, drained and quartered	1
2	small zucchini, sliced	2

Wipe chicken with damp cloth. Combine oregano, marjoram, mustard, salt, pepper and cayenne; rub over chicken. Cover and refrigerate for 1 hour.

❦ In large skillet, heat 1 tbsp (15 mL) of the oil over medium-high heat; cook sausage for about 10 minutes or until well browned. With slotted spoon, remove and drain on paper towel. Add remaining oil to same skillet; cook chicken in batches for 4 to 6 minutes on each side or until browned. Transfer to large shallow casserole.

❦ Drain fat from skillet; cook garlic and carrots over medium heat, covered and stirring occasionally, for 7 to 9 minutes or just until carrots are tender. Add yellow and red peppers; cook for 2 minutes. Arrange vegetables and sausage around chicken. Add tomatoes to skillet and bring to boil, scraping up brown bits; pour over chicken.

❦ Bake, covered, in 400°F (200°C) oven for 30 minutes, basting often. Add zucchini; cover and bake, basting often, for 15 minutes or until juices run clear when chicken thigh is pierced and breast is no longer pink inside. *(Stew can be cooled, covered and refrigerated for up to 2 days; if making ahead, don't add zucchini until reheating. Reheat in 350°F/180°C oven for 30 to 40 minutes.)* Makes 8 generous servings.

MULLED RED WINE

Set out a steaming pot of mulled red wine and mugs, so that cold skiers can warm up fast. Choose modest house wine. Any leftovers can be refrigerated for up to 2 weeks.

❦ In large pot over medium heat, heat 3 bottles (each 1 L) red wine, 1/2 cup (125 mL) granulated sugar, 4 sliced oranges, 4 sliced lemons, 8 cinnamon sticks and 15 whole cloves to just below boiling. Simmer for 30 minutes. Serve warm in heated mugs. Makes 8 generous servings.

(clockwise from bottom right) Fiesta Chicken and Sausage Stew; Corn Bread (recipe, p. 34); salad of mixed greens

PASTA-MEATBALL STEW

This quick meal-in-a-pot is guaranteed to appease hungry cold-weather appetites.

1 tbsp	vegetable oil	15 mL
2	onions, chopped	2
2 tbsp	all-purpose flour	25 mL
1	clove garlic, minced	1
1 cup	beef stock	250 mL
1	can (19 oz/540 mL) tomatoes	1
1 tbsp	tomato paste	15 mL
1/2 tsp	dried thyme	2 mL
1	bay leaf	1
4	carrots	4
1	zucchini	1
1	sweet green or red pepper	1
1 cup	rotini noodles	250 mL
	Pepper	

	MEATBALLS:	
1 lb	lean ground beef	500 g
1/4 cup	fine dry bread crumbs	50 mL
1/4 cup	milk	50 mL
1	egg, lightly beaten	1
1 tbsp	chopped fresh parsley	15 mL
1/2 tsp	each salt, pepper and dry mustard	2 mL
1 tbsp	vegetable oil	15 mL

MEATBALLS: In bowl, combine beef, bread crumbs, milk, egg, parsley, salt, pepper and mustard; mix thoroughly. Shape into 1-inch (2.5 cm) balls. In Dutch oven or baking dish, heat oil over medium-high heat. Cook meatballs in batches, turning, for 5 to 10 minutes or until browned. Drain on paper towels.

❧ Add oil to same Dutch oven; cook onions, stirring frequently, for 5 to 10 minutes or until golden. Add flour and garlic; cook, stirring, for 30 seconds. Gradually stir in beef stock; bring to boil. Add tomatoes, tomato paste, thyme, bay leaf and meatballs; cover, reduce heat to low and simmer for 30 minutes.

❧ Meanwhile, slice carrots diagonally. Slice zucchini and green pepper. Add carrots to stew; cover and simmer for 10 minutes. Add zucchini and green pepper; cover and simmer for 5 minutes longer or until vegetables are tender-crisp.

❧ Meanwhile, in pot of boiling salted water, cook rotini until tender but firm. Drain; stir into stew. Remove bay leaf. Season with pepper to taste. Makes about 4 servings.

MEDITERRANEAN FISH AND PASTA STEW

Although the ingredient list is long, this stew is not hard to prepare—and it makes an impressive company supper.

1 cup	dry white wine or chicken or fish stock	250 mL
2 cups	chicken or fish stock	500 mL
1/4 tsp	each dried thyme, oregano and basil	1 mL
1/4 lb	corkscrew pasta	125 g
1 lb	fish fillets	500 g
	Salt and pepper	

TOPPING:		
2 tbsp	mayonnaise	25 mL
2 tbsp	plain yogurt	25 mL
1	clove garlic, minced	1
1/4 tsp	hot pepper sauce	1 mL
8	whole wheat toast rounds	8
1/4 cup	chopped fresh parsley	50 mL

1/2 lb	scallops	250 g
1/4 lb	shrimp	125 g
1/4 lb	mussels	125 g
2 tsp	vegetable oil	10 mL
1	onion, chopped	1
3	cloves garlic, minced	3
1	carrot, chopped	1
1	stalk celery, chopped	1
1/4 tsp	hot pepper flakes	1 mL
1	sweet red pepper, cut in 1-inch (2.5 cm) chunks	1
1/2 lb	mushrooms, quartered	250 g
1	can (28 oz/796 mL) plum tomatoes, puréed	1

Halve scallops. Peel and clean shrimp; cut in half. Scrub mussels under cold water, removing any beards. Discard any mussels that do not close. Set seafood aside.

❧ In Dutch oven, heat oil over medium heat; add onion, garlic, carrot, celery and hot pepper flakes. Cover and cook for about 10 minutes or until tender, stirring occasionally.

❧ Add red pepper, mushrooms, tomatoes, wine and stock; bring to boil. Add thyme, oregano and basil; reduce heat and simmer for 10 minutes. Add pasta; cook for about 8 minutes or until almost tender.

❧ Add fish fillets, breaking up into chunks; cook for 5 minutes. Add scallops, shrimp and mussels; cover and cook for 5 minutes. Discard any mussels that do not open. Season with salt and pepper to taste.

❧ TOPPING: Combine mayonnaise, yogurt, garlic and hot pepper sauce. Spread 1/2 tbsp (7 mL) on each toast round; sprinkle with parsley.

❧ Ladle stew into warmed bowls; top each with 1 toast round. Makes 8 servings.

CHILI IN CORN BREAD RING

Make our spicy chili even heartier by using half ground beef and half lean chuck cut into 1/2-inch (1 cm) cubes to serve in a peppery corn bread ring. This corn bread can also be baked in a greased 8-inch (2 L) square baking pan.

2 tbsp	vegetable oil	25 mL
1	onion, chopped	1
2	cloves garlic, chopped	2
2 tsp	cumin	10 mL
2 tsp	dried oregano	10 mL
2 tsp	(approx) chili powder	10 mL
1 tsp	paprika	5 mL
1 lb	ground beef	500 g
1	can (14 oz/398 mL) tomatoes	1
1/2 cup	beef stock	125 mL
Half	sweet green pepper, diced	Half
1	green chili pepper, diced (optional)	1
1	can (19 oz/540 mL) kidney beans, drained	1
	Salt	
	Corn Bread Ring (recipe follows)	

In heavy saucepan, heat oil over medium heat; cook onion, garlic, cumin, oregano, 2 tsp (10 mL) chili powder and paprika for 5 minutes or until onion is softened. Add meat and cook, stirring to break up, until no longer pink. Add tomatoes and their juices, stock, sweet green pepper, and chili pepper (if using); simmer, uncovered, for 1 hour.

❦ Add kidney beans; cook until heated through. Season with salt and more chili powder to taste. Spoon into center of hot Corn Bread Ring. Makes 4 servings.

CORN BREAD RING:		
1 cup	all-purpose flour	250 mL
1 cup	cornmeal	250 mL
3/4 cup	shredded old Cheddar cheese	175 mL
1 tbsp	baking powder	15 mL
1/4 tsp	salt	1 mL
2	eggs	2
3/4 cup	milk	175 mL
1/3 cup	vegetable oil	75 mL
3/4 cup	corn	175 mL
1 tbsp	chopped pickled jalapeño pepper (optional)	15 mL

Grease 8-inch (1.5 L) ring mould. Line bottom with waxed paper; grease. Set aside.

❦ In large bowl, stir together flour, cornmeal, cheese, baking powder and salt. In separate bowl, beat together eggs, milk and oil; stir into dry ingredients just until blended. Stir in corn, and jalapeño pepper (if using); spoon into prepared pan.

❦ Bake in 375°F (190°C) oven for 35 minutes or until tester inserted in center comes out clean. Let cool in pan for 5 minutes. Loosen edges and unmould onto serving plate. Makes 1 ring.

HEARTY CHICKEN POT PIE

Make the crust for this classic pot pie by using heart-shaped cookie cutters to stamp out heart motifs.

1	**chicken (2-1/2 lb/1.25 kg)**	1
1	**onion, quartered**	1
1 tsp	**salt**	5 mL
4	**peppercorns**	4
1	**bay leaf**	1
1/3 cup	**butter**	75 mL
2	**large carrots, julienned**	2
1 cup	**sliced green beans**	250 mL
1 cup	**sliced mushrooms**	250 mL
1/4 cup	**all-purpose flour**	50 mL
1/2 cup	**light cream**	125 mL
	Salt and pepper	
8 to 10	**small cooked onions**	8 to 10
	Pastry for single-crust pie	
1	**egg, lightly beaten**	1

In large saucepan, combine chicken, quartered onion, salt, peppercorns and bay leaf; pour in enough water to cover chicken. Bring just to boil; skim off any froth. Reduce heat, cover and simmer for 1-1/2 to 2 hours or until chicken is tender. Strain, reserving stock. Discard onion, peppercorns and bay leaf.

❦ Remove and discard skin and bones from chicken. Cut meat into large chunks; set aside.

❦ In saucepan, melt half of the butter over medium-low heat; cook carrots,

green beans and mushrooms for 5 minutes. With slotted spoon, remove vegetables and set aside.

❦ Add remaining butter to saucepan; stir in flour and cook, stirring constantly, for 1 minute. Stir in 2-1/2 cups (625 mL) reserved stock; cook, stirring, until thickened and smooth. Add cream and heat through but do not boil. Season with salt and pepper to taste.

❦ Gently stir chicken, reserved vegetables and cooked onions into sauce; spoon into 8-cup (2 L) shallow casserole. Roll out pastry and cover casserole; brush with egg. Bake in 400°F (200°C) oven for about 20 minutes or until hot and bubbly and pastry is golden. Makes 6 servings.

SIMPLE CASSOULET

*Cassoulet is a wonderfully fragrant and meaty version of baked beans—guaranteed to satisfy hearty cold-weather
appetites. For a crusty topping, add 1-1/2 cups (375 mL) fresh bread crumbs tossed with 2 tbsp (25 mL) butter about
45 minutes before end of baking time.*

2 cups	dried Great Northern or navy (pea) beans	500 mL
3	cloves	3
1	onion	1
2 cups	chicken stock	500 mL
2 cups	water	500 mL
1/4 lb	slab bacon (unsliced)	125 g
3	cloves garlic, crushed	3
	Bouquet garni*	
3/4 lb	boneless pork, cut in 1-1/2 inch (4 cm) cubes	375 g
1/2 lb	boneless lamb shoulder, cut in 1-1/2 inch (4 cm) cubes	250 g
1/4 tsp	each salt and pepper	1 mL
1/4 cup	vegetable oil	50 mL
1	onion, chopped	1
1/2 cup	tomato sauce	125 mL
1/2 lb	kielbasa, cut in 1/2-inch (1 cm) thick slices	250 g

Soak beans (see Preparing Beans, p. 39). Drain. Push cloves into onion; place in large saucepan along with beans, stock, water, bacon, garlic and bouquet garni. Bring to boil and skim off any foam; cover and simmer for 1 to 1-1/2 hours or until beans are tender. Drain, reserving cooking liquid. Remove bacon and cut into 4 pieces; set aside. Discard bouquet garni and onion.

❦ Sprinkle pork and lamb with salt and pepper. In large skillet, heat oil over medium-high heat; cook pork and lamb for 5 to 7 minutes or until browned. With slotted spoon, remove meat and set aside. Add chopped onion to skillet; cook for 2 minutes or until tender. Add reserved cooking liquid, tomato sauce and reserved pork and lamb; cover and simmer for 40 minutes. Drain and reserve cooking liquid, adding enough water if necessary to make 2 cups (500 mL).

❦ In 20-cup (5 L) casserole or Dutch oven, spread one-third of the beans. Top with pork and lamb, then one-third of the beans, then kielbasa and bacon. Cover with remaining beans. Pour in reserved cooking liquid. Bake, uncovered, in 350°F (180°C) oven for 1-1/2 hours or until bubbly but still fairly liquid, adding more water if necessary. Makes 4 to 6 servings.

*In double-thickness square of cheesecloth, tie together 1 bay leaf, 2 parsley sprigs and pinch of dried thyme.

CHICKEN POT-AU-FEU

A rainbow array of vegetables, flavorful broth, chunks of chicken and a zesty herb sauce make this a first-class choice for family and friends.

6 cups	chicken stock	1.5 L
2	potatoes, peeled	2
2	carrots	2
1	rutabaga, peeled	1
2	parsnips	2
1	leek (white part only)	1
1	onion, cut in chunks	1
Quarter	green cabbage, cut in chunks	Quarter
1/4 tsp	dried thyme	1 mL
1/4 tsp	(approx) pepper	1 mL
1-1/2 lb	chicken breasts, skinned	750 g
	Salt	
1 cup	drained canned red kidney beans	250 mL
	Salsa Verde (recipe follows)	

In Dutch oven, bring chicken stock to boil. Meanwhile, cut potatoes, carrots and rutabaga into 2-inch (5 cm) chunks; cut parsnips and leek into 1-inch (2.5 cm) pieces. Add to chicken stock along with onion, cabbage, thyme and pepper. Reduce heat and simmer for 30 to 40 minutes or until vegetables are almost tender.

❧ Cut chicken into large chunks; add to vegetables and simmer for 10 to 15 minutes or until chicken is no longer pink inside. Season with salt and pepper to taste. Add beans and heat through. Top each serving with some of the Salsa Verde. Makes 4 servings.

SALSA VERDE:		
1 cup	fresh basil or parsley	250 mL
1	slice white bread	1
2	anchovy fillets	2
1/3 cup	olive oil	75 mL
2 tbsp	red wine vinegar	25 mL
1/4 tsp	pepper	1 mL

In food processor, combine basil, bread, anchovies, oil, vinegar and pepper. Makes 3/4 cup (175 mL).

REALLY GOOD BEEF STEW

There's no more perfect welcome for a gang of frozen skaters or skiers than this hearty stew.

2 tbsp	vegetable oil	25 mL
3 lb	lean stewing beef, cut in 2-inch (5 cm) cubes	1.5 kg
2	cloves garlic, minced	2
4	onions, quartered	4
2 tbsp	all-purpose flour	25 mL
2-1/2 cups	beef stock*	625 mL
1	can (19 oz/540 mL) tomatoes (undrained)	1
4	carrots, chopped	4
2	stalks celery, chopped	2
1 tsp	Worcestershire sauce	5 mL
1/2 tsp	dried basil	2 mL
5	potatoes, peeled and quartered	5
	Salt and pepper	

In large heavy saucepan, heat oil over medium-high heat; add beef and brown all over. Reduce heat to medium-low. Add garlic and onions; cook until softened, about 4 minutes.

❧ Sprinkle flour over meat and onions; cook, stirring, until flour browns.

❧ Add stock, tomatoes, carrots, celery, Worcestershire sauce and basil; bring to boil. Cover and reduce heat; simmer for about 1-1/2 hours or until beef is tender. Add potatoes; cook for 30 to 45 minutes or until tender. Season with salt and pepper to taste. Makes 6 to 8 servings.

*If you prefer an equally tasty but more soup-like consistency, add an extra cup of beef stock.

COMFY BAKED BEANS

Nothing is more welcoming on a crisp winter day than the aroma of hearty baked beans. The marriage of tomatoes,
bacon and molasses is what makes the sauce so flavorful and rich. Baked beans are not only deliciously comforting,
they are also nutritious, since white pea beans, or navy beans, are a good source of protein and fiber.

3 cups	white pea beans	750 mL
1/4 lb	slab bacon or salt pork	125 g
1	can (28 oz/796 mL) tomatoes	1
2 cups	chopped onions	500 mL
3/4 cup	ketchup	175 mL
3/4 cup	fancy molasses	175 mL
1/3 cup	packed brown sugar	75 mL
1 tbsp	dry mustard	15 mL
1/2 tsp	salt	2 mL
1/4 tsp	pepper	1 mL

Rinse beans and sort, if necessary, discarding any blemished ones and any grit.

❦ In large Dutch oven or stockpot, cover beans with 3 times their volume of water. Bring to boil; boil gently for 2 minutes. Remove from heat; cover and let stand for 1 hour. Drain, discarding liquid.

❦ Return soaked beans to pot along with 3 times their volume of fresh water. Bring to boil; reduce heat and simmer, covered, for 30 to 45 minutes or until tender. Drain, reserving 2 cups (500 mL) cooking liquid.

❦ Meanwhile, dice bacon; set aside. In bowl, and using potato masher, mash tomatoes in their juice.

❦ In bean pot or 16-cup (4 L) casserole, combine beans, reserved cooking liquid, bacon, tomatoes, onions, ketchup, molasses, sugar, mustard, salt and pepper.

❦ Bake, covered, in 300°F (150°C) oven for 2-1/2 hours. Uncover and bake for 1 to 1-1/2 hours longer or until sauce is thickened and coats beans well. Makes about 10 cups (2.5 L) or 6 to 8 servings.

VARIATIONS

SALSA BAKED BEANS: Substitute bottled taco sauce for ketchup. Add 1 tsp (5 mL) cumin and 1 tbsp (15 mL) dried oregano along with crushed tomatoes. Increase salt to 1 tsp (5 mL) and pepper to 1/2 tsp (2 mL). Stir in 2 chopped sweet green or red peppers for last hour of cooking time.

MAPLE-APPLE BEANS: Substitute maple syrup for molasses. Add 3 cups (750 mL) diced peeled apples and 1 tbsp (15 mL) cider vinegar along with crushed tomatoes.

BLACK BEAN VEGETARIAN CHILI

This chili can be made in a faster version with 4 cups (1 L) drained canned black beans or white kidney beans; omit soaking and reduce water to 1 cup (250 mL). Add beans with red peppers and simmer, uncovered, for 30 minutes or until chili is thickened.

2 cups	black turtle beans (13-1/2 oz/400 g)	500 mL
2 tsp	vegetable oil	10 mL
2	onions, chopped	2
4	cloves garlic, minced	4
3 tbsp	chili powder	50 mL
1 tsp	cumin	5 mL
1 tsp	paprika	5 mL
1 tsp	dried oregano	5 mL
1	can (28 oz/796 mL) plum tomatoes, puréed	1
3	jalapeño peppers, diced	3
3	sweet red peppers, diced	3
2 cups	corn	500 mL
2 tbsp	chopped fresh parsley or coriander	25 mL
1 tsp	salt	5 mL
Pinch	pepper	Pinch
	GARNISHES:	
1 cup	plain yogurt	250 mL
1/2 cup	grated mozzarella cheese	125 mL
1/4 cup	chopped fresh parsley or coriander	50 mL
1/2 cup	diced mild green chilies	125 mL

In saucepan, cover beans with water and soak for 3 hours; drain. Cover again with water and bring to boil; reduce heat to medium-low and simmer for 30 to 40 minutes or just until tender. Set aside.

❧ In Dutch oven, heat oil over medium heat; cook onions and garlic for 5 minutes or until tender and fragrant. Stir in chili powder, cumin, paprika and oregano; cook, stirring, for 30 seconds. Stir in tomatoes and jalapeño peppers; cook for 10 minutes.

❧ Drain beans and add to tomato mixture. Add up to 2 cups (500 mL) fresh water, if necessary, to cover beans with 1 inch (2.5 cm) of liquid. Cover and bring to boil; reduce heat to medium-low and simmer for 1 hour.

❧ Add red peppers; simmer for 30 minutes or until beans are tender. Add corn; cook for 10 minutes. Add parsley, salt and pepper; taste and adjust seasoning. Serve with garnishes to spoon onto chili. Makes 8 servings.

PREPARING BEANS

Before being cooked, beans must be soaked in water. Here are two methods.

❧ **Quick soak:** Cover dried beans with 3 times their volume of water; bring to boil and boil gently for 2 minutes. Remove from heat, cover and let stand for 1 hour. Drain and cook as directed.

❧ **Long soak:** Cover dried beans with 3 times their volume of water and let stand for 8 hours or overnight. Drain and cook as directed.

SUNDAY DINNERS

It's the aroma of everyone's favorite roast chicken filling the house. It's setting the table with the best china and buffing up the heirloom candlesticks. It's Sunday dinner — a time to regroup, to talk about the week, to be together over food that's special without being extravagant or elaborate. It's building family memories, whether the menu is nostalgic with roast beef and steaming popovers or up-to-date with southwestern-flavored chicken.

❧

SKY-HIGH POPOVERS

Unlike Yorkshire pudding, which must be made at the last minute, these crisp and easy popovers are made ahead and reheated just before serving — leaving you free for last-minute gravy making.

2	eggs	2
1 cup	milk	250 mL
1 cup	all-purpose flour	250 mL
1/2 tsp	salt	2 mL

In large bowl, beat eggs with milk; stir in flour and salt until blended but still lumpy. Fill 8 well-greased muffin cups three-quarters full; place on center rack in cold oven. Set oven at 450°F (230°C) and bake for 25 minutes. With skewer, puncture each popover; bake for 10 minutes longer or until golden brown, crisp and puffed. *(Popovers can be cooled, covered with clean tea towel and stored at room temperature for up to 8 hours; reheat in 325°F/160°C oven for 5 to 10 minutes or until heated through.)* Makes 8 servings.

❧

ROAST BEEF

To simplify carving, ask the butcher to remove the chine bone (part of the backbone). When carving, remove string and set meat upright. Holding roast steady with a carving fork, cut away rib bones at base. Then, turn meat on its side and carve into slices across the grain.

1	rib roast of beef (about 7 lb/3.15 kg)	1
1	clove garlic, slivered	1
	Pan Gravy (recipe, p. 45)	

Cut slits in roast and insert garlic slivers; let roast stand at room temperature for 30 minutes.

❧ Place, rib side down, on greased rack in roasting pan; roast in 325°F (160°C) oven for about 2 hours and 20 minutes for rare or until meat thermometer registers 140°F (60°C) or until desired doneness (see Roasting Chart). Transfer roast to warm platter, reserving pan juices for gravy. Cover with foil and let stand for 20 minutes before carving and serving with Pan Gravy. Makes about 12 servings.

ROASTING CHART

	Oven Temperature	Roasting Time	Internal Meat Temperature
Roast Beef	325°F (160°C)	20 minutes per lb (500 g)	**rare:** 140° F (60°C) **medium:** 160°F (70°C) **well done:** 170°F (75°C)
Chicken	325°F (160°C)	35 minutes per lb (500 g)	185°F (85°C)
Pork	325°F (160°C)	30 to 35 minutes per lb (500 g)	160°-170°F (70-75°C)

Roast Beef and Sky-High Popovers

STUFFED PORK TENDERLOIN

Serve this easy stuffed pork tenderloin with applesauce.

2	pork tenderloins (about 1-1/2 lb/750 g total)	2
4 tsp	olive oil	20 mL
2/3 cup	chopped onions	150 mL
3 tbsp	raisins	50 mL
Pinch	each salt, pepper, dried basil, sage and thyme	Pinch
1-3/4 cups	diced fresh bread	425 mL
4	slices bacon	4

Trim tenderloins; slice in half lengthwise.

❦ In skillet, heat oil over medium heat; cook onions until softened, 4 to 5 minutes. Add raisins, salt, pepper, basil, sage and thyme; transfer to bowl and toss with bread.

❦ Lay out 2 bottom halves of tenderloin on work surface. Slide four 12-inch (30 cm) lengths of string crosswise under each tenderloin, spacing them at 2-inch (5 cm) intervals.

❦ Mound stuffing on top of tenderloin; cover with remaining tenderloin, placing narrow ends over wide ends. Cover each with 2 strips bacon; tie strings firmly.

❦ Roast on rack in roasting pan in 350°F (180°C) oven for 55 to 60 minutes or until bacon is crisp and meat thermometer in pork registers 160-170°F (70-75°C). Cover loosely with foil and let stand for 5 minutes before removing string. Makes 4 to 6 servings.

ROAST CAPON WITH WHOLE GARLIC, HERBS AND POTATOES

The aroma of chicken and sweet whole garlic cloves roasting in the oven will magically draw everyone to the table. For a wonderful first course, serve the garlic with French bread and cream cheese (squeeze cloves of garlic gently to pop out pulp). Accompany the capon and potatoes with Nutty Pecan Squash (recipe, p. 95) and sautéed spinach.

1	capon (about 8 lb/3.5 kg)	1
2 tsp	each finely chopped fresh thyme and rosemary (or 1/2 tsp/ 2 mL dried)	10 mL
1 tsp	salt	5 mL
1/2 tsp	pepper	2 mL
1/3 cup	butter, melted	75 mL
1/3 cup	olive oil	75 mL
8	heads garlic	8
16	small red potatoes (unpeeled)	16

Wipe capon inside and out with damp cloth. Combine thyme, rosemary, salt and pepper; rub half of the mixture on inside and outside of capon. Place on rack in shallow roasting pan, breast side up.

❦ Stir together butter and oil; drizzle half of the mixture over capon. Roast, uncovered, in 300°F (150°C) oven for 1-1/2 hours, basting frequently.

❦ Remove loose outer skin from garlic; cut thin slice from top of each head, exposing cloves. Arrange garlic and potatoes around capon. Sprinkle with remaining herb mixture and drizzle with remaining butter mixture.

❦ Roast, basting frequently, for 1-1/2 to 1-3/4 hours or until meat thermometer registers 185°F (85°C).

❦ Transfer capon to cutting board and cover loosely with foil; let stand for 15 minutes before carving and serving with potatoes. Serve garlic separately. Makes about 8 servings.

SOUTHWESTERN CHICKEN

Assorted spices turn a whole chicken into a dinner worth waiting for.

1	large chicken (about 4 lb/2 kg)	1
4 tsp	vegetable oil	20 mL
1 tsp	paprika	5 mL
3/4 tsp	chili powder	4 mL
1/2 tsp	black pepper	2 mL
1/2 tsp	cumin	2 mL
1/4 tsp	dried coriander	1 mL
1/4 tsp	cayenne pepper	1 mL

Truss chicken; place in shallow dish. Combine oil, paprika, chili powder, black pepper, cumin, coriander and cayenne pepper; brush over chicken. Marinate in refrigerator for at least 1 or up to 8 hours.

❦ Set chicken, breast side up, on greased rack in shallow roasting pan. Roast in 325°F (160°C) oven for about 2 hours and 20 minutes or until juices run clear when pierced with fork and meat thermometer registers 185°F (85°C). Transfer to platter; cover with foil and let stand for 10 minutes before carving. Makes 6 servings.

PERFECT POT ROAST

Tantalizing aromas waft through the house as an old-fashioned pot roast simmers to succulent perfection. Add a new flavor twist using our variations with either lots of onions or spicy Cajun seasonings. Each of these one-pot dinners is economical, tasty and easy to prepare.

4 lb	beef cross rib or blade roast	2 kg
1/3 cup	all-purpose flour	75 mL
3 tbsp	vegetable oil	50 mL
1-1/2 cups	chopped onions	375 mL
3/4 cup	chopped carrots	175 mL
3/4 cup	chopped celery	175 mL
1	clove garlic, minced	1
1 cup	chopped drained tomatoes	250 mL
1/2 tsp	dried thyme	2 mL
1	bay leaf	1
1 cup	beef stock	250 mL
6	small onions	6
6	carrots, halved crosswise	6
6	potatoes, quartered	6

Pat meat dry and dredge with 1/4 cup (50 mL) of the flour; brush off any excess. In Dutch oven, heat oil over medium-high heat; brown meat all over for about 7 minutes, turning with wooden spoons. Remove meat and set aside.

🥄 Add chopped onions, carrots, celery and garlic; cook, stirring often, for 3 to 5 minutes or until softened. Sprinkle with remaining flour and cook, stirring, for 1 minute.

🥄 Add tomatoes, thyme and bay leaf; pour in stock and bring to simmer. Return meat to pan; cover and cook over low heat in 325°F (160°C) oven for 1 hour and 45 minutes.

🥄 Add whole onions, carrots and potatoes; cover and cook for 45 to 75 minutes or until meat and vegetables are tender, turning roast every 30 minutes. Remove roast, whole onions, carrots and potatoes; cover and keep warm.

🥄 To make gravy, discard bay leaf from cooking liquid. Tip pan and skim off all fat.

🥄 Pour cooking liquid into blender, food processor or food mill; purée until smooth. Slice roast and arrange on serving platter; surround with vegetables. Pour gravy into sauceboat and pass separately. Makes 6 to 8 servings.

VARIATIONS

ONION POT ROAST: Substitute 4 cups (1 L) thinly sliced onions for the chopped onions. Omit chopped carrots and celery. Increase garlic to 2 cloves.

SPICY CAJUN POT ROAST: Increase garlic to 2 cloves. Omit chopped carrots and celery. Substitute tomato sauce for tomatoes and add 1/2 cup (125 mL) chili sauce, 2 tbsp (25 mL) Dijon mustard, 1 tbsp (15 mL) vinegar and 1/4 tsp (1 mL) hot pepper sauce. Omit thyme and bay leaf.

For pot roasts, choose economical cuts of beef such as cross rib, blade or boneless brisket point. The slow cooking in liquid tenderizes their tough connective tissues. Select roasts that are lean and have as little gristle as possible.

🥄 Never pierce the roast while cooking because this will release juices that keep it moist. Instead, turn it with wooden spoons.

CORN SPOON BREAD

This dish is delicious with any simple roast chicken and Mushroom Gravy (recipe, this page).

1/4 cup	butter	50 mL
1/3 cup	minced onion	75 mL
1 cup	cornmeal	250 mL
1 tsp	salt	5 mL
1 tsp	granulated sugar	5 mL
1/4 tsp	pepper	1 mL
1/4 tsp	cinnamon	1 mL
3-1/2 cups	milk, scalded	875 mL
1/2 cup	light cream	125 mL
3	eggs	3

In saucepan, melt butter over medium heat; cook onion for 2 to 3 minutes or until softened. Stir in cornmeal, salt, sugar, pepper and cinnamon; cook, stirring, for 1 to 2 minutes to coat cornmeal.

Gradually whisk in hot milk; cook, stirring constantly, until thickened and smooth, about 5 minutes. Remove from heat; stir in cream and let cool to lukewarm.

Beat eggs well and stir rapidly into cornmeal mixture. Pour into greased 8-cup (2 L) casserole. Bake in 350°F (180°C) oven for 50 to 60 minutes or until puffed and golden brown. Makes about 8 servings.

SIMPLY THE BEST PAN GRAVY

This master method, with that extra touch of onion, works for beef, pork and chicken. Use carrot cooking liquid when making beef gravy, apple juice for pork gravy and chicken stock (or equal amounts of dry white wine and chicken stock) for chicken gravy.

	Pan drippings	
1	onion, minced	1
2 tbsp	all-purpose flour	25 mL
1-1/2 cups	(approx) liquid	375 mL
	Salt and pepper	

Skim fat from pan drippings; add onion and cook over medium heat, stirring frequently, for 3 minutes or until softened. Stir in flour; cook for 1 minute, stirring constantly. Gradually whisk in liquid and cook, stirring, for about 5 minutes or until sauce boils and thickens. Thin with more liquid if desired. Strain if desired. Season with salt and pepper to taste. Makes about 2 cups (500 mL), enough for 8 servings.

MUSHROOM GRAVY

Pair this creamy gravy with everything from chicken to burgers and baked potatoes.

1/4 cup	butter	50 mL
1	small onion, minced	1
2 cups	chopped mushrooms	500 mL
2 tbsp	all-purpose flour	25 mL
1 cup	chicken stock	250 mL
1 cup	sour cream	250 mL
2 tsp	chopped fresh dill	10 mL
	Salt and pepper	

In skillet, melt butter over medium heat; cook onion until softened. Add mushrooms; cook for about 10 minutes or until tender. Stir in flour; cook, stirring, for 2 minutes. Pour in stock; cook, stirring constantly, for about 4 minutes or until thickened and smooth. Stir in sour cream; cook over medium-low heat for about 2 minutes or just until heated through. Remove from heat; stir in dill. Season with salt and pepper to taste. Makes 2-1/2 cups (625 mL).

LEMON ROAST POTATOES

*Lemon juice and oregano make these melt-in-your-mouth potatoes the perfect accompaniment
to roast lamb or chicken.*

4 lb	potatoes, peeled (8 to 10)	2 kg
1 cup	water	250 mL
1/2 cup	lemon juice	125 mL
1/3 cup	olive oil	75 mL
3	cloves garlic, minced	3
2 tsp	salt	10 mL
2 tsp	dried oregano	10 mL
1 tsp	pepper	5 mL

Cut potatoes lengthwise into thick wedges; place in 13- × 9-inch (3 L) baking dish. Whisk together water, lemon juice, oil, garlic, salt, oregano and pepper; pour over potatoes, turning to coat evenly.

❧ Bake in 325°F (160°C) oven, gently turning occasionally to keep potatoes well moistened, for about 2 hours or until potatoes are very tender and most of the liquid has evaporated. Makes 8 generous servings.

❧

ROAST LEG OF LAMB

*Tender, succulent spring lamb bathed in velvety gravy is the perfect dish to herald in spring. Whether it's
the highlight of a celebration dinner or the main attraction of a Sunday supper, roast leg of lamb
flavored with rosemary and garlic is sure to please everyone.*

1	short-cut leg of lamb (about 4 lb/2 kg)	1
3	cloves garlic, slivered	3
2 tbsp	olive oil	25 mL
1 tbsp	lemon juice	15 mL
1/2 tsp	dried rosemary	2 mL
	RED WINE GRAVY:	
1	small onion, minced	1
1/2 cup	red wine	125 mL
1 cup	beef stock	250 mL
1 tbsp	cornstarch	15 mL
1 tsp	tomato paste	5 mL
	Salt and pepper	

Using sharp knife, remove fell (thin membrane) and most of the fat from lamb. Cut about 25 tiny slits all over lamb; insert garlic slivers. Combine oil, lemon juice and rosemary; brush over lamb. Let stand at room temperature for 30 minutes.

❧ On greased rack in roasting pan, roast lamb in 325°F (160°C) oven for 1-3/4 to 2 hours, 25 to 30 minutes per pound (500 g), or until meat thermometer registers 140°F (60°C) for rare or 160°F (70°C) for medium. Remove lamb to platter; cover loosely with foil and let stand for 15 minutes.

❧ RED WINE GRAVY: Meanwhile, skim fat from pan. Add onion and cook over medium heat, stirring often, for 4 minutes or until softened. Pour in wine and bring to boil over medium-high heat; boil for 1 minute, stirring to scrape up brown bits. Add stock and return to boil; cook for 2 to 3 minutes or until reduced to about 1 cup (250 mL).

❧ Stir cornstarch with 1 tbsp (15 mL) water; stir into stock mixture and cook, stirring, for 1 minute or until thickened. Blend in tomato paste. Taste and adjust seasoning with salt and pepper. Strain if desired.

❧ Place lamb on carving board with narrow shank end away from you. Insert fork in thick meaty end to hold roast securely. With knife at slight angle, carve thin slices toward shank end, carving to bone in center.

❧ Carve thin slices lengthwise from each side. Turn leg over and carve remaining meat in same way as top of roast. Pour gravy into sauceboat and pass separately along with meat. Makes 4 to 6 servings.

❧ If you prefer to omit the wine from the gravy, substitute 2 tbsp (25 mL) red wine vinegar for the wine and increase the beef stock to 1-1/2 cups (375 mL).

❧ For all roasts, you should warm the platter, gravy boat and plates.

GLAZED HAM WITH HOT CIDER SAUCE

*For a buffet or any festive gathering, a large ham provides both excellent value and excellent eating. Serve with
asparagus, fiddleheads or tender green beans and puréed sweet or white potatoes.*

1	cooked ham, bone-in (8 lb/4 kg)	1
2-1/2 cups	cider or apple juice	625 mL
1 cup	packed brown sugar	250 mL
1 tsp	ground cloves	5 mL
1 tsp	cinnamon	5 mL
	Rind and juice of 1 lemon	
1 cup	sultana raisins	250 mL
1 tsp	dry mustard	5 mL
1 tbsp	cornstarch	15 mL
2 tbsp	cold water	25 mL

Remove all but 1/4-inch (5 mm) fat from ham; place, fat side up,
in roasting pan. Combine cider, 1/2 cup (125 mL) brown sugar,
cloves, cinnamon, and lemon rind and juice; pour over ham. Cover
and bake in 325°F (160°C) oven, basting frequently, for 1-1/2 hours.
Add raisins; bake for 30 minutes longer.

❦ Combine remaining 1/2 cup (125 mL) sugar with mustard;
press onto ham. Bake, uncovered, for about 30 minutes longer
or until glaze is set.

❦ Remove ham to heated platter. Skim off fat in pan. Stir in cornstarch with water; blend into pan juices and cook, stirring, until
thickened. Serve with ham. Makes about 12 servings.

❦

ROAST PORK LOIN WITH SAGE

*When it's cold outside, serve with Clementine and Sweet Potato Bake (recipe, p. 97). In the spring, start off with
asparagus and add parsleyed new potatoes to the platter holding this spectacular roast.*

1	pork loin roast (about 5 lb/2.2 kg)	1
2 tsp	dried sage	10 mL
2 tsp	vegetable oil	10 mL
	Pepper	
1/4 cup	fresh bread crumbs	50 mL
1/4 cup	chopped fresh parsley	50 mL
	Pan Gravy (recipe, p. 45)	

Remove string from roast and trim off thin outer layer of fat; retie
with butcher's string. Place pork, bone side down, on greased
rack in shallow roasting pan. Combine sage with oil; brush over
pork. Season with pepper. Let stand at room temperature for 30
minutes.

❦ Roast in 325°F (160°C) oven for 1 hour. Combine bread crumbs
with parsley; press onto fat side of pork. Roast for 1-1/2 to 1-3/4
hours longer or until crumbs are crisp and meat thermometer
registers 160-170°F (70-75°C). Transfer to warm platter; cover
with foil and let stand for 15 minutes before carving and serving
with Pan Gravy. Makes 8 servings.

Ask your butcher to remove the backbone to make carving
easier. Before carving, cut close along the flat bottom bone,
leaving as little meat on it as possible. Place the roast with
the rib bones facing the carver. Carve slices by cutting close
along each side of the ribs. One slice will contain a rib;
the next will be boneless. For thicker chop-size servings,
cut through the meat halfway between the ribs.

BRAISED PORK LOIN

Look for a pork loin with the backbone removed and the bones frenched, or a boneless loin or a lean butt.

1 tbsp	vegetable oil	15 mL
1	pork loin or butt (about 4 lb/2 kg)	1
1 cup	dry white wine or chicken stock	250 mL
2 tsp	paprika	10 mL
1 tsp	caraway seeds	5 mL
2	cloves garlic, slivered	2
8	small onions	8
Pinch	each salt and pepper	Pinch
2 tsp	butter	10 mL
2 tsp	all-purpose flour	10 mL
1/4 cup	sour cream	50 mL

In Dutch oven, heat oil over medium-high heat; brown pork well all over. Drain off fat.

❧ Reduce heat to medium-low; add wine, paprika, caraway seeds and garlic. Cover and simmer for 1 hour, turning pork once. Add onions, salt and pepper. Cover and simmer for 40 to 60 minutes or until meat is fork-tender, turning halfway through. Remove pork and place on platter along with onions; keep warm.

❧ Skim off fat from pan juices. Blend butter with flour; whisk into pan juices. Cook, whisking, over low heat until smooth and thickened, about 5 minutes. Whisk in sour cream and warm through without boiling. Taste and adjust seasoning. Strain if desired. Makes 6 to 8 servings.

FAMILY SUPPERS

It's the little things that count — like coming home for supper and opening the door to aromas that announce your favorite cheesy pizza or crispy fried chicken are on the menu. Family suppers can be as quick and comfy as macaroni and cheese or slow-simmered, like our easy corned beef dinner, where time (not the cook!) does all the work.

SPINACH AND SAUSAGE LASAGNA

Thawed, chopped frozen spinach can be substituted for fresh, if desired, in this spicy, colorful lasagna.

3/4 cup	spinach lasagna noodles	375 g
1/4 cup	freshly grated Parmesan cheese	50 mL
	MEAT SAUCE:	
1-1/2 lb	spicy Italian sausage	750 g
2 tbsp	olive oil	25 mL
1	onion, chopped	1
2	sweet red peppers, diced	2
1	can (28 oz/796 mL) plum tomatoes, puréed with juices	1
1 tsp	salt	5 mL
1/4 tsp	pepper	1 mL

	BESCIAMELLA SAUCE:	
1/4 cup	butter	50 mL
1/4 cup	all-purpose flour	50 mL
4 cups	milk	1 L
1 tsp	salt	5 mL
1/2 tsp	pepper	2 mL
1/4 tsp	nutmeg	1 mL
1	pkg (300 g) spinach, cooked, squeezed dry and chopped	1
1 cup	shredded mozzarella cheese	250 mL

MEAT SAUCE: Remove sausage from casings; break into 1-inch (2.5 cm) chunks. In Dutch oven, heat oil over medium heat; cook onion for 3 to 4 minutes or until tender. Add sausage; cook for 5 to 8 minutes or until browned. Add red peppers; cook for 5 minutes. Add tomatoes, salt and pepper; simmer for 20 to 25 minutes or until thickened.

❧ BESCIAMELLA SAUCE: In saucepan, melt butter over medium heat; whisk in flour and cook, stirring, for 2 minutes without browning. Whisk in milk and bring to boil; reduce heat to medium-low and cook, stirring, for 10 minutes or until thickened. Stir in salt, pepper, nutmeg, spinach and mozzarella. Taste and adjust seasoning.

❧ Meanwhile, cook noodles (see sidebar, this page). Arrange one-quarter of the noodles in single layer in greased 13- × 9-inch (3 L) baking dish. Spread with half of the Meat Sauce, one-quarter of the noodles and half of the Besciamella Sauce. Top with one-quarter of the noodles and remaining Meat Sauce, noodles and Besciamella Sauce. Sprinkle with Parmesan. Bake in 375°F (190°C) oven for 40 to 45 minutes or until bubbling. Let stand for 10 minutes. Makes 8 servings.

LASAGNA LOWDOWN

Cook noodles, a few at a time, in large pot of boiling salted water until almost tender, 2 minutes for fresh and 6 to 8 minutes for dried. Refresh in cold water and arrange in single layer on wet tea towel until ready to use.

❧ Assemble dish ahead, if desired, and refrigerate, unbaked, for up to 1 day or freeze for up to 2 months.

❧ To cook refrigerated lasagna, add 5 minutes to conventional cooking time.

❧ To cook frozen lasagna, thaw in refrigerator for 24 hours, then bake or microwave as usual.

❧ Let oven-baked lasagna stand for 10 minutes before serving.

STUFFED CABBAGE ROLLS

These lightly steamed cabbage rolls are delicious topped with sour cream and/or Easy Tomato Sauce (recipe, p. 63).

1	large head cabbage	1
2 tbsp	vegetable oil	25 mL
1/2 cup	finely chopped onion	125 mL
1	clove garlic, minced	1
1/2 cup	finely chopped sweet red or green pepper	125 mL
1/2 lb	lean ground beef	250 g
1/2 lb	ground pork	250 g
1 cup	cooked rice	250 mL
2 tbsp	finely chopped fresh parsley	25 mL
1/2 tsp	salt	2 mL
1/4 tsp	pepper	1 mL
1	can (28 oz/796 mL) sauerkraut, drained and rinsed	1
1 cup	chicken stock	250 mL

Using sharp knife, remove core from cabbage. Blanch cabbage in large pot of boiling salted water to cover for 5 to 6 minutes or until leaves are softened. Drain; rinse under cold water, carefully separating leaves. (If inner leaves are not softened, repeat blanching until leaves separate easily.) Drain on paper towels; set aside.

In heavy skillet, heat oil over medium-high heat; cook onion and garlic until softened, about 3 minutes. Add red pepper; cook until softened, about 1 minute. Transfer to large bowl and set aside.

In same skillet, cook beef with pork until browned, about 5 minutes. Drain excess fat; add meat mixture to onion mixture. Stir in rice, parsley, salt and pepper until well mixed. Set aside.

Spread sauerkraut in large heavy saucepan or Dutch oven; pour chicken stock over. Set aside.

Place about 1/4 cup (50 mL) rice mixture on each cabbage leaf; roll up, tucking in sides. Arrange rolls, seam side down, over sauerkraut. Cover and bring to boil; reduce heat and simmer for about 20 minutes or until cabbage rolls are heated through. Makes about 6 servings.

FETTUCCINE WITH SAUSAGES AND TOMATOES

Highly seasoned Italian sausage adds spice to this dish. You might like to sprinkle it with freshly grated Parmesan cheese. Serve with Marinated Vegetable Salad (recipe, p. 88).

1 lb	Italian sausage	500 g
1 tbsp	olive oil	15 mL
1	sweet green pepper, chopped	1
1	onion, chopped	1
1	can (28 oz/796 mL) tomatoes (undrained)	1
	Salt and pepper	
3/4 lb	fettuccine or linguine	375 g

Prick sausage all over. In large skillet, cover sausage with water; bring to boil. Reduce heat and simmer for 10 minutes or until cooked through. Drain and cut sausage into 1/2-inch (1 cm) thick slices.

Add oil to skillet and heat over medium heat; add sausages and brown lightly. Add green pepper and onion; cook for 5 minutes or until softened.

Pour in tomatoes and break up with fork; bring to boil. Reduce heat and simmer, stirring occasionally, for 25 minutes or until thickened. Season with salt and pepper to taste.

Meanwhile, in large pot of boiling salted water, cook fettuccine until tender but firm. Drain and toss with sauce. Makes 4 servings.

SAUTÉED SAUSAGE WITH CABBAGE AND APPLES

Prepare this easy, hearty main dish the night before. It's ready in just the time it takes to cook noodles to serve with it.

1-1/2 lb	farmer's sausage	750 g
8 cups	coarsely shredded cabbage (about half a head)	2 L
2	apples, chopped	2
1	small onion, chopped	1
1/2 tsp	nutmeg	2 mL
2 tbsp	cider vinegar	25 mL
2 tsp	granulated sugar	10 mL
Pinch	cayenne pepper	Pinch
	Salt and pepper	
1 cup	sour cream	250 mL
	Chopped fresh parsley	

Prick sausage in several places. Place in large deep skillet with enough water to just cover bottom of pan, about 1/4 cup (50 mL); bring to boil. Reduce heat to medium-low; cover and cook for 10 minutes. Uncover and increase heat to medium-high; cook sausage for about 5 minutes or until browned all over. Remove sausage and set aside.

❧ Pour off all but 1/4 cup (50 mL) pan drippings. Add cabbage, apples, onion and nutmeg to skillet; cook over medium heat, stirring occasionally, for about 10 minutes or until cabbage starts to wilt. Return sausage to pan, pushing down into cabbage; reduce heat to medium-low, cover and cook for 20 minutes, stirring often.

❧ Combine vinegar, sugar, cayenne, and salt and pepper to taste; stir until sugar dissolves. Stir into cabbage mixture; cook, uncovered, for 5 minutes. *(Recipe can be prepared to this point, cooled, covered and refrigerated for up to 24 hours. Heat through over medium-low heat before continuing.)*

❧ Reduce heat to low and stir in sour cream; heat through but do not boil. Taste and adjust seasoning. Sprinkle with parsley to serve. Makes 4 to 6 servings.

PORK AND SAUERKRAUT SKILLET SUPPER

Serve this hearty supper with mustard, mashed or baked potatoes and your favorite tossed salad.

1 tbsp	vegetable oil	15 mL
4	pork chops	4
	Salt and pepper	
1	can (14 oz/398 mL) sauerkraut	1
2	apples, cored	2
1/2 cup	apple juice	125 mL
1 tsp	caraway seeds	5 mL

❧ Drain and rinse sauerkraut; drain again. Slice apples crosswise. Add sauerkraut, apples, apple juice and caraway seeds to skillet; bring to boil. Nestle pork chops into sauerkraut mixture; add any juices accumulated on plate. Cover and simmer over low heat for 15 to 20 minutes or until pork chops are tender and no longer pink inside. Makes 4 servings.

In skillet, heat oil over medium-high heat; cook pork chops for about 2 minutes per side or until lightly browned. Season with salt and pepper to taste. Remove to plate and set aside. Pour off fat from skillet.

SPICY PATTIES

These curried beef turnovers freeze and reheat admirably, making them ideal for meals when everyone gets home
at a different time. Just heat them in a 350°F (180°C) oven for about 15 minutes or until heated through.
Serve with Marinated Vegetable Salad (recipe, p. 88).

PASTRY:

4 cups	all-purpose flour	1 L
4 tsp	baking powder	20 mL
2 tsp	curry powder	10 mL
1 tsp	salt	5 mL
1 tsp	turmeric	5 mL
1-1/3 cups	shortening	325 mL
1/2 cup	butter	125 mL
1 cup	cold water	250 mL

CURRIED BEEF FILLING:

2 tbsp	vegetable oil	25 mL
2	large onions, finely chopped	2
2	cloves garlic, minced	2
2 lb	ground beef	1 kg
1 tbsp	curry powder	15 mL
1-1/2 tsp	salt	7 mL
1-1/2 tsp	dried thyme	7 mL
1 tsp	black pepper	5 mL
Pinch	cayenne pepper	Pinch
2 cups	water	500 mL
1 cup	fresh bread crumbs	250 mL

PASTRY: In large bowl, stir together flour, baking powder, curry powder, salt and turmeric. Cut in shortening and butter until mixture resembles fine crumbs with a few large pieces. Stirring with fork, pour in water; stir to make soft dough. Gather into ball; wrap and chill for 1 hour. *(Pastry can be refrigerated for up to 5 days or frozen for up to 3 weeks.)*

❧ CURRIED BEEF FILLING: In large skillet, heat oil over medium heat; cook onions and garlic until softened, about 5 minutes. Remove onion mixture; set aside.

❧ Increase heat to high. Cook beef, stirring to break up pieces, until no longer pink, about 5 minutes. Drain off fat. Stir in onion mixture, curry powder, salt, thyme, and black and cayenne peppers; cook over medium heat for 3 minutes. Pour in water and bring to boil; reduce heat to simmer and cook for 5 to 10 minutes or until most of the water is absorbed. Stir in bread crumbs to make moist but not runny mixture. Taste and adjust seasoning. Let cool. *(Filling can be covered and frozen for up to 2 months.)*

❧ ASSEMBLY: Divide pastry in half and roll into 2 long sausage shapes. Slice each roll crosswise into 12 equal pieces.

❧ Separate filling into 24 equal mounds; roll out each piece into 6-inch (15 cm) circle. Spoon each mound into center of pastry round. Wet edges with water and fold in half, making edges meet. Using fork, press edges together; prick twice. Trim into neat half-moon shape. Place patties on ungreased baking sheets; bake in 375°F (190°C) oven for 25 to 30 minutes or until crisp and lightly browned. Makes 24 patties.

MEAT LOAF MUFFINS

Delight the family with individual little meat loaves which you can pair with baked potatoes and creamed corn.
For extra flavor, serve with a spoonful of Tomato-Apple Chutney (recipe, p. 175).

1/2 cup	chopped green onions	125 mL
1 lb	lean ground beef	500 g
1	egg	1
1	clove garlic, minced	1
2 tbsp	tomato paste	25 mL
1 tsp	dried oregano	5 mL
1/4 tsp	salt	1 mL
	Pepper	

Remove 1 tbsp (15 mL) onion; set aside. In bowl, mix together remaining onion, beef, egg, garlic, tomato paste, oregano, salt, and pepper to taste. Form into 4 balls and place into ungreased muffin cups; sprinkle with reserved onion. Bake in 425°F (220°C) oven for 15 to 20 minutes or until no longer pink inside. Makes 4 servings.

Spicy Patties

HAMBURGER STROGANOFF

This tried-and-true dish needs only one pot for its preparation. Serve with your favorite green vegetable.

1 lb	ground beef	500 g
2	onions, chopped	2
1	can (19 oz/540 mL) stewed tomatoes	1
1 tbsp	Worcestershire sauce	15 mL
2 cups	small pasta shells or macaroni (1/2 lb/250 g)	500 mL
1 cup	sour cream	250 mL
	Salt and pepper	

In large heavy saucepan or Dutch oven, cook beef and onions for 5 minutes or until meat is no longer pink, breaking up meat with wooden spoon. Pour off fat. Stir in tomatoes, 1 cup (250 mL) water and Worcestershire sauce; bring to boil.

Add pasta and reduce heat to low; cover and simmer, stirring frequently, for 20 minutes or until pasta is tender but firm. Stir in sour cream; heat through but do not boil. Season with salt and pepper to taste. Makes 4 servings.

MICROWAVE METHOD

In 12-cup (3 L) casserole, combine beef and onions; microwave, uncovered, at High for 5 minutes or until meat is no longer pink, stirring once. Pour off fat.

Stir in tomatoes, 1 cup (250 mL) water, Worcestershire sauce and pasta; mix well. Cover and microwave at High for 12 to 14 minutes or until pasta is tender but firm, stirring 3 times. Let stand for 5 minutes. Stir in sour cream; microwave at High for 2 minutes or just until heated through but not boiling. Season with salt and pepper to taste.

BEEF AND KIDNEY PIE

This Warkworth, Ontario prize-winning pie takes a little time but is worth every second.

	Pastry for 9-inch (23 cm) double-crust pie	
	FILLING:	
1	beef kidney (about 1/2 lb/250 g), trimmed	1
1 tbsp	vegetable oil	15 mL
1 lb	lean ground beef	500 g
1	onion, finely chopped	1
1/2 cup	finely chopped celery	125 mL
2	potatoes, peeled and cubed	2
1 cup	beef stock	250 mL
1/4 cup	minced fresh parsley	50 mL
1 tbsp	Worcestershire sauce	15 mL
1/2 tsp	dried sage	2 mL
1/2 tsp	salt	2 mL
1/4 tsp	pepper	1 mL
1 tbsp	all-purpose flour	15 mL
1 tbsp	butter	15 mL

	GLAZE:	
1	egg yolk	1
1 tbsp	water	15 mL

FILLING: Cut kidney into 1/2-inch (1 cm) cubes. In bowl, cover kidney with cold water; let soak for 1 hour. Drain well and pat dry.

In large skillet, heat oil over medium-high heat; brown kidney and beef, stirring frequently to break up beef. Add onion and celery; cook for 3 minutes or until softened. Drain off any fat.

Transfer meat mixture to saucepan. Add potatoes, stock, parsley, Worcestershire sauce, sage, salt and pepper; bring to boil. Cover tightly and reduce heat to low; simmer for 1 hour or until kidney is tender. Blend flour with butter; stir into meat mixture and cook, stirring, for 2 to 3 minutes or until thickened. Taste and adjust seasoning if necessary. Let cool.

On lightly floured surface, roll out half of the pastry and fit into 9-inch (23 cm) pie plate; do not trim. Spoon in filling. Roll out remaining pastry. Moisten rim of shell and cover with top pastry. Trim and flute edge.

GLAZE: Mix egg yolk with water; brush over pastry. Cut steam vents in top. Bake in 425°F (220°C) oven for 15 minutes. Reduce heat to 350°F (180°C) and bake for about 35 minutes longer or until filling steams and pastry is golden. Makes about 6 servings.

CHEESE MEAT LOAF PINWHEEL

The spinach-mushroom filling adds a company touch to a rolled beef-and-pork meat loaf.

1 lb	ground beef	500 g
1/2 lb	lean ground pork	250 g
1 cup	shredded Cheddar cheese	250 mL
1/2 cup	fine dry bread crumbs	125 mL
1	egg, beaten	1
2 tsp	Worcestershire sauce	10 mL
3/4 tsp	salt	4 mL
1/4 tsp	pepper	1 mL
	SPINACH-MUSHROOM FILLING:	
1	pkg (10 oz/300 g) spinach	1
1/4 cup	butter	50 mL
1 cup	sliced mushrooms	250 mL
1/2 cup	chopped onions	125 mL
1/2 cup	fine dry bread crumbs	125 mL
1/4 cup	chopped fresh parsley	50 mL
1	egg	1
1/2 tsp	salt	2 mL
Pinch	each pepper and nutmeg	Pinch

SPINACH-MUSHROOM FILLING: Steam spinach until wilted; refresh with cold water. Drain and squeeze out excess moisture; chop coarsely and set aside.

❧ In skillet, melt butter over medium heat; cook mushrooms and onions until onions are translucent. Transfer to bowl. Add spinach, bread crumbs, parsley, egg, salt, pepper and nutmeg; mix well.

❧ In bowl, combine beef, pork, cheese, bread crumbs, egg, Worcestershire sauce, salt and pepper; mix well. Place meat mixture between 2 sheets of waxed paper and roll into 18- × 8-inch (45 × 20 cm) rectangle. Remove top sheet. Spread spinach mixture evenly over meat, leaving 1/2-inch (1 cm) border. Roll up meat from short end. Ease into 9- × 5-inch (2 L) loaf pan. Bake in 350°F (180°C) oven for about 1 hour or until browned and meat thermometer registers 160-170°F (71-75°C). Transfer to serving platter and serve hot or cold. Makes about 6 servings.

CORNED BEEF DINNER

*For a warming winter supper, simmer a corned beef brisket with root vegetables. Serve with grainy mustard
thinned with cooking liquid.*

1	corned beef brisket (about 3 lb/1.5 kg)	1
16 cups	water	4 L
2	stalks celery, chopped	2
1	bay leaf	1
4	whole cloves	4
3	cloves garlic	3
1/2 tsp	dried thyme	2 mL
4	each carrots, potatoes, parsnips and onions	4
Half	small rutabaga	Half
Half	small cabbage	Half

Rinse brisket; place in large stock pot along with water, celery, bay leaf, cloves, garlic and thyme. Bring to boil, reduce heat and simmer, covered, just until tender, 2-1/2 to 3 hours. Skim off fat.

❦ Peel carrots, potatoes, parsnips and onions; peel rutabaga and cut into finger-size sticks. Add carrots, potatoes, parsnips, onions and rutabaga to pot; bring to gentle boil. Reduce heat to simmer; cover and cook for 10 to 15 minutes or until vegetables are tender-crisp. Cut cabbage into 4 wedges; lay over vegetables and simmer for 10 to 15 minutes or until vegetables and beef are fork tender.

❦ Remove beef and slice. Arrange in center of warm platter, with vegetables around edge. Strain about 1 cup (250 mL) cooking liquid and serve as sauce if desired. Makes 8 servings.

MEAT LOAF SANDWICHES WITH SPICY SAUCE

The old-fashioned meat loaf sandwich is making a big comeback. This meat loaf, which is great hot or cold, works especially well for sandwiches because it slices easily. If you don't need this many sandwiches, freeze the remainder for another time.

2 tbsp	vegetable oil	25 mL
1	onion, chopped	1
2	cloves garlic, chopped	2
2 lb	lean ground beef	1 kg
2	eggs	2
1-1/2 cups	fresh bread crumbs	375 mL
1/2 cup	tomato juice	125 mL
2 tbsp	chopped fresh parsley	25 mL
1 tbsp	Dijon mustard	15 mL
1 tbsp	Worcestershire sauce	15 mL
1 tsp	salt	5 mL
1/2 tsp	hot pepper sauce	2 mL
1/2 tsp	pepper	2 mL
12	large crusty Italian buns, halved	12

SPICY SAUCE:		
2 tbsp	olive oil	25 mL
1	onion, chopped	1
2	cloves garlic, minced	2
1/4 tsp	hot pepper flakes	1 mL

1	can (28 oz/796 mL) tomatoes (undrained)	1
2 tbsp	chopped hot pickled peppers (optional)	25 mL
	Salt and pepper	

In skillet, heat oil over medium heat; cook onion and garlic until tender, about 5 minutes. Meanwhile, in bowl, combine meat, eggs, bread crumbs, tomato juice, parsley, mustard, Worcestershire sauce, salt, hot pepper sauce and pepper. Mix in onion mixture.

❧ Line 9- × 5-inch (2 L) loaf pan with parchment paper or foil. Pat meat mixture into pan; cover with foil. Bake in 350°F (180°C) oven for 1 hour. Remove foil and bake for 30 minutes longer. Remove meat loaf from pan; let cool.

❧ SPICY SAUCE: Meanwhile, in deep skillet, heat oil over medium heat; cook onion, garlic and hot pepper flakes until onion is tender, about 5 minutes. Add tomatoes, breaking up with fork; cook for about 20 minutes or until thickened. Stir in hot pickled peppers (if using), and salt and pepper to taste.

❧ Arrange 1/2-inch (1 cm) slice of meat loaf on bottom halves of buns. Top with about 2 tbsp (25 mL) sauce and remaining halves of buns. Makes 12 sandwiches.

SAUTÉ OF LIVER AND ONIONS

Soaking the liver in milk before cooking removes its strong flavor and leaves it melt-in-your-mouth tender. Serve with fluffy rice and Refrigerator Slaw (recipe, p. 92).

1 lb	calves' liver	500 g
1 cup	milk	250 mL
3 tbsp	olive oil	50 mL
6	onions, thinly sliced	6
2 tsp	red wine vinegar	10 mL
	Salt and pepper	

Trim and cut liver into strips 3 inches (8 cm) long and 1/2 inch (1 cm) wide. In bowl, pour milk over liver; cover and refrigerate for 30 minutes.

❧ Meanwhile, in large skillet, heat 2 tbsp (25 mL) of the oil over medium-low heat; cook onions, stirring occasionally, for 30 minutes or until lightly golden and very soft. With slotted spoon, remove onions and set aside. Wipe out skillet.

❧ Drain liver and discard milk; pat liver dry. Add remaining oil to skillet and heat over medium-high heat; cook liver, stirring constantly, for about 3 minutes or until browned outside but still pink inside. Return onions to skillet along with vinegar; cook until heated through. Season with salt and pepper to taste. Makes 4 servings.

PLUMP PEROGIES

Comfort food that warms the soul as well as the body is one of today's fashionable trends. But to many of us, there's nothing new about the most comfy of all foods — satisfyingly plump, filled dumplings. Whether you know them as perogies, pyrohy *or* varenyky, *they are a real Canadian tradition, especially on the Prairies.*

2 tbsp	butter	25 mL
1	onion, sliced	1
	Sour cream	
	DOUGH:	
3 cups	all-purpose flour	750 mL
1-1/2 tsp	salt	7 mL
1	egg	1
3/4 cup	(approx) water	175 mL
4 tsp	vegetable oil	20 mL
	FILLING:	
1 tbsp	butter	15 mL
1/3 cup	finely chopped onion	75 mL
1 cup	cold mashed potatoes	250 mL
3/4 cup	shredded Cheddar cheese	175 mL
1/2 tsp	salt	2 mL
1/4 tsp	pepper	1 mL

> You can cover the perogies with a damp towel and refrigerate them for up to 8 hours before cooking. Freeze uncooked perogies with the potato filling and the mushroom filling on baking sheets, then pack them in freezer bags and freeze for up to 1 month. Do not thaw them before cooking.

DOUGH: In bowl, combine flour with salt. Beat together egg, water and oil; stir into flour mixture to make soft but not sticky dough that holds together in ball. If necessary, add 1 tbsp (15 mL) more water at a time, being careful not to make dough sticky.

❧ Turn out dough onto lightly floured surface; knead about 10 times or just until smooth. Halve dough; cover with plastic wrap or damp cloth. Let rest for 20 minutes.

❧ FILLING: Meanwhile, in skillet, heat butter over medium heat; cook onion for 3 to 5 minutes or until tender. Transfer to bowl and mix in potatoes, cheese, salt and pepper.

❧ Working with one portion of dough at a time and keeping remaining dough covered, roll out on lightly floured surface to about 1/16-inch (1.5 mm) thickness. Using 3-inch (8 cm) round cutter, cut dough into rounds.

❧ Place 1 tsp (5 mL) filling on each round. Lightly moisten edge of one half of dough with water; pinch edges together to seal and crimp attractively. Place on cloth; cover with damp cloth to prevent drying out. Repeat with remaining portion of dough.

❧ In large pot of boiling salted water, cook perogies, in batches, for 1-1/2 to 2 minutes or until they float to top, stirring gently to prevent perogies from sticking together or to bottom of pot. With slotted spoon, remove to colander to drain.

❧ In large heavy skillet, melt butter over medium heat; cook onion for about 5 minutes or until golden. Add perogies and toss to coat and warm through. Serve with sour cream. Makes about 30 perogies.

VARIATIONS

COTTAGE CHEESE: Combine 1 cup (250 mL) pressed cottage cheese, 1 beaten egg, 1/2 tsp (2 mL) salt, 1/4 tsp (1 mL) pepper and 1 tbsp (15 mL) chopped green onion.

MUSHROOM: In skillet, melt 2 tbsp (25 mL) butter over medium heat; cook 3 cups (750 mL) chopped mushrooms and 1/3 cup (75 mL) finely chopped onion for 7 to 9 minutes or until moisture has evaporated. Remove from heat; stir in 1 egg yolk and 1 tbsp (15 mL) chopped fresh dill. Season with salt and pepper to taste.

MEAL IN A POTATO

Three of the four food groups are stuffed into this tasty potato entrée. Complete the meal with a cucumber salad and whole wheat rolls.

4	baking potatoes (2 lb/1 kg total)	4
1 cup	cottage cheese	250 mL
1/2 cup	chopped celery	125 mL
1/4 cup	chopped green onion	50 mL
3 tbsp	chopped fresh dill or parsley	50 mL
1	can (7.5 oz/213 g) red salmon, drained	1

Pierce potatoes in several places; bake in 400°F (200°C) oven for about 1 hour or until tender. Cut thin slice from top of each potato; scoop out pulp, leaving 1/4-inch (5 mm) thick shell.

❦ In bowl, mash potato; mix in cheese, celery, onion and 2 tbsp (25 mL) of the dill. Gently fold in salmon; season with salt and pepper to taste. Spoon into potato shells, mounding tops. *(Recipe can be prepared to this point, covered and refrigerated for up to 1 day.)* On baking sheet, bake stuffed potatoes in 400°F (200°C) oven for 15 to 25 minutes

or until heated through. Sprinkle with remaining dill. Makes 4 servings.

MICROWAVE METHOD

Pierce potatoes in several places and arrange in circle on paper towel; microwave at High for 10 to 15 minutes.

❦ Scoop out potatoes and stuff following conventional method. Arrange in circle on microwaveable plate; microwave at Medium (50%) for 8 minutes or until heated through, rotating once.

QUICK AND COMFY MACARONI AND CHEESE

With this quick and easy recipe, you don't have to make the cheese sauce separately. Add diced sweet red pepper or peas, if desired, and serve with sliced tomatoes and cucumbers.

2 cups	macaroni (1/2 lb/250 g)	500 mL
2 cups	shredded mozzarella or Cheddar cheese	500 mL
1-1/2 cups	sour cream or plain yogurt	375 mL
1-1/3 cups	diced ham (1/2 lb/250 g)	325 mL
1 cup	cottage or ricotta cheese	250 mL
1	egg, lightly beaten	1
1/4 tsp	each salt and pepper	1 mL

In large pot of boiling salted water, cook macaroni until tender but firm; drain.

❦ In large bowl, combine 1-1/2 cups (375 mL) of the mozzarella, sour cream, ham, cottage cheese, egg, salt and pepper. Add macaroni and mix well.

❦ Pour mixture into greased 8-inch (2 L) square baking dish; sprinkle with remaining mozzarella. Bake, uncovered, in 350°F (180°C) oven for 30 minutes or until bubbly. (Alternatively, pour mixture into 12-cup (3 L) microwaveable and ovenproof casserole; cover with waxed paper and microwave at Medium (50%) for 10 to 12 minutes or until heated through, stirring twice. Sprinkle with remaining mozzarella.) Broil for 2 minutes or until lightly golden. Makes 4 servings.

EASY TOMATO SAUCE

Nothing could be simpler than this tomato and herb sauce. Cook 3/4 lb (375 g) penne or spaghetti to serve with this sauce and pass 1/2 cup (125 mL) freshly grated Parmesan cheese separately.

2 tbsp	vegetable oil or butter	25 mL
1	large onion, chopped	1
2	cloves garlic, minced	2
1/4 cup	finely chopped carrot	50 mL
1	can (28 oz/796 mL) tomatoes	1
1	bay leaf	1
1/2 tsp	each dried basil and oregano	2 mL
1/4 tsp	granulated sugar	1 mL

	Salt and pepper	
1/4 cup	minced fresh parsley	50 mL

In large skillet, heat oil over medium heat; cook onion, garlic and carrot until softened, about 5 minutes.

❦ Add tomatoes, mashing with fork into small chunks. Stir in bay leaf, basil, oregano and sugar. Bring to boil; reduce heat and simmer, uncovered, for 20 to 30 minutes or until thickened. Season with salt and pepper to taste. Stir in parsley. Remove bay leaf. Makes 4 servings.

RATATOUILLE LASAGNA

You'll never miss the meat in this colorful, vegetable-packed dish.

2 tbsp	olive oil	25 mL
2	onions, minced	2
3	cloves garlic, minced	3
1/4 tsp	hot pepper flakes	1 mL
2	zucchini, diced	2
1	eggplant, diced (about 1 lb/500 g)	1
2	sweet red peppers, diced	2
1	can (28 oz/796 mL) plum tomatoes	1
1	bay leaf	1
1 tsp	salt	5 mL
1/2 tsp	pepper	2 mL
1/2 tsp	dried thyme	2 mL
3/4 lb	lasagna noodles	375 g
3 cups	shredded mozzarella cheese (about 12 oz/375 g)	750 mL
1 cup	freshly grated Parmesan cheese	250 mL
2 tbsp	butter	25 mL

In Dutch oven, heat oil over medium heat; cook onions, garlic and hot pepper flakes, stirring, for about 5 minutes or until fragrant. Add zucchini, eggplant, sweet peppers and tomatoes, breaking up tomatoes with spoon. Add bay leaf, salt, pepper and thyme; bring to boil. Reduce heat to medium-low and simmer, stirring occasionally, for about 30 minutes or until vegetables are tender and sauce is thickened. Discard bay leaf.

❦ Cook noodles (see sidebar, p. 50). Arrange one-third of the noodles in single layer in greased 13- × 9-inch (3 L) baking dish. Cover with one-third of the sauce; sprinkle with one-third of the mozzarella and one-third of the Parmesan. Repeat layers twice. Dot with butter. Bake in 375°F (190°C) oven for 30 minutes or until bubbling. Let stand for 10 minutes. Makes 8 servings.

LASAGNA IN THE MICROWAVE

❦ Lasagna dishes can be cooked in the microwave with a few small changes. Increase amount of noodles to 1 lb (500 g), and boil noodles about 2 minutes longer. Assemble lasagna dish in two 8-inch (2 L) baking dishes. Cover with waxed paper and microwave at High for 5 minutes, then Medium (50%) for 10 minutes or until heated through, rotating once. Let stand, covered, for 5 minutes. Brown under conventional broiler for 2 minutes, if desired.

BASIC PIZZA DOUGH

This pizza dough uses the kind of yeast that is dissolved in sweet warm water before it's mixed with remaining ingredients. It makes enough for two large pizzas.

1 tsp	granulated sugar	5 mL
1 cup	warm water	250 mL
1	pkg active dry yeast (or 1 tbsp/15 mL)	1
2 tbsp	vegetable or olive oil	25 mL
3 cups	(approx) all-purpose flour	750 mL
1 tsp	salt	5 mL

In large bowl, dissolve sugar in warm water. Sprinkle in yeast; let stand for 10 minutes or until foamy. Stir in oil.

❦ Combine flour with salt; stir about half into yeast mixture. Mix in enough of the remaining flour until dough can be gathered into slightly sticky ball. On lightly floured surface, knead dough for about 5 minutes or until smooth and elastic.

❦ Cut dough in half; cover and let rest for 10 minutes. On lightly floured surface, roll out each half into 12-inch (30 cm) circle.

❦ Transfer pizza rounds to two cornmeal-dusted or lightly greased 12-inch (30 cm) pizza pans or baking sheets. With fingers, carefully stretch and pull dough to fit pans; let rise for 15 minutes. For slightly thicker crust, let dough rise for about 30 minutes. Makes two 12-inch (30 cm) pizza rounds.

VARIATIONS

WHOLE WHEAT PIZZA DOUGH: Use 1-1/2 cups (375 mL) all-purpose flour and 1 cup (250 mL) whole wheat flour.

FOOD PROCESSOR PIZZA DOUGH: Dissolve yeast as directed in above recipe; add oil. In food processor fitted with metal blade, combine 2-1/2 cups (625 mL) of the flour with salt. With motor running, gradually pour in yeast mixture and process just until dough sticks together; don't overprocess.

❦ On lightly floured surface, knead dough for 1 minute, adding just enough of the remaining flour to prevent sticking. Continue with recipe.

PIZZA TOPPINGS

Pizza toppings can be tried-and-true family favorites — meatballs, ham, tomato sauce, hot peppers, anchovies, bacon bits, sausage slices, mushrooms, green peppers and double mozzarella — or downright trendy with goat cheese and sun-dried tomatoes. When buying mozzarella, partly skim will save calories but it isn't as creamy or stretchy as regular mozzarella. If topping with Parmesan, look for the real thing — a block of Parmigiano-Reggiano — and grate your own as you need it. Or, replace Parmesan's intense flavor with a freshly grated romano or asiago.

TRY THESE TASTY COMBINATIONS:

❦ Thin layer of tomato sauce topped with thinly sliced tomatoes, mushrooms and onions, sprinkled with oregano and mozzarella.

❦ Slices of eggplant, red onions and zucchini, brushed with olive oil, then grilled and arranged on base. Sprinkle with fresh basil, mozzarella and a sprinkle of Parmesan, too, for oomph.

❦ Ratatouille with black olives and Parmesan.

❦ Pesto with thinly sliced tomatoes and creamy goat cheese.

❦ Thinly sliced red onions and tomatoes. Top with crumbled feta cheese and some mozzarella, then pitted black olives and oregano.

❦ Roasted red and yellow peppers, peeled and cut into strips, then arranged on pizza base and topped with mozzarella and Parmesan.

❦ Herbed cream cheese with dill and shrimps.

❦ Generous amounts of thinly sliced onions, sautéed in butter until golden, with a flourish of thyme and shredded Cheddar.

❦ Lots of mushrooms, sliced and sautéed in butter or olive oil, then sprinkled with rosemary, some slivered red pepper and Swiss cheese.

❦ Thinly sliced tomatoes and onions with a hint of slivered jalapeño pepper and chili powder. Top with Monterey Jack cheese.

CHEESY CHEESE AND PEPPERONI PIZZA

You can use as many toppings as you like on this classic pizza. For our photo, we added sliced tomatoes, chopped green and yellow peppers, chopped black or green olives, a few hot peppers, sliced artichoke hearts and sliced mushrooms.

1	can (14 oz/398 mL) tomato sauce	1
1 tsp	each crumbled oregano and basil	5 mL
2	cloves garlic, minced	2
2	rounds Pizza Dough (recipe, p. 64)	2
3 cups	shredded mozzarella cheese	750 mL
1 cup	thinly sliced pepperoni	250 mL

Combine tomato sauce, oregano, basil and garlic; mix well. Pour half over each pizza round and spread evenly. Sprinkle with cheese; arrange pepperoni on top.

☙ Bake on lowest rack in 450°F (230°C) oven for 16 to 18 minutes or until crust is golden brown and cheese is bubbly. Makes two 12-inch (30 cm) pizzas.

QUICK CHUNKY TOMATO PIZZA

Not a typical pizza crust, this one is an easy quick bread flavored with rosemary and cornmeal.

2 cups	all-purpose flour	500 mL
1 cup	whole wheat flour	250 mL
1/2 cup	cornmeal	125 mL
1 tbsp	chopped fresh rosemary (or 1/2 tsp/2 mL dried)	15 mL
1 tbsp	granulated sugar	15 mL
2 tsp	baking powder	10 mL
1 tsp	baking soda	5 mL
1 tsp	salt	5 mL
1-2/3 cups	plain yogurt	400 mL
1/3 cup	olive oil	75 mL
	TOPPING:	
4	tomatoes	4
1/2 cup	chopped fresh basil	125 mL
2	cloves garlic, minced	2
1 tsp	salt	5 mL
1/4 tsp	pepper	1 mL
Pinch	hot pepper flakes	Pinch

1	jar (4 oz/110 g) marinated artichokes	1
1/2 cup	black olives	125 mL
2 cups	shredded mozzarella cheese	500 mL
1/2 cup	freshly grated Parmesan cheese	125 mL

In large bowl, stir together all-purpose and whole wheat flours, cornmeal, rosemary, sugar, baking powder, baking soda and salt. Combine yogurt with oil; pour over flour mixture, stirring with fork. On lightly floured surface, knead dough lightly into ball. Cover and let stand while preparing topping.

❧ TOPPING: Core, halve and seed tomatoes; chop coarsely and drain well in colander. Pat dry on paper towels. In bowl, combine tomatoes, basil, garlic, salt, pepper and hot pepper flakes. Drain and halve artichokes. Halve and pit olives.

❧ Press dough evenly into greased 15- × 10-inch (2 L) jelly roll pan. Sprinkle on half of the mozzarella. Top with tomato mixture, artichokes, olives, remaining mozzarella and Parmesan.

❧ Bake in 400°F (200°C) oven for 20 to 30 minutes or until cheese is lightly browned and bottom of crust is golden. Makes 6 to 8 servings.

PARMESAN CHICKEN

Bake potatoes and Gilded Onions (recipe, p. 90) alongside and serve with a broccoli salad.

3/4 cup	freshly grated Parmesan cheese	175 mL
1/2 cup	fresh bread crumbs	125 mL
1-1/2 tsp	finely chopped fresh thyme (or 1/2 tsp/2 mL dried)	7 mL
1/3 cup	Dijon mustard	75 mL
2 tbsp	lemon juice	25 mL
3 lb	chicken pieces	1.5 kg

In sturdy plastic bag, combine cheese, bread crumbs and thyme. Stir together mustard and lemon juice; brush over chicken. Add chicken to bag and shake to coat.

❧ Place chicken, skin side up, on greased foil-lined baking sheet. *(Chicken can be prepared to this point, covered and refrigerated for up to 8 hours.)* Bake in 375°F (190°C) oven for about 45 minutes or until golden brown, chicken is no longer pink inside, and juices run clear when chicken is pierced. Makes about 4 servings.

❧

CHICKEN WITH ROSEMARY AND LEMON

Although this recipe seems very simple, the combined flavors are sophisticated and intriguing. For an elegant dinner, use chicken breasts; for a budget meal, buy inexpensive chicken legs.

6	chicken breasts	6
1/3 cup	lemon juice	75 mL
2 tbsp	chopped fresh rosemary (or 1 tsp/5 mL dried)	25 mL
2 tbsp	olive oil	25 mL
2 tbsp	Dijon mustard	25 mL
1/2 tsp	each salt and pepper	2 mL
1/2 tsp	hot pepper sauce	2 mL

1/4 tsp	hot pepper flakes	1 mL
2	cloves garlic, minced	2

Pat chicken dry. Place in shallow glass bowl or plastic bag. Whisk together lemon juice, rosemary, oil, mustard, salt, pepper, hot pepper sauce, hot pepper flakes and garlic; pour over chicken, turning to coat all pieces. Cover bowl or seal bag; marinate in the refrigerator for up to 24 hours.

❧ Arrange chicken pieces, skin side up, on foil-lined baking sheet. Bake in 375°F (190°C) oven for 35 to 40 minutes or until chicken is no longer pink inside. Makes 4 to 6 servings.

❧

CRISPY OVEN-FRIED CHICKEN

A crunchy sesame seed coating keeps chicken thighs juicy. For a summer picnic, pack in a hamper with New Potato Salad (recipe, p. 86) and Annie's Cucumber Salad (recipe, p. 91).

1	egg	1
1/2 cup	milk	125 mL
1/2 cup	all-purpose flour	125 mL
2 tbsp	sesame seeds	25 mL
1 tbsp	baking powder	15 mL
1 tbsp	paprika	15 mL
1 tsp	salt	5 mL

3 lb	chicken thighs	1.5 kg
1/4 cup	butter, melted	50 mL

In bowl, whisk together egg and milk. In large bag, shake together flour, sesame seeds, baking powder, paprika and salt. Dip chicken pieces, one at a time, into egg mixture; add to bag and shake to coat.

❧ Place on foil-lined baking sheet; drizzle with butter. Bake in 350°F (180°C) oven for 1 hour or until crispy outside and juices run clear when chicken is pierced with fork. Makes 6 servings.

DILL CHICKEN BREASTS

This delicious chicken recipe can easily be doubled.

2	boneless skinless chicken breasts	2
1 tbsp	all-purpose flour	15 mL
Pinch	(approx) each salt and pepper	Pinch
1 tsp	butter	5 mL
1 tsp	vegetable oil	5 mL
1/4 cup	white wine or chicken stock	50 mL
1/3 cup	whipping cream	75 mL
1 tbsp	chopped fresh dill	15 mL
2 tsp	chopped fresh chives or green onion	10 mL
1/2 tsp	lemon juice	2 mL
	GARNISH:	
	Lemon slices	
	Dill sprigs	

Dredge chicken breasts lightly in flour; season with pinch each of salt and pepper.

❦ In skillet, heat butter with oil over medium-high heat; cook chicken, turning once, for about 6 minutes or until golden brown and no longer pink inside. Remove from pan and keep warm.

❦ Pour off all fat from pan. Pour in wine and bring to boil over high heat; cook, stirring to scrape up any brown bits in pan, for about 1 minute or until reduced and syrupy. Add cream; boil for about 1 minute or until thick enough to coat spoon. Stir in dill, chives, lemon juice, and salt and pepper to taste.

❦ Stir any accumulated juices from chicken back into pan; pour sauce over chicken. Garnish with lemon slices and dill. Makes 2 servings.

CHICKEN BREASTS WITH HONEY AND THYME

Marinated chicken bakes to juicy tenderness with a sweet hot glaze. Sugar snap peas, asparagus or fiddleheads both look and taste right with the orange and oriental flavors of the glaze. Cook up a pot of rice, too.

8	chicken breasts (about 3 1/4 lb/1.75 kg total)	8
1/2 cup	orange juice	125 mL
2 tbsp	olive oil	25 mL
1 tsp	grated orange rind	5 mL
1/4 tsp	hot pepper flakes	1 mL
1/4 tsp	pepper	1 mL
1/4 tsp	dried thyme	1 mL
	GLAZE:	
1/2 cup	liquid honey	125 mL
2 tbsp	frozen orange juice concentrate, thawed	25 mL
1 tbsp	soy sauce	15 mL
1 tbsp	Dijon mustard	15 mL
1/2 tsp	dried thyme	2 mL
1/2 tsp	pepper	2 mL

1/2 tsp	hot pepper sauce	2 mL
1/4 tsp	dried rosemary (or 2 tsp/10 mL fresh)	1 mL

Pat chicken dry. In large glass bowl, combine orange juice, oil, orange rind, hot pepper flakes, pepper and thyme; add chicken and turn to coat. Cover and marinate for up to 8 hours in refrigerator.

❦ GLAZE: In bowl, combine honey, orange juice concentrate, soy sauce, mustard, thyme, pepper, hot pepper sauce and rosemary.

❦ Remove chicken from marinade; pat dry. Arrange chicken, skin side up, on foil-lined baking sheet; brush with half of the glaze. Bake in 375°F (190°C) oven for 15 minutes; brush with remaining glaze. Bake for 15 to 25 minutes longer or until chicken is no longer pink inside and skin is golden. Makes 8 servings.

Chicken Breasts with Honey and Thyme

SAUCY COD

This easy fish casserole zings with the flavors of the Mediterranean—tomatoes, black olives, oregano and feta cheese.
Serve with tossed greens and rice or crusty bread to mop up the delicious juices.

1 lb	cod fillets, thawed	500 g
3 tbsp	(approx) all-purpose flour	50 mL
2 tbsp	olive oil	25 mL
1 cup	crumbled feta cheese (about 1/4 lb/125 g)	250 mL
1	onion, chopped	1
3	cloves garlic, minced	3
1	sweet green pepper, chopped	1
1	can (19 oz/540 mL) tomatoes (undrained)	1
1/2 cup	pitted black olives	125 mL
1/2 tsp	dried oregano	2 mL
Pinch	each hot pepper flakes and granulated sugar	Pinch
2 tbsp	minced fresh parsley	25 mL
	Salt and pepper	

Cut cod into serving-size portions; pat dry. Dredge lightly in flour.

In large skillet, heat half of the oil over medium-high heat; brown cod lightly on both sides. Arrange cod in 8-inch (2 L) square baking dish; sprinkle with feta.

Pour remaining oil into skillet; cook onion, garlic and green pepper, stirring, until softened, about 4 minutes. Add tomatoes, crushing with fork; stir in olives, oregano, hot pepper flakes and sugar. Bring to boil; reduce heat to medium-low and simmer, stirring often, until thickened, about 10 minutes.

Add parsley; season with salt and pepper to taste. Spoon over fish. *(Dish can be prepared to this point, cooled, covered and refrigerated for up to 8 hours. Add 5 minutes to baking time.)* Bake, uncovered, in 375°F (190°C) oven for about 15 minutes or until bubbling. Makes 4 servings.

ACADIAN COD CAKES

These hearty fish and potato cakes are delicious for supper or lunch. Serve with a dollop of
Classic Chili Sauce (recipe, p. 174).

3/4 lb	boneless salt cod	375 g
6	large potatoes, peeled	6
1/4 cup	butter or lard	50 mL
2 cups	finely chopped onions	500 mL
2	eggs, beaten	2
	Salt and pepper	
2 tbsp	all-purpose flour	25 mL

In large bowl, soak cod in cold water for 12 hours in refrigerator, changing water 3 times. Drain and transfer to saucepan. Pour in enough water to cover cod; bring to boil. Reduce heat to medium-low; simmer, covered, for 10 minutes or until cod flakes easily when tested with fork. Drain and flake cod with fork, discarding any bones.

Meanwhile, in saucepan of boiling salted water, cook potatoes until tender, 20 to 25 minutes. Drain and return potatoes to saucepan; heat for a few seconds to dry. Remove from heat, rice or mash finely to make about 4 cups (1 L); transfer to large bowl.

In skillet, melt half of the butter over medium heat; cook onions, stirring, until softened, about 5 minutes. Add to potatoes along with cod and eggs; mix to combine. Season with salt and pepper to taste.

Form into 12 patties; dredge in flour, gently shaking off excess. *(Cod can be prepared to this point, placed on rack on baking sheet, covered and refrigerated for up to 8 hours.)*

In large skillet, melt half of the remaining butter over medium-high heat; fry cakes, in batches, until golden brown on both sides, about 6 minutes, adding butter as needed. Makes 6 servings.

BAKED STUFFED COD

We've simplified a traditional Newfoundland recipe for whole baked cod by using 2 equal-size fillets,
each about 1/2 inch (1 cm) thick.

2	cod fillets (each about 3/4 lb/375 g)	2
2 tbsp	butter, melted	25 mL
	Salt and pepper	
	SAVORY DRESSING:	
2 tbsp	butter	25 mL
1	onion, minced	1
1	small carrot, diced	1
2 tsp	dried savory	10 mL
1/2 tsp	salt	2 mL
1/4 tsp	pepper	1 mL
1-1/2 cups	coarse slightly dry bread crumbs	375 mL

SAVORY DRESSING: In small skillet, melt butter over medium heat; cook onion and carrot until softened, about 5 minutes. Stir in savory, salt and pepper; cook for 2 minutes. Remove from heat; stir in bread crumbs.

❧ Place one fillet in greased shallow ovenproof dish. Top evenly with dressing. Place remaining fillet over top. Drizzle with butter; season with salt and pepper to taste. Bake, uncovered, in 400°F (200°C) oven for 15 to 20 minutes or until fish flakes easily when tested with fork. Makes 4 to 6 servings.

LAMB AND VEGETABLE BROIL

Crusty potatoes, tender tomatoes and juicy pink lamb lightly brushed with mustard make a delightfully simple and
tasty meal. For our cover, we garnished the platter with red peppers, zucchini and spring onions.

4	potatoes, cut in wedges	4
3 tbsp	butter, melted	50 mL
	Salt and pepper	
8	loin (or 4 shoulder) lamb chops	8
2	tomatoes, halved	2
2 tbsp	Dijon mustard	25 mL
1/2 tsp	dried thyme or rosemary	2 mL

In saucepan of boiling water, cook potatoes for about 10 minutes or until tender; drain and toss with 2 tbsp (25 mL) of the butter. Season with salt and pepper to taste. Arrange in single layer on greased jelly roll pan; broil 4 inches (10 cm) from heat for 5 minutes.

❧ Meanwhile, trim excess fat from lamb chops; slash edges in several places. Add to pan along with tomatoes. Brush remaining melted butter over tomatoes; broil for 4 minutes.

❧ Mix together mustard and thyme. Turn lamb chops over; spread with mustard mixture. Broil for about 4 minutes longer or until chops are lightly browned yet still pink inside and potatoes are golden. Season with salt and pepper to taste. Makes 4 servings.

SIMMERED LAMB WITH WINTER VEGETABLES

Lamb simmered to perfection with leeks is delicious served with a fresh herb sauce.

2 lb	boneless lamb shoulder, trimmed	1 kg
2 tbsp	olive oil	25 mL
2	onions, sliced	2
2 cups	dry white wine	500 mL
1 cup	chicken stock	250 mL
2	cloves garlic, minced	2
2	bay leaves	2
1 tbsp	finely grated orange rind	15 mL
1/2 tsp	fennel seeds	2 mL
1/2 tsp	dried rosemary	2 mL
4	leeks (white parts only)	4
3	white turnips	3
5	large carrots	5
	Salt and pepper	
	Fresh Herb Sauce (recipe follows)	

Cut lamb into 2-inch (5 cm) cubes, trimming fat; pat dry with paper towels. In large saucepan or Dutch oven, heat oil over medium-high heat; cook lamb, in batches, until well browned all over. Remove to plate.

❦ Add onions to saucepan. Reduce heat to medium and cook, stirring constantly, for 3 to 4 minutes or just until softened. Pour in wine and chicken stock, stirring to scrape up any brown bits from bottom of pan. Return lamb to pan. Add garlic, bay leaves, orange rind, fennel seeds and rosemary. Reduce heat to low and simmer, covered, for 1 hour.

❦ Meanwhile, trim roots from leeks. Make 6 to 8 lengthwise cuts on each leek to within 1 inch (2.5 cm) of root end without cutting through end. Separate leaves enough to thoroughly wash while keeping leek whole. Peel and quarter turnips; cut carrots into 2-inch (5 cm) lengths.

❦ Add leeks, turnips and carrots to pan. Simmer, covered, for 45 minutes or until lamb and vegetables are tender. Using slotted spoon, transfer lamb and vegetables to heated platter; cover and keep warm.

❦ Remove bay leaves from liquid. Skim off any fat; cook liquid over high heat for 5 to 10 minutes or until it has thickened slightly. Add salt and pepper to taste. Pour over lamb and vegetables. Serve with Fresh Herb Sauce. Makes 4 to 6 servings.

FRESH HERB SAUCE:		
1/3 cup	fresh parsley leaves	75 mL
1/4 cup	fresh mint leaves	50 mL
1/4 cup	chopped fresh chives or green onions	50 mL
1/3 cup	olive oil	75 mL
2 tbsp	white wine vinegar	25 mL

In blender, purée parsley, mint, chives, oil and vinegar. Makes about 3/4 cup (175 mL).

PEPPERED LAMB CHOPS

This recipe can easily be doubled for four.

4	lamb chops (about 3/4 lb/375 kg total)	4
2 tbsp	soy sauce	25 mL
1 tbsp	olive oil	15 mL
1 tbsp	red wine vinegar	15 mL
2 tsp	coarsely crushed black peppercorns	10 mL
1 tsp	Dijon mustard	5 mL
1/4 tsp	dried thyme	1 mL
1	clove garlic, minced	1
	Salt	

Simmered Lamb with Winter Vegetables

Trim all but 1/4-inch (5 mm) thickness of fat from chops; nick fat at 1/2-inch (1 cm) intervals.

❦ In shallow glass dish, combine soy sauce, oil, vinegar, peppercorns, mustard, thyme and garlic; add chops, turning to coat all over. Cover and marinate at room temperature for up to 30 minutes or in refrigerator for up to 12 hours. *(If refrigerated, bring back to room temperature before proceeding with recipe.)*

❦ Transfer chops to broiler rack, reserving any marinade; broil about 4 inches (10 cm) from heat until crisp and brown, about 3 minutes. Turn, brushing with remaining marinade; broil about 3 minutes longer or until pink and juicy inside but crisp on outside. Season with salt to taste. Makes 2 servings.

OVER THE COALS

Barbecuing is a warm-weather way of life. On weeknights, fill the grill with burgers or wings tangy with lemon. And when the weekend comes, welcome the gang with ribs lavished with honey and mustard, or butterflied leg of lamb redolent with ginger and mint. Included here are many ways to bring out new flavors with this old way of cooking.

MAPLE SYRUP-GLAZED PEAMEAL BACON DINNER

Grill sweet potatoes, bacon and a packet of apple slices for an easy meal done on the barbecue.

4	sweet potatoes or yams (unpeeled) (about 1-3/4 lb/875 g total)	4
1-1/2 lb	peameal bacon	750 g
2	apples (unpeeled)	2
1/3 cup	maple syrup	75 mL
2 tsp	Dijon mustard	10 mL
Pinch	cloves	Pinch

Prick potatoes and place on greased grill over medium-hot coals or medium setting; cook for 25 minutes, turning occasionally.

❦ Meanwhile, cut bacon into 3/4-inch (2 cm) thick slices. Core apples and cut into eighths. Combine maple syrup, mustard and cloves. Place apples on large buttered square of foil; drizzle with 2 tbsp (25 mL) of the maple syrup mixture. Seal packet and set aside.

❦ Place bacon slices on grill and cook for 10 minutes. Turn and brush with some of the maple syrup mixture. Add apple packet to grill; cook for about 10 minutes longer or until apples and potatoes are tender. Slash each potato just enough to drizzle in 1 tsp (5 mL) maple syrup mixture. Makes 4 servings.

GINGER, MINT AND SPICED LEG OF LAMB

Yogurt is a great meat tenderizer and, combined with mint, gingerroot and spices, provides a marinade worthy of butterflied leg of lamb. Serve with rice and Tomato-Apple Chutney (recipe, p. 175).

1	butterflied leg of lamb (about 3-1/2 lb/1.6 kg)	1
1	small onion, minced	1
2	cloves garlic, minced	2
2 tbsp	minced fresh mint (or 2 tsp/10 mL dried)	25 mL
2 tbsp	vegetable oil	25 mL
1 tsp	minced gingerroot	5 mL
1 tsp	cumin	5 mL
1/2 tsp	each ground coriander, turmeric, chili powder and pepper	2 mL
1 cup	plain yogurt	250 mL
	Salt	

Remove membrane and all but 1/4-inch (5 mm) thickness fat from lamb; wipe and set aside.

❦ In shallow bowl large enough to hold lamb, blend together onion, garlic, mint, oil, ginger, cumin, coriander, turmeric, chili powder and pepper; stir in yogurt. Add lamb, turning to coat all over; cover and marinate in refrigerator for at least 8 or up to 24 hours.

❦ Place on greased grill or in grill basket, over medium-hot coals or at medium-high setting; cover and grill, brushing with any remaining marinade, for 12 to 15 minutes per side or until meat thermometer registers 140°F (60°C) for rare or 160°F (70°C) for medium. Season with salt to taste. Let stand for 10 minutes before carving. Makes 6 to 8 servings.

Maple Syrup-Glazed Peameal Bacon Dinner

LEMONADE CHICKEN WINGS

Incredibly easy to make and so tasty, this marinade is perfect for brushing over wings and other cuts of chicken, too.

3 lb	chicken wings	1.5 kg
	LEMONADE MARINADE:	
1	can (12-1/2 oz/355 mL) frozen lemonade concentrate, thawed	1
1/2 cup	soy sauce	125 mL
3	cloves garlic, minced	3

Remove tips from wings and reserve for stock. Separate wings at joint; place in heavy plastic bag and set in shallow dish.

❧ LEMONADE MARINADE: In bowl, combine lemonade concentrate, soy sauce and garlic. Pour over wings in plastic bag; press air out of bag and secure with twist tie. Marinate for at least 4 or up to 24 hours in refrigerator.

❧ Remove wings from marinade, reserving marinade. Place wings on lightly greased grill over medium-hot coals or at medium setting; grill, turning occasionally, for 10 minutes. Baste wings with reserved marinade; grill, basting often, for 5 to 10 minutes or until browned and no longer pink inside. Makes about 4 servings.

LEMON AND MINT CHICKEN LEGS

A buttermilk marinade keeps the chicken moist and succulent.

1-1/2 cups	buttermilk	375 mL
3 tbsp	lemon juice	50 mL
1/2 tsp	pepper	2 mL
4	chicken legs, thighs attached	4
1/3 cup	mint leaves, lightly crushed	75 mL
	Lemon slices	
	Fresh mint sprigs	

In heavy plastic bag, combine buttermilk, lemon juice and pepper; add chicken and mint leaves. Tie bag closed, pressing out as much air as possible. Refrigerate for at least 2 hours or up to 8 hours, turning bag occasionally.

❧ Remove chicken from buttermilk mixture, scraping off excess. Place on greased grill over medium-hot coals or medium-high setting; cover and cook for 15 minutes. Turn chicken over; top each piece with 2 or 3 lemon slices and mint sprigs. Cook for 15 to 20 minutes longer or until juices run clear when chicken is pierced. Serve garnished with more lemon and mint. Makes 4 servings.

BEEF AND HORSERADISH BURGERS

Serve these zesty patties with mayonnaise and marinated onions.

1	egg	1
1/3 cup	fresh bread crumbs	75 mL
1/3 cup	minced green onion	75 mL
1/4 cup	minced fresh parsley	50 mL
2 tbsp	horseradish	25 mL
2 tbsp	cold water	25 mL
2 tsp	Dijon mustard	10 mL
1/2 tsp	salt	2 mL
1/4 tsp	pepper	1 mL
1 lb	ground beef	500 g
4	English muffins, split and toasted	4

In large bowl, beat egg lightly; mix in bread crumbs, onion, parsley, horseradish, water, mustard, salt and pepper. Mix in beef; shape into 4 patties, about 3/4 inch (2 cm) thick.

❧ Grill on greased grill or in grill basket over medium-hot coals or at medium-high setting for 7 minutes. Turn and grill for 7 to 10 minutes longer or until no longer pink inside. Serve on English muffins. Makes 4 servings.

BARBECUED PORK SANDWICHES

These sandwiches are perfect for a big family barbecue. Add corn (see sidebar, p. 98) and a big bowl of summer greens.

4 lb	pork butt roast	2 kg
12	kaiser rolls, halved	12
	BARBECUE SAUCE:	
1 cup	ketchup	250 mL
1 cup	chili sauce	250 mL
1/4 cup	Dijon mustard	50 mL
2 tbsp	vinegar	25 mL
1 tbsp	Worcestershire sauce	15 mL
1 tsp	hot Chinese chili paste	5 mL
3	cloves garlic, minced	3
1	onion, chopped	1

BARBECUE SAUCE: In saucepan, combine ketchup, chili sauce, mustard, vinegar, Worcestershire sauce, chili paste, garlic and onion. Bring to boil and cook over medium heat for about 10 minutes or until thickened. Let cool.

❦ In large bowl, combine sauce and 1-1/2 cups (375 mL) water; add pork and marinate overnight in refrigerator. Wrap pork in foil, reserving sauce in refrigerator. Barbecue, with lid closed, 4 inches (10 cm) from medium-hot coals or on medium-high setting for 2-1/2 to 3 hours or until meat thermometer registers 160-170°F (71-75°C), brushing with remaining sauce every 45 minutes. (Alternatively, brush 1/2 cup (125 mL) sauce over pork. Place roast on rack in roasting pan; add 1-1/2 cups (375 mL) water. Cover and roast in 350°F (180°C) oven for 2 hours, adding more water every half-hour if pork is dry. Brush with another 1/2 cup (125 mL) sauce; roast, uncovered, for 30 minutes longer or until meat thermometer registers 160-170°F (71-75°C).

❦ Let pork stand for 15 to 20 minutes before slicing. Meanwhile, in saucepan, combine remaining sauce with pan juices; cook, stirring occasionally, for 15 to 20 minutes or until thickened. Skim off fat. Slice pork; trim off fat. Spoon 2 to 3 tbsp (25 to 50 mL) sauce over bottom half of each roll; top with 2 or 3 slices of pork and top half of roll. Makes 12 sandwiches.

HONEY-MUSTARD BARBECUED RIBS

For the tenderest, juiciest barbecue, buy back ribs, which are meatier than side ones. Serve alongside Grill-Roasted
Onion Potatoes (recipe, p. 82) and skewers of sweet peppers and corn.

3 lb	pork spareribs	1.5 kg
1/4 cup	liquid honey	50 mL
1/4 cup	Dijon mustard	50 mL
2 tbsp	vegetable oil	25 mL
1/4 tsp	crumbled dried rosemary	1 mL

Cut spareribs into serving-size pieces; place in large pot of boiling water. Reduce heat and simmer, covered, for about 45 minutes or until meat is fork-tender and no longer pink inside. (Alternatively, place ribs in 12-cup/3 L microwaveable casserole, add 1/4 cup/50 mL water. Cover and microwave at High for 5 minutes. Microwave, covered, at Medium (50%) for 15 to 20 minutes or until meat is fork-tender and no longer pink inside, turning ribs halfway through.)

❦ Drain ribs and pat dry. Combine honey, mustard, oil and rosemary.

❦ On greased grill over medium-hot coals or on medium-high setting, cook ribs, turning often and brushing with honey mixture, for 15 to 20 minutes or until browned and glazed. Makes about 4 servings.

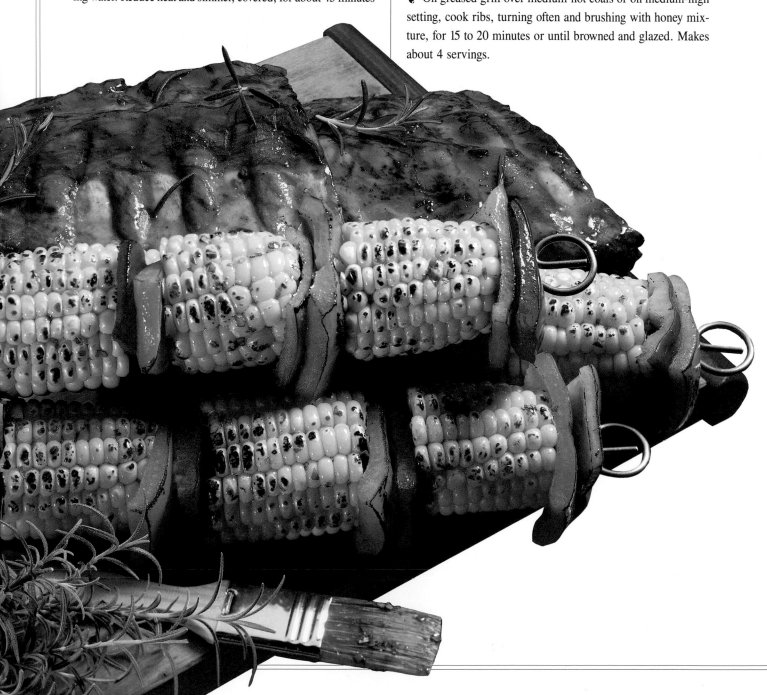

BEEF ROAST IN COOKED WINE MARINADE

A cooked marinade is needed to tenderize a less expensive roast of beef. It also lets the subtle flavors of vegetables and herbs emerge more forcefully. This is an excellent choice for a spring or fall family barbecue. Bake large potatoes right on the barbecue and toss up a big bowl of Refrigerator Slaw (recipe, p. 92).

3 lb	cross rib or boneless blade roast	1.5 kg
	MARINADE:	
1-1/2 cups	red wine	375 mL
1/3 cup	wine vinegar	75 mL
1/4 cup	olive oil	50 mL
1	small onion, finely chopped	1
2 tbsp	finely chopped celery	25 mL
2 tsp	chopped fresh thyme (or 1/2 tsp/2 mL dried)	10 mL
1/2 tsp	pepper	2 mL
1	clove garlic, crushed	1
1	bay leaf	1

MARINADE: In saucepan, combine wine, wine vinegar, oil, onion, celery, thyme, pepper, garlic and bay leaf; bring to boil. Reduce heat to low; cover and simmer for 20 minutes. Let cool.

❧ Place roast in sturdy plastic bag; pour in marinade. Squeeze out air; seal bag tightly. Place in bowl and refrigerate for at least 12 or up to 24 hours. Remove from refrigerator and let stand for 30 minutes. Drain meat, reserving marinade for basting.

❧ Place roast on greased grill over drip pan and arrange coals around pan. Or, place roast on opposite side of medium-low burner to avoid flare-ups. Close lid or tent with foil; cook, basting occasionally, for 1-1/2 hours or until meat thermometer registers 140°F (60°C) for rare, 160°F (70°C) for medium or 170°F (75°C) for well done. Makes about 10 servings.

BEEF STEAK WITH SESAME OIL MARINADE

Oriental sesame oil, made from toasted sesame seeds, has become a flavor favorite in recent years. Let its nutty flavor go to work on beef. A slice of flank steak or top round, about 1-1/2 inches (4 cm) thick, is ideal. Be sure to allow at least 8 hours for marinade to tenderize these cuts. This steak is great for a barbecue picnic with Tomato and Red Pepper Pasta Salad (recipe, p. 84) and tossed greens.

1/4 cup	dry white wine	50 mL
2 tbsp	white wine vinegar	25 mL
2 tbsp	sesame oil	25 mL
1 tbsp	vegetable oil	15 mL
2	large cloves garlic, minced	2
2 tsp	minced gingerroot	10 mL
1/4 tsp	each pepper and dried thyme	1 mL
1	flank or top round steak (about 1-1/2 lb/750 g)	1
	Salt	

In large shallow nonmetallic dish, stir together wine, vinegar, sesame and vegetable oils, garlic, ginger, pepper and thyme. Add steak, turning to coat both sides; cover and marinate in refrigerator for at least 8 or up to 24 hours.

❧ Place on greased grill over medium-hot coals or at medium-high setting; grill, brushing with any remaining marinade and turning once, for 10 to 14 minutes or until browned on outside but still pink inside. Season with salt to taste. Let stand for 5 minutes before cutting diagonally across the grain into thin slices. Makes 4 to 6 servings.

CHERRY TOMATOES WITH FRESH BASIL

Fresh-from-the-garden tomatoes sprinkled with basil make a simple and delicious accompaniment to any meal. Divide 2 cups (500 mL) cherry tomatoes among 4 greased pieces of foil. Sprinkle 1 tbsp (15 mL) chopped fresh basil evenly over each. Fold up foil loosely around tomatoes and seal tightly to form packets. Place on greased grill over hot coals or on medium-high setting and cook for 5 to 10 minutes or until heated through. Makes 4 servings.

BARBECUED SIRLOIN STEAK

If you're a traditionalist who thinks that white wine and red meat don't mix, you'll be pleasantly surprised with this marinated steak. Potatoes baked alongside the meat and a green salad round out this easy Saturday-night barbecue.

1-1/2 lb	sirloin steak, about 1 inch (2.5 cm) thick	750 g
	Cracked black peppercorns	
1/4 cup	white wine	50 mL
2 tbsp	vegetable oil	25 mL
2 tsp	dry mustard	10 mL

In shallow nonmetallic dish, cover steak generously with peppercorns; sprinkle with half of the wine, oil and mustard. Turn steak over and repeat. Cover and marinate in refrigerator for at least 2 or up to 12 hours, turning occasionally. Bring to room temperature before grilling.

❦ Remove steak from marinade; slash any fat around edges. Place on greased grill over medium-hot coals or at medium setting; grill steak for 1 minute on each side. Grill for about 5 minutes per side for rare, 6 to 7 minutes for medium, or until desired doneness. To serve, cut across the grain into 1/2-inch (1 cm) thick slices. Makes about 6 servings.

LEMON AND THYME BEEF KABOBS

Piquant lemon and fresh herbs give a summery flavor to a bargain cut of beef. Grill sliced onions, eggplant and zucchini, brushed with olive oil, to serve with the kabobs, along with rice or couscous.

2 lb	boneless blade or chuck short rib steak (1-inch/2.5 cm thick)	1 kg
	Salt	

	MARINADE:	
1/2 cup	lemon juice	125 mL
1/4 cup	olive oil	50 mL
2 tbsp	liquid honey	25 mL
2 tsp	each chopped fresh mint and thyme (or 3/4 tsp/4 mL dried)	10 mL
2	cloves garlic, crushed	2
1/2 tsp	pepper	2 mL

Trim steak; cut meat into 1-inch (2.5 cm) cubes.

❦ MARINADE: In nonmetallic bowl, whisk together lemon juice, oil, honey, mint, thyme, garlic and pepper until well blended; add beef, stirring to coat. Cover and refrigerate for at least 8 or up to 24 hours, stirring occasionally.

❦ Drain meat, reserving marinade. Thread meat onto greased metal skewers. Cook on greased grill over medium-hot coals or at medium setting, turning once and basting occasionally with marinade, for 7 to 10 minutes or until brown and glazed outside and pink inside. Sprinkle with salt to taste. Makes 6 servings.

GRILLING ADDITIONS

To simplify barbecued meals and to cut down on cooking time, you can grill vegetables alongside the main course.

❦ To steam vegetables on the barbecue: Slice, dice or julienne large vegetables; small vegetables can be grilled whole. Place vegetables on large greased pieces of foil; sprinkle with herbs, minced garlic, olive oil, butter, soy sauce or grated cheese. Fold up foil to form sealed packets.

❦ Vegetables such as carrots, beans, onions and potatoes take longer to cook than vegetables such as mushrooms, tomatoes and zucchini and should be placed in separate sealed packets.

❦ To grill vegetable brochettes: Thread an assortment of vegetables onto greased metal or soaked wooden skewers. Mushrooms, peppers and snow peas are a great combination; so are parboiled potatoes, carrots and onions.

Lemon and Thyme Beef Kabobs

GRILL-ROASTED ONION POTATOES

Potatoes cooked on the barbecue are wonderful and go well with everything from burgers to T-bones.

8	baking potatoes	8
3	onions, thinly sliced	3
3 tbsp	butter, melted	50 mL
	Salt and pepper	
2 tbsp	chopped chives	25 mL

Scrub potatoes well. Carefully slash each potato crosswise at 1/4-inch (5 mm) intervals, cutting almost through. Insert onion slices into slashes.

❦ Center each potato on square of heavy-duty foil; drizzle with melted butter. Sprinkle with salt and pepper to taste, then with chopped chives. Fold up foil around potato, sealing loosely to leave room for steam.

❦ Grill over medium-hot coals or on medium-high setting for 25 minutes. Fold back foil so top of potato can crisp without juices spilling. Grill for 10 to 15 minutes longer or until potatoes are tender. Makes 8 servings.

GRILLED PICKEREL

Moist and juicy pickerel is threaded onto skewers and served as an appetizer or main course on a bed of spring greens tossed with vinaigrette. Soak wooden skewers in water for 30 minutes before using.

1 lb	pickerel fillets	500 g
1 tbsp	vegetable oil	15 mL
Pinch	each salt and pepper	Pinch
	CHIVE AND LEMON MAYO:	
1/4 cup	mayonnaise	50 mL
1/4 cup	sour cream	50 mL
1 tbsp	minced fresh chives or green onion tops	15 mL
1/2 tsp	grated lemon rind	2 mL
2 tsp	lemon juice	10 mL
1/2 tsp	Dijon mustard	2 mL
Dash	hot pepper sauce	Dash
	Salt and pepper	

CHIVE AND LEMON MAYO: In bowl, blend together mayonnaise, sour cream, chives, lemon rind and juice, mustard and hot pepper sauce; season with salt and pepper to taste. *(Mayo can be covered and refrigerated for up to 2 days.)*

❦ Cut pickerel into 3/4-inch (2 cm) wide strips; thread each strip onto soaked wooden skewer. Brush with oil and sprinkle with salt and pepper.

❦ Place pickerel on greased grill about 4 inches (10 cm) from hot coals or on high setting; grill for 1 to 3 minutes or until beginning to turn opaque. Using lifter, carefully turn over and grill for 1 to 3 minutes longer or until golden and opaque. Pass Chive and Lemon Mayo separately. Makes 8 appetizer or 4 main-course servings.

BARBECUING FISH

❦ Compensate for the lack of natural fat in fish by using marinades and basting sauces to prevent drying out. These can be as simple as lemon juice or oil or melted butter. Add flavor and color with fresh garden herbs.

❦ Oil barbecue surfaces, especially if cooking fish directly on grill. Baste fish frequently and keep a glass of water nearby to douse flare-ups when basting oils hit coals.

❦ Don't overcook fish. Winds and outside temperatures will affect cooking time but a general rule is to barbecue fish over hot coals or at high setting for 10 minutes per inch (2.5 cm) of thickness, measured at thickest point of fish.

❦ Fish is naturally tender and tends to break easily when cooked so handle it carefully when serving.

MARINATED SALMON STEAKS

Salmon is king at April Point Lodge on British Columbia's Quadra Island. Owner Eric Peterson grills thick salmon steaks just outside the open doors of the dining room and lets the delicious aroma entice guests in for dinner. Either marinade makes for memorable grilled salmon steaks.

4	salmon steaks (about 2-1/4 lb/1.25 kg total)	4
	Teriyaki or Fennel Marinade (recipes follow)	

Arrange salmon in shallow dish; pour marinade over. Cover and marinate for 30 minutes at room temperature or 1 hour in refrigerator, turning once.

❦ Place fish on greased grill over medium-hot coals or medium-high setting; grill, turning once, for 10 minutes per inch (2.5 cm) of thickness or until fish is opaque and flakes easily when tested with fork. Makes 4 servings.

TERIYAKI MARINADE:

1/4 cup	olive oil	50 mL
1/4 cup	rye whisky	50 mL
2 tbsp	soy sauce	25 mL
1 tsp	Worcestershire sauce	5 mL
1/4 tsp	dry mustard	1 mL
1/4 tsp	pepper	1 mL
1	clove garlic, minced	1

In bowl, whisk together oil, whisky, soy sauce, Worcestershire sauce, mustard, pepper and garlic. Makes about 3/4 cup (175 mL).

FENNEL MARINADE:

1/4 cup	dry white vermouth	50 mL
2 tbsp	lemon juice	25 mL
2 tbsp	olive oil	25 mL
1 tbsp	fennel seeds, crushed	15 mL
1/2 tsp	coarsely ground pepper	2 mL

In bowl, whisk together vermouth, lemon juice, oil, fennel seeds and pepper. Makes about 1/2 cup (125 mL).

FROM THE GARDEN

If spring is asparagus and fiddleheads, summer must be shelling peas still moist with dew or slicing into a tomato filled with August sunshine. Autumn brings ears of corn to slather with butter, and winter is the season to look forward to the comfort of earthy potatoes, rutabaga and squash. Here's how to get the most out of fresh vegetables — whether they come from the backyard garden, a local pick-your-own or a carefully tended produce section.

TOMATO AND RED PEPPER PASTA SALAD

Pasta salads are a great way to enjoy vegetables. For a nutritious main course, just add cooked meat, poultry, fish or seafood (barbecued leftovers are particularly good).

3	sweet red peppers	3
4	red potatoes	4
4	large tomatoes	4
1/4 cup	pitted black olives, halved	50 mL
1/4 cup	sliced sun-dried tomatoes (optional)	50 mL
1/4 cup	chopped fresh basil or parsley	50 mL
1 lb	penne noodles	500 g
1	small head radicchio or red-tipped leaf lettuce, shredded	1
	DRESSING:	
1/2 cup	olive oil	125 mL
2 tbsp	red wine vinegar	25 mL

1	clove garlic, minced	1
1 tsp	anchovy paste	5 mL
1/2 tsp	salt	2 mL
1/4 tsp	hot pepper flakes	1 mL
1/4 tsp	pepper	1 mL

Halve red peppers; remove seeds and membranes. Place skin side up on baking sheet; broil until blistered and blackened. Let cool; peel and cut into chunks. Place in large bowl.

❦ In pot of boiling salted water, cook potatoes until tender. Let cool; cut into chunks and add to red peppers.

❦ Core tomatoes; cut into chunks and add to bowl. Add olives, sun-dried tomatoes (if using) and basil.

❦ DRESSING: In bowl, whisk together oil, vinegar, garlic, anchovy paste, salt, hot pepper flakes and pepper; pour over tomato mixture and toss lightly.

❦ In large pot of boiling salted water, cook pasta until tender but firm, 8 to 10 minutes. Drain well; toss immediately with tomato mixture. Taste and adjust seasoning. Serve warm or at room temperature on bed of radicchio. Makes 8 to 10 servings.

TASTY TOMATOES

❦ Look for pink, orange and golden yellow tomatoes at harvesttime and let them add a dash of color to your meals.

❦ Use round or pear-shaped mini-tomatoes to dress up a salad or barbecue.

❦ Plum tomatoes (Roma or San Marzano) are best for sauces since they are pulpier than regular tomatoes.

❦ To ripen tomatoes, arrange in a single layer on trays and let ripen at room temperature away from direct sunlight.

❦ A 4 L basket of tomatoes weighs about 6 lbs (2.5 kg); 1 chopped tomato yields about 1 cup.

NEW POTATO SALAD WITH BUTTERMILK DRESSING

This chunky potato salad is a great way to enjoy tiny new potatoes and garden beans. Be sure to keep it chilled
en route to a picnic.

4 lb	new red potatoes, halved or quartered	2 kg
1/4 cup	vegetable oil	50 mL
1/4 cup	cider vinegar	50 mL
2 tsp	granulated sugar	10 mL
1 tsp	dry mustard	5 mL
1/2 tsp	pepper	2 mL
1/2 tsp	salt	2 mL
1 cup	diagonally sliced yellow wax beans	250 mL
1 cup	frozen green peas	250 mL
1/2 cup	coarsely chopped green onions	125 mL
	BUTTERMILK DRESSING:	
1/2 cup	buttermilk	125 mL
1/2 cup	sour cream	125 mL
1/4 cup	chopped fresh dill	50 mL
1 tbsp	horseradish	15 mL

In large saucepan of boiling salted water, cook potatoes for 10 to 12 minutes or just until tender. Drain; transfer to large bowl.

❧ Meanwhile, whisk together oil, vinegar, sugar, mustard, pepper and salt; pour over warm potatoes and toss gently.

❧ In large pot of boiling salted water, cook beans for 3 to 5 minutes or until tender-crisp. Add peas; cook for 1 minute. Drain and refresh beans and peas under cold water; drain again and pat dry. Add to potatoes along with green onions.

❧ BUTTERMILK DRESSING: In bowl, whisk together buttermilk and sour cream; stir in dill and horseradish. Add to potato salad and toss well to coat. Serve immediately or cover and refrigerate for up to 8 hours. Makes about 6 servings.

OLD-FASHIONED SALAD DRESSING

For cabbage and potato salads, no salad dressing is as right as this tried and true one. Combine with sour cream and/or yogurt, if desired, when dressing vegetables.

1 cup	granulated sugar	250 mL
2 tbsp	all-purpose flour	25 mL
2 tsp	dry mustard	10 mL
1 tsp	salt	5 mL
1	egg, lightly beaten	1
1 cup	milk	250 mL
1 cup	white vinegar	250 mL
1 tbsp	butter	15 mL

In saucepan, combine sugar, flour, mustard and salt; beat in egg. Gradually stir in milk and vinegar until smooth. Cook over medium heat, stirring constantly, for 5 minutes or until mixture comes to boil. Stir in butter; cook, stirring constantly, for 3 to 4 minutes or until bubbly and thickened.

❧ Let cool at room temperature for about 5 minutes, stirring frequently to prevent skin from forming. *(Dressing can be refrigerated in jar with tight-fitting lid for up to 2 weeks.)* Makes about 2-1/2 cups (625 mL).

CONFETTI MIXED BEAN SALAD

Corn and chopped sweet red and green peppers add flavor and color to this picnic-perfect salad.

1 lb	green beans	500 g
1	can (19 oz/540 mL) chick-peas	1
1	can (19 oz/540 mL) red kidney beans	1
1	each sweet red and green pepper, diced	1
1	small red onion, diced	1
1 cup	cooked corn kernels	250 mL
1/4 cup	chopped fresh parsley	50 mL
1	small head iceberg lettuce, shredded	1
	DRESSING:	
1/4 cup	red wine vinegar	50 mL
1	shallot, minced	1
1 tsp	dry mustard	5 mL
1 tsp	salt	5 mL
1/4 tsp	pepper	1 mL
2/3 cup	olive or vegetable oil	150 mL

❧ In bowl, combine green beans, chick-peas, kidney beans, red and green peppers, onion, corn and parsley.

❧ DRESSING: In small bowl, combine vinegar, shallot, mustard, salt and pepper; whisk in oil. Taste and adjust seasoning if necessary. Pour over salad and toss to coat well. Marinate for 2 hours at room temperature or cover and refrigerate overnight.

❧ Just before serving, arrange lettuce in serving bowl; mound salad in center. Makes 4 to 6 servings.

Cut green beans into 1-inch (2.5 cm) lengths. In large pot of boiling water, cook beans for 2 to 3 minutes or until tender-crisp. Chill in bowl of cold water; drain and pat dry. Drain and rinse chick-peas and kidney beans.

MARINATED VEGETABLE SALAD

Every cook needs a make-ahead salad for potlucks, picnics, barbecues and buffets. Here's a colorful one with a pleasing mustardy vinaigrette. For our cover, we garnished the salad with green and red-tipped leaf lettuce and sprinkled it with herbs.

1	small cauliflower	1
1/2 lb	green beans, trimmed*	250 g
1/2 lb	mushrooms	250 g
1	sweet red pepper	1
2 cups	julienned carrots	500 mL
2 cups	julienned peeled rutabaga or parsnip	500 mL
1/2 cup	chopped red onion	125 mL
	MUSTARD VINAIGRETTE:	
3/4 cup	vegetable oil	175 mL
1/3 cup	cider vinegar	75 mL
1 tbsp	grainy mustard	15 mL
1	clove garlic, minced	1
	Salt and pepper	
	GARNISH:	
	Cherry tomatoes	
	Watercress	

MUSTARD VINAIGRETTE: In large bowl, combine oil, vinegar, mustard, garlic, and salt and pepper to taste.

❧ Divide cauliflower into florets; cut beans into bite-size pieces. Halve large mushrooms. Cut red pepper into chunks.

❧ In saucepan of lightly salted boiling water, steam or boil green beans just until tender-crisp; drain. Rinse under cold water and pat dry; wrap in clean tea towel and refrigerate overnight.

❧ In same saucepan of boiling water, steam or boil cauliflower, then carrots, then rutabaga, just until tender-crisp; drain.

❧ Add cauliflower, carrots, rutabaga, mushrooms, red pepper and onion to vinaigrette; toss lightly until well coated. Cover and refrigerate overnight.

❧ Just before serving, add beans to vegetable mixture; toss gently. Transfer to salad bowl or remove with slotted spoon to platter and arrange as desired. Garnish with cherry tomatoes and watercress. Makes about 12 servings.

*To prevent beans from discoloring, don't marinate them in vinaigrette overnight.

CHICKEN-ASPARAGUS SALAD

You can use leftover roast chicken, or poach chicken especially for this fresh-tasting spring salad.

4 cups	cubed cooked chicken	1 L
1 lb	cooked asparagus, sliced	500 g
1 cup	sliced celery	250 mL
1 cup	walnuts, toasted*	250 mL
1/2 cup	chopped green onions	125 mL
1 cup	mayonnaise	250 mL
1/4 cup	sour cream	50 mL
2 tbsp	lemon juice	25 mL
1 tbsp	Dijon mustard	15 mL
1/2 tsp	hot pepper sauce	2 mL
	Salt and pepper	

In bowl, toss together chicken, asparagus, celery, walnuts and onions. Combine mayonnaise, sour cream, lemon juice, mustard and hot pepper sauce; stir into chicken mixture. Season with salt and pepper to taste. Makes 6 servings.

*To toast walnuts, bake on baking sheet in 350°F (180°C) oven for 5 to 8 minutes or until fragrant.

Marinated Vegetable Salad

CORN, RICE AND BEAN SALAD

*Enjoy this delicious salad chilled as a summer salad or warm as a side dish. Pack for picnics
or carry out to the backyard for barbecues.*

1/3 cup	parboiled rice	75 mL
3 cups	corn	750 mL
1	can (14 oz/398 mL) kidney beans, drained and rinsed	1
1 cup	chopped sweet red pepper	250 mL
1/2 cup	chopped celery	125 mL
1/3 cup	chopped green onions	75 mL
1/4 cup	chopped fresh parsley	50 mL
1 tbsp	chopped jalapeño pepper (optional)	15 mL
	DRESSING:	
1/4 cup	white wine vinegar	50 mL
2 tbsp	olive oil	25 mL
1 tsp	cumin	5 mL
1/2 tsp	salt	2 mL
1/4 tsp	pepper	1 mL
Dash	hot pepper sauce	Dash

In saucepan, bring 1 cup (250 mL) water to boil; add rice. Reduce heat to low; cover and cook for 20 minutes or until tender.

❦ Meanwhile, in separate saucepan, cook corn in boiling water for 5 minutes or until tender; drain well. In serving bowl, combine rice and corn.

❦ Add beans, red pepper, celery, onions, parsley, and jalapeño (if using).

❦ DRESSING: Whisk together vinegar, oil, cumin, salt, pepper and hot pepper sauce; drizzle over salad and toss lightly. Makes 6 servings.

GILDED ONIONS

*Onions glazed with this honey-mustard combination are delectable, especially when arranged around Roast Pork Loin
with Sage (recipe, p. 48). Make the brown sugar variation to serve with Southwestern Chicken (recipe, p. 43).*

4	onions	4
	HONEY-MUSTARD GLAZE:	
1/4 cup	liquid honey	50 mL
1 tsp	soy sauce	5 mL
1 tsp	Dijon mustard	5 mL

Cut off tops and bottoms of onions; remove outer skin. Place onions in saucepan and add enough water to come to depth of 1 inch (2.5 cm); cover and bring to boil. Reduce heat to medium and cook for 30 minutes or until tender. Drain and transfer onions to small greased casserole.

❦ HONEY-MUSTARD GLAZE: In small saucepan, combine honey, soy sauce and mustard; cook over medium heat, stirring, for 5 minutes. Pour over onions and bake, uncovered, in 350°F (180°C) oven, basting occasionally, for 30 to 40 minutes or until heated through and glazed. Cut each onion in half to serve. Makes 8 servings.

VARIATION

BROWN SUGAR GLAZE: In small saucepan, combine 1/2 cup (125 mL) packed brown sugar, 2 tbsp (25 mL) butter and 2 tbsp (25 mL) water; cook as above and pour over onions before baking.

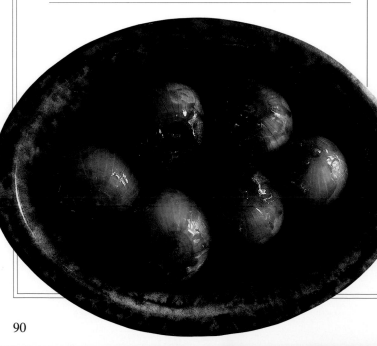

FRESH MOZZARELLA WITH TOMATOES

Available at specialty cheese stores, fresh mozzarella is often shaped into small balls (about 1-1/2 inches/4 cm in diameter) called bocconcini. *Halve cherry tomatoes if they are too large. If cherry tomatoes are unavailable, use regular tomatoes cut into chunks and drained slightly.*

3/4 lb	fresh mozzarella	375 g
1 lb	cherry tomatoes	500 g
1/4 cup	thinly sliced sun-dried tomatoes (optional)	50 mL
1/4 cup	shredded fresh basil or chopped parsley	50 mL
2 tbsp	toasted pine nuts or sliced almonds	25 mL
	DRESSING:	
2 tbsp	red wine vinegar	25 mL
1/4 tsp	pepper	1 mL
1	clove garlic, minced	1
	Salt	
1/2 cup	olive oil	125 mL

Cut cheese into 1 inch (2.5 cm) cubes. In bowl, combine cheese, cherry tomatoes, sun-dried tomatoes (if using), basil and pine nuts.

❦ DRESSING: In small bowl, combine vinegar, pepper, garlic, and salt to taste; whisk in oil. Taste and adjust seasoning if necessary. Pour over salad and toss to coat well.

❦ Marinate for at least 30 minutes at room temperature or cover and refrigerate for up to 2 days. (Remove from refrigerator 30 minutes before serving.) Makes 4 to 6 servings.

ANNIE'S CUCUMBER SALAD

This crunchy salad is always a hit at the annual summer chicken barbecue in Erieau on the shores of Lake Erie. For the best taste, use dill-size cucumbers.

3 lb	cucumbers, peeled and sliced (approx 12)	1.5 kg
1 cup	chopped celery	250 mL
1/4 cup	chopped onion	50 mL
1/4 cup	chopped sweet green pepper	50 mL
1/4 cup	granulated sugar	50 mL
1/4 cup	white vinegar	50 mL
2 tbsp	canola oil	25 mL
1/4 tsp	celery seeds	1 mL
1/4 tsp	each salt and pepper	1 mL
	Chopped fresh dill	

In nonaluminum bowl, combine cucumbers, celery, onion and green pepper. In saucepan, bring sugar, vinegar, oil, celery seeds, salt and pepper to boil, stirring constantly. Pour over vegetables and stir. Refrigerate until cooled, stirring twice. Cover and refrigerate for at least 2 hours or up to 2 days. Just before serving, stir in dill. Makes about 8 servings.

FINISHING TOUCHES FOR GARDEN VEGETABLES

Don't overpower the real flavor of green vegetables such as asparagus, broccoli, green beans, fiddleheads and snap peas with strong sauces or elaborate preparations. Here are three quick and simple sauces that will complement the unique subtle taste of each vegetable. Each recipe makes enough to sauce or toss with 2 cups (500 mL) of cooked greens (4 small servings).

YOGURT HOLLANDAISE:

3/4 cup	plain yogurt	175 mL
2 tsp	lemon juice	10 mL
3	egg yolks	3
1/2 tsp	Dijon mustard	2 mL
1/4 tsp	salt	1 mL
Pinch	white pepper	Pinch
Dash	hot pepper sauce	Dash

In top of double boiler over simmering water, whisk together yogurt, lemon juice, egg yolks, mustard, salt, pepper and hot pepper sauce; cook, stirring constantly, for 8 to 12 minutes or until sauce is thickened and coats back of wooden spoon. Taste and adjust seasoning.

SESAME BUTTER:

1 tbsp	sesame seeds	15 mL
4 tsp	butter	20 mL
4 tsp	lemon juice	20 mL
	Salt and pepper	
Dash	sesame oil (optional)	Dash

In small skillet, heat sesame seeds over low heat, stirring occasionally, until lightly browned, about 5 minutes. Add butter and lemon juice; heat, stirring, until butter melts. Season with salt and pepper to taste, and sesame oil, if using.

LEMON BUTTER:

2 tbsp	minced green onion	25 mL
2 tbsp	lemon juice	25 mL
1	clove garlic, minced	1
3 tbsp	cold butter, in small pieces	50 mL
	Salt and pepper	
1 tbsp	finely grated lemon rind	15 mL
	Thin slices lemon	

In small saucepan, cook onion, lemon juice and garlic over medium heat until onion is softened and liquid almost evaporated, about 3 minutes. Remove from heat. Whisk in butter, one piece at a time, incorporating each piece before adding next. Season with salt and pepper to taste. Whisk in lemon rind. Garnish vegetables with lemon slices.

REFRIGERATOR SLAW

Double this crunchy sweet and sour cabbage salad for easy fall and winter meals.

4 cups	finely shredded cabbage	1 L
1	large onion, thinly sliced	1
1/3 cup	granulated sugar	75 mL
1/2 tsp	salt	2 mL
1/4 cup	white wine vinegar	50 mL
1-1/2 tsp	celery seeds	7 mL
1/2 tsp	dry mustard	2 mL
1/4 cup	vegetable oil	50 mL

In large nonaluminum bowl, combine cabbage, onion, 1/4 cup (50 mL) of the sugar and salt; set aside.

❦ In nonaluminum saucepan, combine remaining sugar, vinegar, celery seeds and mustard; bring to boil. Pour in oil and return to boil. Pour immediately over cabbage mixture and mix thoroughly. Cover and refrigerate until chilled. *(Slaw can be refrigerated for up to 2 weeks.)* Drain well before serving. Makes about 6 servings.

FIDDLEHEAD COUNTRY

PICKING

Be sure you pick only ostrich ferns; all others are unsafe to eat, and may be carcinogenic. Don't pick fronds that have opened out into ferns; they're tough and unpalatable.

❧ Don't overpick; always leave about half the fronds in each clump so as not to weaken it.

❧ Pick in the morning when plants are still crisp, and pick heads that are no more than 4 inches (10 cm) above ground. Good-quality fiddleheads should be tightly curled with short tails, thick and of uniform size, crisp, and good in color with no bruising or rust.

❧ Put picked ferns into burlap bags or old pillowcases so they can "breathe" without drying out.

❧ Pack picked ferns in coolers with ice packs if you're picking very far from home.

❧ Fiddleheads are best eaten as soon as possible. Store them in a paper bag in the refrigerator crisper for up to two days. Freeze for longer storage. Home canning is not recommended.

CLEANING

The best way to remove the thin brown, paper-like scales that encase the baby fiddleheads is to uncurl each head and shake off this husk.

❧ Wash fiddleheads several times in cool water. Trim off any dark ends before cooking.

COOKING

Two cups (500 mL) of fiddleheads weigh about 1/2 lb (500 g) and make 4 servings. If fresh fiddleheads aren't available, use one package (10.6 oz/300 g) of frozen ones to replace 2 cups (500 mL) of fresh ones. Don't thaw before cooking. Cooked fiddleheads should be bright green; over-cooking fades them, robs them of nutrients and flavor, and makes them mushy. Use one of the following easy methods for fresh fiddleheads.

❧ **Boiling:** Cook, uncovered, in large amount of boiling salted water for 5 to 7 minutes or just until tender. Don't be alarmed at the dark color of the water—it's due to the high iron content in fiddleheads.

❧ **Steaming:** Steam in basket set over boiling water for about 8 minutes or just until tender.

❧ **Microwaving:** Microwave at High in small amount of water, covered, for 5 minutes; let stand, covered, for 3 minutes.

BRAISED RED CABBAGE

This is the perfect wintertime dish to serve with roast pork or chicken, grilled sausages or pork chops.

1/4 cup	butter	50 mL
1	onion, chopped	1
1	apple, cored and diced	1
8 cups	shredded red cabbage	2 L
1/3 cup	raisins	75 mL
3 tbsp	packed brown sugar	50 mL
3 tbsp	cider vinegar	50 mL
1 tsp	salt	5 mL
1/2 tsp	caraway seeds	2 mL
1/4 tsp	pepper	1 mL

In large heavy saucepan, melt butter over medium heat; cook onion and apple until softened, about 5 minutes. Add cabbage and toss to combine. Cover and cook for 5 minutes. Stir in raisins, sugar, vinegar, salt, caraway seeds and pepper. Cover and cook until cabbage is tender but not mushy, 10 to 12 minutes. Makes 8 servings.

ZUCCHINI PANCAKES

Savory zucchini pancakes are an easy last-minute side dish to serve with chicken or fish. Double for larger gatherings—or when zucchini threaten to overtake your garden and crisper!

1	egg	1
1 cup	grated (unpeeled) zucchini	250 mL
1/2 cup	minced onion	125 mL
1 tbsp	slivered sweet red pepper	15 mL
1 tbsp	dry bread crumbs	15 mL
1/4 tsp	salt	1 mL
Pinch	dried oregano	Pinch
Dash	hot pepper sauce	Dash
1 tbsp	butter or vegetable oil	15 mL

In bowl, beat egg; mix in zucchini, onion, red pepper, bread crumbs, salt, oregano and hot pepper sauce.

❧ In large skillet, melt butter over medium-high heat; spoon in about 1/4 cup (50 mL) zucchini mixture per pancake, spreading to about 1/4-inch (5 mm) thickness. Cook for 3 to 4 minutes per side or until golden. Serve immediately. Makes 6 pancakes.

ROASTED PEPPERS

If you want to enjoy roasted peppers all year round but hate paying out-of-season prices, here are several ways to roast them for freezing. For a deep roast flavor, the best way is to broil or grill them on the barbecue. If the peppers you're grilling are hot, such as cayenne, jalapeño and banana, be sure to wear rubber gloves and avoid touching any part of your body with them.

❧ Grill peppers for about 15 minutes, turning with tongs as each side browns and puffs. Let cool, peel and remove seeds, reserving any juices.

❧ Broil peppers 4 inches (10 cm) from heat following directions for grilling.

❧ Roast sweet red or yellow peppers only in shallow roasting pan in 375°F (190°C) oven for about 30 minutes, turning once, or until puffed and lightly browned. Let cool, peel and remove seeds, reserving any juices.

❧ Freeze convenient amounts of peppers and juices in freezer bags or containers.

NUTTY PECAN SQUASH

Full of comforting flavor, this vegetable dish is delicious with Peppered Lamb Chops (recipe, p. 73)
or any of the pork or chicken roasts in Sunday Dinners.

1	hubbard squash (about 1 lb/500 g)	1
1/4 cup	butter	50 mL
1/4 cup	chopped pecans	50 mL
2 tbsp	orange juice	25 mL
1 tsp	packed brown sugar (optional)	5 mL
	Salt and pepper	

Cut squash in half lengthwise; remove seeds and cut into 1/2-inch (1 cm) wide slices. In saucepan of boiling water, cook squash for 20 to 25 minutes or just until tender. (Alternatively, place squash in microwaveable dish and cover with vented plastic wrap; microwave at High for 8 to 10 minutes or just until tender, stirring twice.) Drain; cover and set aside.

❧ In small saucepan, melt butter over medium heat; stir in pecans to coat evenly. Cook for about 5 minutes or until nuts are golden and warmed through, being careful not to burn. Stir in orange juice, and sugar (if using). Arrange squash on platter and pour sauce over top. Season with salt and pepper to taste. Makes 4 servings.

❧

THE BEST-EVER SCALLOPED POTATOES

Scalloped potatoes remind us of days gone by. Traditionally, the flour was simply sprinkled over the potato layers. In this updated version, the cream sauce is made first so that it doesn't separate during baking. For extra flavor, sprinkle the top with grated Parmesan, shredded Cheddar cheese or buttered bread crumbs after the first 45 minutes of baking.

6	potatoes (about 2 lb/1 kg total)	6
1/3 cup	finely chopped onions	75 mL
	SAUCE:	
3 tbsp	butter	50 mL
3 tbsp	all-purpose flour	50 mL
1-1/2 tsp	salt	7 mL
1/2 tsp	pepper	2 mL
2-1/2 cups	milk	625 mL

SAUCE: In saucepan, melt butter over medium heat. Add flour, salt and pepper; cook, stirring, for 1 minute. Gradually stir in milk; cook, stirring constantly, for about 5 minutes or until boiling and thickened. Set aside.

❧ Peel and thinly slice potatoes; arrange one-third in greased 8-inch (2 L) square baking dish or 8-cup (2 L) casserole. Pour one-third of the sauce over potatoes; sprinkle with one-third of the onions. Repeat layering twice. Cover and bake in 350°F (180°C) oven for 45 minutes. Uncover and bake for 30 minutes longer or until potatoes are tender and top is lightly browned. Let stand for 5 minutes before serving. Makes 8 servings.

CLEMENTINE AND SWEET POTATO BAKE

Pair this make-ahead classic with Roast Turkey (recipe, p. 20) or Roast Leg of Lamb (recipe, p. 46).

3	large sweet potatoes, peeled (about 2 lb/1 kg total)	3
1 tbsp	grated clementine rind	15 mL
1 cup	clementine juice	250 mL
2 tsp	cornstarch	10 mL
1/4 cup	butter	50 mL
2 tbsp	packed brown sugar	25 mL
2 tbsp	minced preserved ginger	25 mL
1 tbsp	preserved ginger syrup	15 mL
1 cup	chopped pecans or sliced unblanched almonds	250 mL

In large pot of boiling water, cook potatoes for about 20 minutes or until tender but not mushy. Drain and let cool. Cut diagonally into 1/4-inch (5 mm) thick slices; arrange in overlapping circles in 12-inch (30 cm) oval gratin dish. *(Potatoes can be prepared to this point, covered and refrigerated for up to 4 hours.)*

❧ In saucepan, stir together clementine rind and juice and cornstarch; add butter, sugar, ginger and syrup. Bring to boil, stirring until thickened. *(Sauce can be cooled, covered and refrigerated for up to 2 days.)* Drizzle evenly over potatoes; sprinkle with nuts. Bake in 375°F (190°C) oven for about 20 minutes or until sauce is bubbly and nuts are toasted. Makes about 6 servings.

TURNIPS REVISITED

Assertive orange turnips, or rutabaga as this root vegetable is now called, are tamed into a delicious side dish with apples and a crumble topping. Make sure to serve this with Roast Turkey (recipe, p. 20).

1	rutabaga (about 2 lb/1 kg)	1
1/2 cup	packed brown sugar	125 mL
1 tsp	cinnamon	5 mL
4	cooking apples (about 2 lb/1 kg total)	4
3 tbsp	all-purpose flour	50 mL
3 tbsp	butter	50 mL
	Salt and pepper	

Peel and cube rutabaga. In saucepan, cover rutabaga with cold water and bring to boil; cover and cook for 15 to 20 minutes or until tender.

❧ Meanwhile, in large bowl, mix together 1/4 cup (50 mL) of the sugar and cinnamon. Peel and slice apples very thinly; toss with sugar mixture and set aside. In separate bowl, mix together flour and remaining sugar; cut in 2 tbsp (25 mL) of the butter until mixture is crumbly. Set aside.

❧ Drain rutabaga and mash with remaining butter; spread one-third in lightly greased 8-cup (2 L) casserole. Spread one-half of the apple mixture on top. Repeat layers, ending with rutabaga. Sprinkle flour mixture evenly over top. Bake, uncovered, in 350°F (180°C) oven for 30 to 40 minutes or until apples are tender and top is golden brown. Season with salt and pepper to taste. Makes 8 servings.

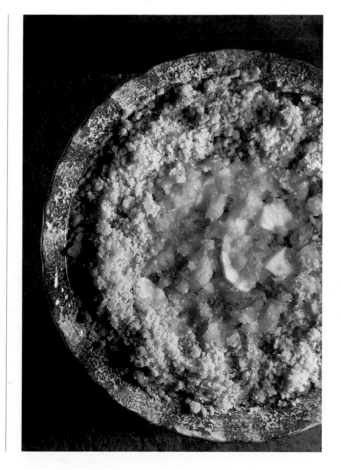

FRESH CORN CUSTARD

Flavored with Cheddar and topped with crispy crumbs, this custard of corn, cream and eggs is a country classic.
It's terrific with roast chicken or duck and all cuts of pork.

4	eggs	4
3/4 cup	light cream	175 mL
2 tbsp	finely chopped fresh chives or green onions	25 mL
1 tbsp	finely chopped fresh parsley	15 mL
1/2 tsp	salt	2 mL
1/4 tsp	pepper	1 mL
1/4 tsp	cayenne pepper	1 mL
2 cups	fresh corn (3 to 4 uncooked cobs)	500 mL
1/2 cup	shredded old Cheddar cheese (preferably white)	125 mL
3/4 cup	fresh bread crumbs	175 mL
2 tbsp	butter, melted	25 mL

In large bowl, beat together eggs and cream; mix in chives, parsley, salt, pepper and cayenne. Stir in corn, cheese and 1/2 cup (125 mL) of the bread crumbs. Combine remaining crumbs with butter; set aside for topping.

❧ Transfer custard to buttered 8-inch (2 L) square baking dish. Place dish in larger shallow pan; pour in enough boiling water to come two-thirds up sides of dish. Bake in 350°F (180°C) oven for 25 to 30 minutes or until tester inserted in center comes out clean.

❧ Remove dish from pan; sprinkle reserved crumbs over custard. Broil for 2 to 3 minutes or until crumbs are golden.

❧ Cut into squares and serve immediately. Makes 6 servings.

CORN ON THE COB

To boil: Bring large pot of water to boil (do not add salt; it toughens the kernel). Add corn, cover and return to boil; cook for 3 to 10 minutes, depending on variety and maturity, until kernels are tender when pierced with a fork.

To barbecue: Peel back husks, leaving them attached at the base; remove all silk. Rewrap corn in husks and secure with string. Soak cobs in cold water for 15 minutes or remove husks and silk and just wrap cobs in foil. Grill 4 inches (10 cm) from hot coals or on high setting, turning occasionally, for 25 minutes or until tender when pierced with fork.

CORN ON THE COB BUTTERS

Corn on the cob is not complete without slices of flavored butters to melt over the cobs. Place the butters in plastic wrap and roll into a log shape before refrigerating.

Basil Butter: Beat 1/2 cup (125 mL) softened butter with 2 tbsp (25 mL) finely chopped fresh basil.

Parmesan Chive Butter: Beat together 1/2 cup (125 mL) softened butter, 3 tbsp (50 mL) grated Parmesan cheese and 1 tbsp (15 mL) chopped chives.

Hot Pepper Butter: Beat together 1/2 cup (125 mL) softened butter, 1 tbsp (15 mL) minced sweet red pepper and 1 tsp (5 mL) hot pepper sauce.

CORN CAKES

Back bacon is a quick, easy accompaniment to these niblet-filled pancakes. All you need to round out supper are hot zucchini slices and a tomato salad.

1/2 cup	all-purpose flour	125 mL
1/2 tsp	baking powder	2 mL
1/4 tsp	salt	1 mL
1/4 tsp	dried thyme	1 mL
Pinch	pepper	Pinch
1	egg	1
1/4 cup	milk	50 mL
2 tbsp	vegetable oil	25 mL
3/4 cup	corn	175 mL
1/4 cup	chopped green onion	50 mL
1/4 cup	shredded old Cheddar cheese	50 mL

In bowl, stir together flour, baking powder, salt, thyme and pepper. Whisk together egg, milk and 1 tbsp (15 mL) of the oil; pour over flour mixture. Add corn, onion and cheese; mix just until combined.

Heat large skillet over medium-high heat; brush with remaining oil. Spoon in batter to make 4 cakes; cook for 5 minutes or until golden brown underneath. Turn and cook for about 4 minutes longer or until set. Makes 2 servings. (To serve 4, double the recipe.)

ASPARAGUS — A SURE SIGN OF SPRING!

Tall and proud in the produce section, Canadian asparagus is a great sign of spring.

Select firm, straight, rich green spears that are uniform in size and have closed tips. Stalks should be well rounded: ridges are a sign of age. The thicker the spear, the tastier and more tender it is.

Refrigerate for up to three days by wrapping the base of the stalks in damp paper towels and placing them in a plastic bag. Or, stand them in 1 inch (2.5 cm) of water and cover with plastic bag.

Brush gently under cold running water to remove sand. Hold spear with both hands and snap off end; the stalk will break at the point where toughness stops.

Cook asparagus by laying spears in a wide saucepan of boiling salted water and cooking for 2 to 5 minutes or until tender-crisp. Or, cook in steamer basket over boiling water for the same time.

ASPARAGUS WITH CREAMY ORANGE VINAIGRETTE

Spring green asparagus piled on a platter and bathed in a creamy vinaigrette makes a terrific first course that tastes superb.

In bowl, combine 3 tbsp (50 mL) orange juice, 1 tbsp (15 mL) grated orange rind and 1/2 tsp (2 mL) Dijon mustard. Season with salt and pepper to taste.

Arrange 1 lb (500 g) cooked asparagus on serving platter; pour dressing over. Sprinkle with 2 tbsp (25 mL) chopped fresh chives or green onion. Makes 4 servings.

LOAF AND LADLE

Loaf and ladle. Bread and soup. This time-honored combination can be as homey and soul-satisfying as homemade chicken soup and a crusty baguette, or as elegant as chilled shrimp and cucumber soup served with thin slices of walnut sesame-seed bread.

❦

GRANARY BUNS

A combination of three flours used in these proportions gives a wonderful flavor along with good volume. Make these small for dinner rolls, large for great hamburger or sandwich buns.

1 cup	milk	250 mL
1/4 cup	packed brown sugar	50 mL
2 tbsp	shortening or butter	25 mL
2 tsp	salt	10 mL
1 tsp	granulated sugar	5 mL
1 cup	warm water	250 mL
1	pkg active dry yeast (or 1 tbsp/15 mL)	1
2 cups	whole wheat flour	500 mL
1 cup	rye flour	250 mL
2 cups	(approx) all-purpose flour	500 mL
1	egg yolk	1
2 tbsp	water	25 mL
	Natural bran or rolled oats	

In saucepan, heat milk, brown sugar, shortening and salt until shortening has melted. Let cool to lukewarm.

❦ Dissolve granulated sugar in warm water; sprinkle in yeast and let stand for 10 minutes or until frothy. In large mixing bowl, combine yeast mixture with milk mixture. Using electric mixer, gradually beat in whole wheat and rye flours; beat until smooth, about 3 minutes. With wooden spoon, gradually stir in enough of the all-purpose flour to make stiff dough.

❦ Turn out dough onto lightly floured surface and knead until smooth and elastic, about 10 minutes. Place in lightly greased bowl, turning to grease all over. Cover with plastic wrap and let rise for 1 to 1-1/2 hours or until doubled in bulk. Punch down dough; turn out onto lightly floured surface and knead into smooth ball. Cover and let rest for 10 minutes.

❦ Divide dough into 12 or 16 pieces (depending on size of bun desired). Shape each piece into ball or oval and place 2 inches (5 cm) apart on greased baking sheets. Cover and let rise for about 1 hour or until doubled in bulk. *(Dough has doubled in bulk if indentation remains after lightly pressing two fingertips into dough.)*

❦ Combine egg yolk with water; brush over tops of buns. Sprinkle with bran. Bake in 375°F (190°C) oven for 20 to 25 minutes or until golden brown and buns sound hollow when tapped on bottoms. Transfer to rack and let cool. Makes 12 or 16 buns.

FREEZING DOUGH

Allow dough one rise until doubled in bulk. Punch down and shape as desired. Place in greased baking dish or on greased baking sheet; cover and freeze for up to two months. Frozen individual buns may be transferred to plastic bags for prolonged storage. The day before baking, transfer frozen dough to refrigerator to thaw overnight. (Arrange buns on greased baking sheet if they have been stored in bags.) Remove from refrigerator. Cover and let rise until almost doubled in bulk, 1-1/2 hours. Bake as directed.

(clockwise from bottom) Granary Buns; whole wheat bread; French Baguette (recipe, p. 104)

WALNUT SESAME-SEED BREAD

This easy-to-make bread is fabulous with cheese and makes an excellent snack.

1 tbsp	granulated sugar	15 mL
1-1/4 cups	warm water	300 mL
1	pkg active dry yeast (or 1 tbsp/15 mL)	1
1-1/2 cups	whole wheat flour	375 mL
1-1/4 cups	(approx) all-purpose flour	300 mL
1 tsp	salt	5 mL
2 tbsp	walnut oil or vegetable oil	25 mL
1 cup	coarsely chopped walnuts, toasted*	250 mL
1	egg white, lightly beaten	1
1/2 cup	sesame seeds	125 mL

In bowl, dissolve sugar in 1/4 cup (50 mL) of the warm water; sprinkle in yeast and let stand for 10 minutes or until frothy.

❦ Stir together whole wheat and all-purpose flours and salt; set aside. In large bowl, combine remaining warm water with oil; stir in yeast mixture. By hand or using mixer fitted with dough hook, gradually beat in flour mixture, adding just enough all-purpose flour to make soft dough that does not stick to your hands.

❦ Turn out onto lightly floured surface and knead for 10 minutes by hand or 5 minutes in mixer or until very smooth and elastic. Place dough in lightly greased bowl, turning to grease all over. Cover with plastic wrap; let rise in warm spot for 1 hour or until doubled in bulk.

❦ Punch down dough; knead in walnuts. Cut dough in half; roll out each half into oval about 14 × 16 inches (35 × 15 cm). Roll up lengthwise to form 2 long loaves; pinch seams closed. Brush lightly with egg white; roll in sesame seeds.

❦ Place loaves on well-greased large baking sheet. Cover loosely with greased plastic wrap; let rise in warm place for about 45 minutes or until doubled in bulk. Bake in 375°F (190°C) oven for 30 to 35 minutes or until loaves sound hollow when tapped on bottoms. Remove to rack and let cool. Makes 2 loaves.
* Vacuum-packed or freshly shelled walnuts are recommended. To toast walnuts, bake on baking sheet in 350°F (180°C) oven for 8 to 10 minutes or until fragrant. Let cool completely.

WILD RICE MUFFINS

Wild rice adds to the richness of these fruit-and-nut-filled muffins.

1/3 cup	wild rice	75 mL
2	eggs	2
1 cup	milk	250 mL
1/2 cup	butter, melted and cooled	125 mL
1-1/2 cups	all-purpose flour	375 mL
1/2 cup	natural bran	125 mL
1/3 cup	packed brown sugar	75 mL
1 tbsp	baking powder	15 mL
1/4 tsp	each salt and nutmeg	1 mL
1/2 cup	chopped toasted pecans*	125 mL
1/2 cup	sliced dates	125 mL
1/4 cup	slivered apricots	50 mL
2 tsp	coarsely grated orange rind	10 mL

In small saucepan, bring 2 cups (500 mL) water to boil; add rice, cover and cook over medium heat until very tender and splayed, about 45 minutes. Drain well; let cool. In bowl, whisk eggs; mix in rice, milk and butter.

❦ In large bowl, stir together flour, bran, sugar, baking powder, salt and nutmeg. Pour in rice mixture; sprinkle with pecans, dates, apricots and orange rind. Mix together just until dry ingredients are moistened.

❦ Spoon batter into large paper-lined muffin cups, filling each to top of liner. Bake in 375°F (190°C) oven for about 25 minutes or until golden and firm to the touch. Makes 10 large muffins.
*To toast pecans, bake on baking sheet in 350°F (180°C) oven for 5 to 10 minutes or until golden.

CHUNKY PIZZA SOUP

The only thing better than a slice of pizza on a cold winter's day is a steaming hot bowl of pizza soup. Serve with crusty French bread or our quick and easy Cheese Cookies.

1 tbsp	vegetable oil	15 mL
1	small onion, chopped	1
1/2 cup	sliced mushrooms	125 mL
1/4 cup	slivered sweet green pepper	50 mL
1	can (28 oz/796 mL) plum tomatoes (undrained)	1
1 cup	beef stock	250 mL
1 cup	thinly sliced pepperoni (about 5 oz/150 g)	250 mL
1/2 tsp	dried basil	2 mL
1 cup	shredded mozzarella cheese	250 mL
	Cheese Cookies (recipe follows)	

In saucepan, heat oil over medium heat; cook onion, mushrooms and green pepper, stirring often, until softened but not browned. Add tomatoes, stock, pepperoni and basil; cook until heated through.

❦ Ladle soup into 4 ovenproof or microwaveable bowls; sprinkle with cheese. Broil or microwave at High for 1-1/2 minutes or until cheese melts and is bubbly. Serve immediately with Cheese Cookies. Makes 4 servings.

CHEESE COOKIES:

1/2 cup	butter	125 mL
1/2 cup	shredded Cheddar cheese	125 mL
1 cup	all-purpose flour	250 mL
1-1/2 tsp	milk	7 mL

In bowl, cream together butter and cheese. Mix in flour, then milk; shape into ball. On lightly floured surface, roll out dough to 1/8-inch (3 mm) thickness. Cut into 1-inch (2.5 cm) rounds. Transfer to lightly greased baking sheets; prick each cookie twice with fork. Bake in 350°F (180°C) oven for 10 to 12 minutes or until golden. Let cool on racks. Makes about 36 cookies.

FRENCH BAGUETTE

Canadian all-purpose flour is ideal because the high gluten content produces strong structure for free-form loaves.

2-1/2 cups	lukewarm water	625 mL
1 tsp	granulated sugar	5 mL
1	pkg active dry yeast (or 1 tbsp/15 mL)	1
5-1/2 cups	(approx) all-purpose flour	1.25 L
1/4 cup	skim milk powder	50 mL
1 tbsp	salt	15 mL
	Cornmeal	

In mixing bowl, combine water and sugar; sprinkle in yeast and let stand for 10 minutes or until yeast is dissolved and creamy.

❦ Using electric mixer, gradually beat in 3 cups (750 mL) of the flour, skim milk powder and salt; beat until smooth, about 3 minutes. With wooden spoon, gradually stir in enough of the remaining flour to make stiff dough.

❦ Turn out onto lightly floured surface and knead until smooth and elastic, about 10 minutes. Place in lightly greased bowl, turning to grease all over. Cover with plastic wrap; let rise for 2 to 2-1/2 hours or until almost tripled in bulk. Punch down dough; cover and let rise for 1 to 1-1/2 hours or until doubled in bulk. Grease 2 heavy baking sheets and dust with cornmeal; set aside.

❦ Punch down dough; turn out onto lightly floured surface and knead into smooth ball. Divide dough into 4 equal pieces; roll each into rope about 14 inches (35 cm) long. Place 2 ropes at least 4 inches (10 cm) apart on each prepared baking sheet. Dust tops with flour. Cover with dry tea towel and let rise for about 1 hour or until doubled in bulk.

❦ Fifteen minutes before baking, place inverted baking sheet on middle rack of 425°F (220°C) oven. Place cake pan or pie plate on bottom rack. Just before baking only 2 baguettes at a time, pour 1 cup (250 mL) water into pan. Using serrated knife, cut 3 long diagonal slashes about 1/4 inch (5 mm) deep along top of each baguette. Place baking sheet with baguettes on inverted baking sheet; bake for 20 to 25 minutes or until golden brown and bottoms sound hollow when tapped. Remove to wire rack and let cool. Repeat with remaining loaves. Makes 4 baguettes.

BEGINNER'S BREAD

This basic yeast dough is extremely versatile and is easy enough for a novice to tackle successfully.
(See sidebar next page, for shaping directions.)

1 cup	milk	250 mL
2 tbsp	granulated sugar	25 mL
2 tbsp	shortening or butter	25 mL
2 tsp	salt	10 mL
1 tsp	granulated sugar	5 mL
1 cup	warm water	250 mL
1	pkg active dry yeast (or 1 tbsp/15 mL)	1
5 cups	(approx) all-purpose flour	1.25 L

In small saucepan, heat together milk, 2 tbsp (25 mL) sugar, shortening and salt until shortening has melted. Let cool to lukewarm.

❦ Dissolve 1 tsp (5 mL) sugar in warm water; sprinkle in yeast and let stand for 10 minutes or until frothy.

❦ In large mixing bowl, combine yeast mixture with milk mixture. Using electric mixer, gradually beat in 3 cups (750 mL) of the flour; beat until smooth, about 3 minutes. With wooden spoon, gradually stir in enough of the remaining flour to make moderately stiff dough.

❦ Turn out dough onto lightly floured surface and knead until smooth and elastic, about 10 minutes. Place in lightly greased bowl, turning to grease all over. Cover with plastic wrap; let rise for 1 to 1-1/2 hours or until doubled in bulk.

❦ Punch down dough; turn out onto lightly floured surface. Knead into smooth ball. Cover and let rest for 10 minutes.

❦ Shape as desired. Cover and let rise for about 1 hour or until doubled in bulk. Glaze or finish as desired.

❦ Bake in 400°F (200°C) oven until crusts are golden brown and bottoms of loaves sound hollow when tapped; 35 to 40 minutes for loaves and pull-apart buns, 25 to 30 minutes for mini-loaves, 15 to 20 minutes for individual buns. Remove from pans and let cool on racks.

FRESH FROM THE OVEN

Use these shaping variations and finishing touches to produce a wonderful assortment of delicious baked goods.

LOAVES

Divide dough in half. Knead each portion into smooth ball. Using side of hand, press to form crease halfway through each ball. Fold dough over; roll into ovals and fit into 2 greased 8- × 4-inch (1.5 L) loaf pans. Cover, let rise and bake as directed.

MINI-LOAVES

Divide dough into 12 equal portions. Knead and shape into loaves as above. Fit into twelve 1-cup (250 mL) greased mini-loaf pans. Cover, let rise and bake as directed.

PULL-APART BUNS

Divide dough into 24 equal portions. Knead each piece into smooth ball. Place about 1 inch (2.5 cm) apart in 2 greased 8-inch (2 L) square baking dishes. Cover, let rise and bake as directed.

CLOVERLEAF BUNS

Divide dough in half. Divide each half into 12 equal portions, then each portion into 3 pieces. Knead each piece into small ball; arrange groups of 3 balls in 24 greased muffin cups. Cover, let rise and bake as directed.

BOW KNOTS

Divide dough into 24 portions. Roll each piece into rope about 7 inches (18 cm) long; tie loosely in knot. Place 2 inches (5 cm) apart on greased baking sheets. Cover, let rise and bake as directed.

CRESCENT ROLLS

Divide dough into 4 equal portions. On lightly floured board, roll into 8-inch (20 cm) circles. Cut each circle into 6 wedges. Starting at wide ends, roll into crescents. Place about 2 inches (5 cm) apart on greased baking sheets. Cover, let rise and bake as directed.

FAN TANS

Divide dough in half. On lightly floured surface, roll each piece into 15- × 8-inch (38 × 20 cm) rectangle. Brush with a little melted butter. Cut each rectangle into 6 lengthwise strips. Stack strips and cut into 12 squares. Stand stacks, cut side up, in 24 greased muffin cups. Cover, let rise and bake as directed.

PARKER HOUSE BUNS

Divide dough in half. On lightly floured surface, roll each piece into 15- × 8-inch (38 × 20 cm) rectangle. Using 2-1/2-inch (6 cm) round cookie cutter, cut out circles. Brush tops with a little melted butter. Using dull edge of knife, press crease across center of each round; fold rounds over to form semi-circles. Place 2 inches (5 cm) apart on greased baking sheets. Cover, let rise and bake as directed.

AUTUMN RAREBIT SOUP

Dotted throughout Canada are small inns that care passionately about the food they serve. This velvety fall soup offers a warm welcome to guests at the Orchid Trail Inn near Wiarton, Ontario.

5 cups	cubed pumpkin or squash	1.25 L
2-1/2 cups	chicken stock	625 mL
1-1/2 cups	light beer	375 mL
2 tbsp	butter	25 mL
1	large onion, chopped	1
3	cloves garlic, crushed	3
1 cup	shredded old Cheddar cheese	250 mL
1/4 cup	pumpkin seeds	50 mL
	Salt and pepper	

In large heavy saucepan, bring pumpkin and stock to boil; reduce heat to medium, cover and simmer for 15 minutes or until tender. In blender or food processor, purée in batches.

❦ In clean saucepan, combine pumpkin purée with beer; bring to boil over medium heat, stirring often. Reduce heat and simmer for 5 minutes.

❦ Meanwhile, in small skillet, melt butter over medium-low heat; cook onion and garlic, stirring, until softened, about 5 minutes. Add to pumpkin mixture; stir in cheese and simmer gently, partially covered, for 20 minutes.

❦ Meanwhile, in skillet over medium heat, cook pumpkin seeds, shaking pan often, for 7 to 10 minutes or until golden brown and toasted.

❦ Season soup with salt to taste. Garnish with pepper and pumpkin seeds. Makes 4 to 6 servings.

CABBAGE AND KIELBASA SOUP

Hearty soups often simmer for hours. Not this thick cabbage soup zipped up with kielbasa sausage and made into a whole meal with potatoes and carrots. A bowl with Granary Buns (recipe, p. 101) or Cheese Scones (recipe, p. 129) makes a wonderful cold-weather supper.

2 tsp	vegetable oil	10 mL
1 cup	chopped onions	250 mL
1 cup	thinly sliced carrots	250 mL
1 cup	diced potatoes	250 mL
1/4 lb	kielbasa sausage, sliced and quartered	125 g
1	can (19 oz/540 mL) tomatoes (undrained), coarsely chopped	1
4 cups	shredded cabbage	1 L
2-1/2 cups	hot beef stock	625 mL
1/4 cup	chopped fresh parsley	50 mL
1 tbsp	granulated sugar	15 mL
1/2 tsp	paprika	2 mL
1/2 tsp	pepper	2 mL

In large heavy saucepan, heat oil over medium heat; cook onions, carrots, potatoes and kielbasa for 5 minutes or until onions are softened. Stir in tomatoes, cabbage, beef stock, parsley, sugar, paprika and pepper; cover and bring to boil. Reduce heat to medium-low; cover and simmer for 20 minutes or until vegetables are tender. Makes 4 servings.

Cabbage and Kielbasa Soup

SUMMER SHRIMP SOUP

A bowl of this icy soup is a perfect way to start a summer dinner party or barbecue.

1	English cucumber (about 12 inches/30 cm long)	1
2-1/4 cups	plain yogurt	550 mL
2 cups	chicken stock	500 mL
1 cup	light cream	250 mL
2/3 cup	tomato juice	150 mL
1	clove garlic, minced	1
1/2 lb	cooked peeled small shrimp	250 g
	Salt and white pepper	
	Dill sprigs	

Peel cucumber; grate coarsely. Place in colander set in sink and drain for 30 minutes, pressing occasionally.

❦ In large bowl, stir together yogurt, stock, cream, tomato juice and garlic. Set 6 of the shrimp aside for garnish; stir remaining shrimp into bowl.

❦ Spread cucumber in thin layer on double thickness of paper towels; pat dry with towels. Stir cucumber into soup; season to taste with salt and pepper. Cover and refrigerate for up to 1 day.

❦ Just before serving, taste and adjust seasoning. Garnish each serving with reserved shrimp and dill. Makes 6 servings.

SPLIT PEA SOUP

Split pea soup is a hearty winter tradition and makes a wonderful welcome home to skiers, skaters and snow shovellers alike. For a smooth soup, purée in food processor, blender or food mill. Or, purée 1 cup (250 mL) of the mixture and stir back into the soup.

	Salt and pepper	
	Croutons	

Rinse peas and place in large saucepan. Pour in water, cover and bring to boil, skimming off foam. Stir in savory and bay leaf. Reduce heat and simmer until peas are tender, 55 minutes.

❦ Meanwhile, chop celery, carrots, potato and onion into bite-size pieces.

❦ In large skillet, heat oil over medium-high heat; cook celery, carrots, potato, onion and garlic for 5 to 7 minutes or until softened. Add to saucepan; simmer, covered, for 20 to 30 minutes or until vegetables are tender. Remove bay leaf. Season with salt and pepper to taste.

❦ Ladle soup into warmed bowls; sprinkle with croutons. Makes 6 to 8 servings.

3 cups	split green peas (1-1/2 lb/750 g)	750 mL
8 cups	water	2 L
1/2 tsp	dried savory	2 mL
1	bay leaf	1
3	stalks celery	3
2	carrots	2
1	large potato, peeled	1
1	large onion	1
1/4 cup	olive oil	50 mL
3	cloves garlic, minced	3

CROUTONS

Trim crusts off 4 slices homestyle bread; cut into bite-size cubes. In large skillet, melt 1/3 cup (75 mL) butter over medium-high heat until foam subsides; add bread, stirring to coat evenly. Cook, stirring often, until crisp and golden.

CREAM OF RUTABAGA SOUP

This simple creamy soup features rutabaga at its mildest and sweetest.

1/4 cup	butter	50 mL
1 cup	sliced leeks	250 mL
3 cups	diced peeled rutabaga	750 mL
4 cups	chicken stock	1 L
1 cup	whipping cream or light cream	250 mL
2 tbsp	maple syrup	25 mL
	Salt and pepper	
	Chopped chives or green onion	

In large saucepan, melt butter over low heat; cook leeks, covered, for 5 minutes. Add rutabaga and cook, covered, for 5 minutes. Stir in stock and bring to boil. Reduce heat to low; cook, covered, for about 35 minutes or until rutabaga is very tender.

 Transfer to blender or food processor and purée in batches. Pass through food mill or sieve for an even smoother soup.

 Return to saucepan; stir in cream, maple syrup, and salt and pepper to taste. Gently heat through; serve in warmed soup bowls or tureen. Garnish with chives. Makes 4 to 6 servings.

CREAM OF FIDDLEHEAD SOUP

Fiddleheads, the curled shoots of ostrich ferns, are like wild rice and maple syrup, as distinctly Canadian as can be.
Fresh fiddleheads are naturally best here, but frozen will do as long as they are thawed first.

1/4 cup	butter	50 mL
1 cup	sliced leeks or onions	250 mL
2 tbsp	all-purpose flour	25 mL
2-1/2 cups	chicken stock	625 mL
4 cups	fiddleheads	1 L
2 cups	light cream	500 mL
1 tbsp	lemon juice	15 mL
1/4 tsp	white pepper	1 mL
Pinch	cayenne pepper	Pinch
	Salt	
1/4 cup	sour cream	50 mL

In large saucepan, melt butter over low heat; cook leeks, covered and stirring often, for 10 to 15 minutes or until softened but not browned. Add flour and cook, stirring, for 2 minutes. Gradually stir in stock; increase heat to medium-high and bring to boil, stirring constantly.

 Add fiddleheads and return to boil; reduce heat to medium, cover and simmer for 5 to 6 minutes or until fiddleheads are tender. Remove 6 fiddleheads for garnish. Purée soup in batches in blender or food processor. *(Recipe can be prepared to this point, cooled, covered and refrigerated for up to 2 days.)*

 Return purée to saucepan; whisk in cream. Cook, stirring often, for 5 minutes or just until heated through but not boiling. Stir in lemon juice, white pepper and cayenne; season with salt to taste. Garnish each serving with sour cream and fiddlehead. Makes 6 servings.

CLAM CHOWDER

Potato-based chowders are one of winter's most welcome comfort foods.

2 tbsp	butter	25 mL
1	small onion, chopped	1
1	stalk celery, chopped	1
2 tbsp	all-purpose flour	25 mL
2	cans (each 5 oz/142 g) baby clams (undrained)	2
2 cups	cubed peeled potato	500 mL
2 cups	milk	500 mL
	Salt and pepper	

In large saucepan, melt butter over medium-high heat; cook onion and celery for 3 minutes or until softened. Sprinkle with flour; reduce heat to medium and cook, stirring, for 1 minute.

❦ Drain clams, reserving liquid in measure. Add enough water to clam liquid to make 2 cups (500 mL); stir into onion mixture. Add potatoes and bring to boil; reduce heat and simmer, covered, for 10 to 15 minutes or until potatoes are tender. Stir in milk; season with salt and pepper to taste. Heat through over medium heat but do not boil. Makes about 4 servings.

GALECLIFF CRAB CHOWDER

This recipe is adapted from a Newfoundland Bed and Breakfast where the cod and crab are caught close by.

2 tbsp	butter	25 mL
1	onion, chopped	1
2 tbsp	all-purpose flour	25 mL
3 cups	water	750 mL
2	potatoes, peeled and diced	2
1	carrot, diced	1
1/2 tsp	salt	2 mL
1/2 tsp	dried savory	2 mL
1/4 tsp	pepper	1 mL
Pinch	dried thyme	Pinch
2 cups	milk	500 mL

1 lb	cod fillets, cut in bite-size pieces	500 g
1 cup	snow crab (about 1/4 lb/125 g)	250 mL

In large heavy saucepan, melt butter over medium heat; cook onion until softened, about 3 minutes. Stir in flour to coat onion; cook, stirring, for 1 minute. Add water, potatoes, carrot, salt, savory, pepper and thyme; cover and bring to boil. Reduce heat and simmer until vegetables are tender, about 15 minutes.

❦ Pour in milk; return to simmer. Add cod and return to boil. Immediately remove from heat. Add crab, breaking apart pieces; cover and let stand for 5 minutes. Taste and adjust seasoning. Makes about 4 servings.

PEACH SOUP

This pretty soup is equally delicious as a refreshing starter or a summery dessert.

2	peaches, peeled and halved	2
1 cup	plain yogurt	250 mL
2 tbsp	frozen orange juice concentrate	25 mL
1 tbsp	liquid honey (optional)	15 mL
	Fresh mint leaves	

In blender or food processor, process peaches, yogurt, orange juice concentrate, and honey (if using) until smooth. Garnish each serving with mint and serve immediately. Makes 4 appetizers.

Clam Chowder

HOMEMADE CHICKEN SOUP

Tender chunks of chicken, fresh vegetables and egg noodles in a flavorful broth make this the comforting
chicken soup you loved as a child.

2 tbsp	butter	25 mL
1/2 cup	minced onion	125 mL
1-1/2 cups	sliced carrots	375 mL
1-1/2 cups	sliced celery	375 mL
1 cup	sliced peeled parsnips	250 mL
1-1/2 cups	egg noodles	375 mL
1/4 cup	chopped fresh parsley	50 mL
	Hot pepper sauce	
	Salt and pepper	
	HOMEMADE CHICKEN STOCK:	
5 lb	stewing hen or roasting chicken	2.2 kg
16 cups	water	4 L
2	carrots, chopped	2
2	stalks celery, chopped	2
1	onion, chopped	1
1	leek, chopped (optional)	1
3	sprigs fresh parsley	3

1	bay leaf	1
1 tsp	salt	5 mL
1/2 tsp	dried thyme	2 mL
1/2 tsp	whole black peppercorns	2 mL

HOMEMADE CHICKEN STOCK: Place hen in stock pot or Dutch oven; add water. Bring to boil; skim off froth.

❧ Add carrots, celery, onion, leek (if using), parsley, bay leaf, salt, thyme and peppercorns. Reduce heat and simmer, partially covered, for 2 to 2-1/2 hours for hen, 1 to 1-1/2 hours for chicken, or until juices run clear when thigh is pierced.

❧ Remove chicken and refrigerate. Strain liquid through cheesecloth-lined sieve into large shallow bowl, pressing vegetables to extract as much liquid as possible before discarding. Let stock cool.

❧ Cover and refrigerate stock for at least 6 hours or overnight; remove fat from surface. Set 8 cups (2 L) aside. Refrigerate remaining 7 cups (1.75 L) stock for up to 3 days or freeze for up to 4 months for another use.

Continued on next page

In large saucepan, melt butter over medium heat; cook onion for 3 minutes or until softened.

Add reserved 8 cups (2 L) chicken stock; bring to boil. Stir in carrots, celery and parsnips; cover and cook over medium-high heat for 5 minutes.

Add egg noodles; cook, uncovered, for 8 to 10 minutes or until noodles and vegetables are tender.

Remove skin and bones from cooked chicken. Dice meat and add 2 cups (500 mL) to soup; heat through. Stir in parsley; season with hot pepper sauce, salt and pepper to taste. Refrigerate remaining chicken for another use. Makes 6 to 8 servings.

VARIATION

ORIENTAL CHICKEN SOUP: Follow recipe for Homemade Chicken Soup but add 1 tbsp (15 mL) chopped gingerroot to onions while softening. Reduce carrots and celery to 1 cup (250 mL) each diagonally sliced. Substitute 1 cup (250 mL) diagonally sliced bok choy for the parsnips. Omit egg noodles and cook soup for 10 to 15 minutes or until vegetables are softened. Substitute slivered chicken for diced. Add 1 cup (250 mL) snow peas, 1/4 cup (50 mL) sherry and 2 tbsp (25 mL) soy sauce along with the chicken. Omit parsley and hot pepper sauce.

HARVEST CORN CHOWDER

You can substitute carrots for red pepper, and parsley for coriander. Serve with Cheese Scones (recipe, p. 129).

1 tbsp	olive oil	15 mL
1 cup	chopped onion	250 mL
1/4 tsp	hot pepper flakes	1 mL
2 cups	diced peeled potatoes	500 mL
1 cup	chopped celery	250 mL
1/2 cup	chopped sweet red pepper	125 mL
3 cups	chicken stock	750 mL
2 cups	corn	500 mL
1	can (10 oz/284 mL) creamed corn	1
1 cup	milk	250 mL
2 tbsp	finely chopped fresh coriander	25 mL
	Salt and pepper	

In large saucepan, heat oil over high heat; cook onion and hot pepper flakes, stirring, for 1 minute. Add potatoes, celery and sweet red pepper; cook, stirring, for 2 minutes. Pour in chicken stock; cover and bring to boil.

Reduce heat; simmer for 5 to 8 minutes or until vegetables are tender-crisp. Add corn, creamed corn and milk; cook until heated through. Stir in coriander; season with salt and pepper to taste. Makes 4 servings.

AGRIBITION LENTIL SOUP

This flavorful soup is an annual tradition at Agribition, Canada's international agricultural fair in Regina.

1 tbsp	vegetable oil	15 mL
2 cups	chopped onions	500 mL
8 cups	chicken or beef stock	2 L
1	can (19 oz/540 mL) tomatoes	1
1 cup	dried lentils, rinsed	250 mL
1 cup	thinly sliced carrots	250 mL
1/2 tsp	each dried thyme and marjoram	2 mL
	Salt and pepper	
1/4 cup	dry sherry	50 mL
1 cup	shredded Cheddar cheese	250 mL

In 16-cup (4 L) stockpot or Dutch oven, heat oil over medium heat; cook onions until softened, about 3 minutes. Add stock, tomatoes, lentils, carrots, thyme and marjoram; simmer, covered, for 45 minutes or until lentils and vegetables are tender. Season with salt and pepper to taste. Stir in sherry. Place 1 to 2 tbsp (15 to 25 mL) of the cheese in each soup bowl; ladle soup into bowls. Makes about 10 servings.

COUNTRY MORNINGS

Weekend mornings hold the promise of the day — a pot of coffee steaming on the table overlooking the garden, fresh currant-studded scones lying in wait under a napkin, and an easy-to-put-together frittata to take you into the afternoon. Weekends and a leisurely breakfast — what better way to slow down and catch up!

SPEEDY CINNAMON-SWIRL LOAF

Using instant yeast and a food processor, this loaf takes much less time and effort than a traditional yeast bread, yet has the same delicious flavor.

3-1/4 cups	all-purpose flour	800 mL
1/4 cup	granulated sugar	50 mL
1/4 cup	butter, cut in 1-inch (2.5 cm) pieces	50 mL
1 tsp	salt	5 mL
1	pkg quick-rising instant yeast (or 1 tbsp/15 mL)	1
3/4 cup	(approx) milk	175 mL
2	eggs, lightly beaten	2
	FILLING:	
1/2 cup	packed brown sugar	125 mL
1/4 cup	chopped pecans	50 mL
1/4 cup	raisins	50 mL
1 tbsp	cinnamon	15 mL
1/4 cup	butter, softened	50 mL
	GLAZE:	
1	egg yolk	1
1 tbsp	milk	15 mL
	Icing sugar	

In food processor, process flour, sugar, butter, salt and yeast for 30 seconds. Heat milk until hot (125 to 130°F/50 to 54°C). With motor running, alternately pour in eggs and enough of the milk through feed tube to form dough into ball. Process for 1 minute to knead. Place dough in greased bowl, turning to grease all over. Cover and let rest for 10 minutes.

❧ FILLING: In small bowl, combine sugar, pecans, raisins and cinnamon.

❧ On lightly floured surface, roll out dough into 12- × 9-inch (30 × 23 cm) rectangle. Spread with butter, leaving 1/2-inch (1 cm) border uncovered. Sprinkle sugar mixture over butter. Starting at long side, roll up dough jelly roll-style; pinch ends together to seal. Place on greased rimmed baking sheet. Cover and let rise until doubled in bulk, about 1 hour.

❧ GLAZE: Beat egg yolk with milk; brush over loaf. Bake in 375°F (190°C) oven for 15 minutes; cover with foil to prevent overbrowning. Bake for 15 to 20 minutes longer or until golden and bottom of loaf sounds hollow when tapped. Let cool on rack; dust with icing sugar. Makes 1 loaf.

(clockwise from top): Speedy Cinnamon-Swirl Loaf; Quick Orange-Cream Croissants (recipe, p. 116); Two-Salmon Pâté (recipe, p. 13); Mushroom Frittata (recipe, p. 122)

QUICK ORANGE-CREAM CROISSANTS

Each light croissant holds a nugget of orange-flavored cream cheese. This easy quick bread dough makes croissants possible for at-home bakers in a hurry.

1-3/4 cups	all-purpose flour	425 mL
1 tbsp	baking powder	15 mL
1 tsp	granulated sugar	5 mL
1/2 tsp	salt	2 mL
1/3 cup	butter	75 mL
2/3 cup	(approx) milk	150 mL
	FILLING:	
4 oz	cream cheese, softened	125 g
2 tbsp	granulated sugar	25 mL
2 tsp	grated orange rind	10 mL
	GLAZE:	
1	egg yolk	1
1 tbsp	milk	15 mL
	Icing sugar	

FILLING: In small bowl, beat cream cheese with sugar; stir in orange rind. Set aside.

In large bowl, stir together flour, baking powder, sugar and salt. Using pastry blender or 2 knives, cut in butter until mixture resembles coarse crumbs. Using fork, stir in enough milk to make soft, slightly sticky dough; gather into ball.

Turn out dough onto lightly floured surface and knead gently about 8 times or until smooth. Divide dough in half. On lightly floured surface, roll out each portion into 9-inch (23 cm) circle. Cut each circle into 6 wedges.

Place 2 tsp (10 mL) filling about 1 inch (2.5 cm) from curved edge of each wedge. Roll up dough toward narrow end to form croissant. Place on lightly greased baking sheet.

GLAZE: Beat egg yolk with milk; brush on croissants. Bake in 375°F (190°C) oven for about 20 minutes or until golden brown. Let cool. Dust with icing sugar. Makes 12 croissants.

BLUEBERRY MUFFINS

A pot of coffee, a basket of blueberry muffins and a jar of honey—there's no better start to a lazy weekend morning!

2 cups	all-purpose flour	500 mL
2 tsp	baking powder	10 mL
1/4 tsp	salt	1 mL
1/2 cup	butter, softened	125 mL
1 cup	granulated sugar	250 mL
2	eggs	2
3/4 cup	milk	175 mL
1-1/2 cups	fresh blueberries	375 mL

In bowl, combine flour, baking powder and salt. In separate bowl, cream butter with sugar; beat in eggs one at a time. Stir in milk. Make a well in center of dry ingredients; pour in milk mixture. Sprinkle with blueberries and stir just until moistened.

Spoon into large deep well-greased or paper-lined muffin tins, filling to top. Bake in 375°F (190°C) oven for about 25 minutes or until golden and firm to the touch. Makes 12 muffins.

BLUEBERRIES AT THEIR BEST

Blueberries range in size from the small flavorful wild or lowbush variety (found in Eastern Canada) to the larger highbush berries (cultivated mainly in British Columbia), and in color from soft blue to deep blackish blue. The silvery bloom on the skin of some berries is a natural protective waxy coating. Choose well-colored berries (red or green berries will not ripen) of fairly uniform size. Refrigerate and use within two or three days. Just before serving, wash berries, remove any stems and drain.

BIG SCOOP ORANGE BRAN MUFFINS

A zester makes quick work of the tangy orange rind for these big batch muffins. Use a large ice-cream scoop for filling muffin cups. The batter keeps for up to a week in the refrigerator, so you can bake these muffins in batches for a fresh-from-the-oven treat. The muffins freeze well, too.

5 cups	100% bran cereal	1.25 L
4 cups	natural bran	1 L
3 cups	raisins	750 mL
1 cup	rolled oats	250 mL
1/2 cup	coarsely grated orange rind (4 large oranges)	125 mL
2-1/2 cups	boiling water	625 mL
5	eggs	5
4 cups	buttermilk	1 L
1-1/2 cups	packed brown sugar	375 mL
1 cup	vegetable oil	250 mL
1 cup	fancy molasses	250 mL
1/2 cup	orange juice	125 mL
4 cups	all-purpose flour	1 L
2 cups	whole wheat flour	500 mL
2 tbsp	baking soda	25 mL
1 tbsp	salt	15 mL
1 tsp	nutmeg	5 mL

In large bowl, stir together bran cereal, natural bran, raisins, rolled oats and orange rind; pour in water, stirring well. Let stand for 10 minutes.

Meanwhile, in separate bowl, whisk eggs; add buttermilk, sugar, oil, molasses and orange juice. Stir into bran mixture. Combine all-purpose and whole wheat flours, baking soda, salt and nutmeg. Add to bran mixture, stirring until just mixed. *(Batter can be covered and refrigerated for up to 1 week.)*

Scoop batter into large greased or paper-lined muffin cups, filling to top. Bake in 375°F (190°C) oven for about 25 minutes or until tops are firm to the touch. Makes about 48 muffins.

BANANA CHOCOLATE CHIP MUFFINS

Bananas meet chocolate in scrumptious muffins that are perfect for a brunch, brown bag or munching with a glass of cold milk.

2 cups	all-purpose flour	500 mL
1/4 cup	granulated sugar	50 mL
2 tsp	baking powder	10 mL
1 tsp	baking soda	5 mL
Pinch	salt	Pinch
1 cup	chocolate chips	250 mL
2 cups	mashed ripe bananas (about 3 large)	500 mL
1/2 cup	butter, melted	125 mL
1/4 cup	milk	50 mL
2	eggs	2

In large bowl, stir together flour, sugar, baking powder, baking soda and salt; add chocolate chips. Blend together bananas, butter, milk and eggs; with fork, stir into flour mixture just until blended. Don't overmix.

❧ Fill greased muffin cups three-quarters full. Bake in 350°F (180°C) oven for 25 minutes or until golden brown and firm to the touch. Makes 18 muffins.

APPLE-CINNAMON MULTIGRAIN CEREAL

Naturally sweetened with apple juice and crunchy with granola and chopped apple, this hot cereal turns breakfast into an event! If you like your cereal sweeter, use all apple juice.

2 cups	unsweetened apple juice	500 mL
1 cup	water	250 mL
1 cup	multigrain cereal	250 mL
1/2 tsp	salt	2 mL
1/2 tsp	cinnamon	2 mL
1/3 cup	raisins	75 mL
1	apple (unpeeled), chopped	1
1/2 cup	plain yogurt	125 mL
1/2 cup	granola	125 mL

In large saucepan, combine apple juice, water, cereal, salt and cinnamon; bring to boil, stirring frequently. Reduce heat to medium and boil for 3 minutes. Add raisins and apple; cook for about 2 minutes or until desired consistency.

❧ Top each serving with dollop of yogurt; sprinkle with granola. Makes 4 to 6 servings.

BERRY BREAKFAST PUFF

For a summer weekend brunch treat, fill the center of this skillet-baked pancake with the best of the season's strawberries, blueberries, raspberries or blackberries. If the handle of your skillet is not ovenproof, wrap it in foil. To serve 4, make the recipe twice.

3	eggs	3
1/2 cup	all-purpose flour	125 mL
1/2 cup	milk	125 mL
2 tbsp	granulated sugar	25 mL
1 tsp	vanilla	5 mL
	Icing sugar	
1-1/2 cups	berries	375 mL
	Yogurt or whipped cream	

In bowl, whisk eggs with flour; gradually whisk in milk. Whisk in granulated sugar and vanilla. Pour into greased 8-inch (20 cm) skillet; bake in 425°F (220°C) oven for 15 to 20 minutes or until puffed and golden. Dust with icing sugar; mound berries in center. Serve immediately with yogurt. Makes 2 servings.

QUICK CINNAMON BUNS AND CHEESE AND HERB CRESCENTS

This recipe makes two batches—make one of whole wheat cinnamon buns and another of savory cheese and herb crescent rolls. If you wish all cinnamon buns, double the cinnamon filling.

	Quick Dough (recipe follows)	
	CINNAMON BUNS:	
2 tbsp	butter	25 mL
2 tbsp	apricot jam	25 mL
2 tbsp	packed brown sugar	25 mL
1 tsp	cinnamon	5 mL
1/4 cup	sliced almonds	50 mL
1 tbsp	butter, melted	15 mL
	CHEESE AND HERB CRESCENTS:	
2 tbsp	butter, softened	25 mL
1/3 cup	freshly grated Parmesan cheese	75 mL
1 tsp	dried basil	5 mL
	Pepper	
1	egg yolk	1
1 tbsp	water	15 mL

CINNAMON FILLING: Roll out 1 portion of dough into 16- × 8-inch (40 × 20 cm) rectangle. Combine butter and jam; spread over dough. Combine sugar and cinnamon; sprinkle over butter mixture. Top with almonds. Roll up, jelly roll-style, from long side. Cut into 16 slices; place in greased 9-inch (1.5 L) round cake pan.

🌰 CHEESE AND HERB CRESCENTS: Roll out 1 portion of dough into 12-inch (30 cm) circle. Spread with butter; sprinkle with cheese, basil, and pepper to taste. Cut into 16 triangles. From base of triangle, roll up each toward narrow end to form crescent-shaped roll; place, seam side down, on lightly greased baking sheet. Beat egg yolk with water; brush over dough.

🌰 Cover buns and crescents; let rise in warm place for 30 to 40 minutes or until doubled in bulk. Bake in 400°F (200°C) oven; bake crescents for 10 minutes, buns for 20 minutes, or until lightly browned. Brush cinnamon buns with melted butter. Serve warm. Makes 16 buns and 16 crescents.

	QUICK DOUGH:	
2 cups	whole wheat flour	500 mL
1-1/2 cups	(approx) all-purpose flour	375 mL
1/4 cup	granulated sugar	50 mL

1	pkg quick-rising instant yeast (or 1 tbsp/15 mL)	1
1/2 tsp	salt	2 mL
1-1/4 cups	milk	300 mL
2 tbsp	butter	25 mL
1	egg	1

In large bowl, combine whole wheat flour, 1 cup (250 mL) of the all-purpose flour, sugar, yeast and salt. Heat milk and butter until hot (125 to 130°F/52 to 54°C). Stir into flour mixture, along with egg, beating well with wooden spoon. Mix in enough of the remaining flour until dough is no longer sticky.

🌰 Turn out onto floured surface and knead for 10 minutes until smooth and elastic. Cover; let rest for 10 minutes in warm place. Divide into 2 portions.

BUTTERMILK BUCKWHEAT PANCAKES

No collection of country recipes would be complete without a long-standing breakfast favorite—buckwheat pancakes.
Serve with the classic accompaniments of maple syrup and sausages or peameal bacon.

2	eggs	2
2-1/2 cups	buttermilk	625 mL
2 tbsp	butter, melted	25 mL
1 tbsp	molasses or honey	15 mL
1-1/2 cups	buckwheat flour	375 mL
1/2 cup	all-purpose flour	125 mL
3/4 tsp	baking soda	4 mL
3/4 tsp	salt	4 mL
	Butter for cooking	

In large bowl, whisk together eggs, buttermilk, melted butter and molasses. Stir together buckwheat and all-purpose flours, baking soda and salt; sprinkle over buttermilk mixture and stir just enough to moisten.

In skillet, melt just enough butter over medium heat to coat surface of pan. Cook batter, 1/4 cup (50 mL) for each pancake, for 1-1/2 to 2 minutes or until bubbles on top break but do not fill in and pancakes are golden brown on bottom. Turn pancakes and cook for 30 to 60 seconds or until golden brown. Makes 16 to 20 pancakes.

BLUEBERRY YOGURT PANCAKES OR WAFFLES WITH LEMON-HONEY BUTTER

With this versatile batter, it's easy to make delicious fruit-filled pancakes or waffles.

1-1/2 cups	all-purpose flour	375 mL
3 tbsp	granulated sugar	50 mL
1 tsp	baking powder	5 mL
1 tsp	baking soda	5 mL
1/2 tsp	salt	2 mL
1 cup	plain yogurt	250 mL
1/2 cup	milk	125 mL
3	eggs, separated	3
3 tbsp	butter, melted	50 mL
3/4 cup	blueberries	175 mL
2 tbsp	unsalted butter, melted	25 mL
	LEMON-HONEY BUTTER:	
1/2 cup	unsalted butter	125 mL
1/4 cup	liquid honey	50 mL
1-1/2 tsp	grated lemon rind	7 mL
1 tsp	lemon juice	5 mL

LEMON-HONEY BUTTER: In small bowl, whip butter until light; blend in honey, lemon rind and juice. Set aside.

In large bowl, mix together flour, sugar, baking powder, baking soda and salt. Stir together yogurt, milk, egg yolks and butter; mix into flour mixture with a few quick strokes. Beat egg whites until stiff, but not dry, peaks form; fold into batter. Fold in blueberries.

PANCAKES: In nonstick skillet, heat unsalted butter over medium heat; cook batter, 1/4 cup (50 mL) for each pancake, for 1 to 1-1/2 minutes or until bubbles break but do not fill in and pancakes are golden on bottom. Turn and cook for 30 seconds or until set.

WAFFLES: Brush heated waffle iron with unsalted butter. Pour in enough batter to fill about two-thirds full. Close lid and cook, turning once, for 3 minutes or until no longer steaming and waffles are golden. Repeat with remaining batter.

Serve pancakes or waffles with Lemon-Honey Butter. Makes 14 pancakes or 8 large waffles.

Blueberry Yogurt Pancakes with Lemon-Honey Butter

MUSHROOM FRITTATA

Weekend guests won't miss bacon and eggs when this savory frittata comes to the table.

1 tbsp	butter	15 mL
2 cups	sliced mushrooms	500 mL
8	eggs	8
1/4 cup	sour cream	50 mL
2 cups	shredded Swiss cheese	500 mL
3/4 cup	fresh bread crumbs	175 mL
4	green onions, chopped	4
1/3 cup	chopped fresh parsley	75 mL
3/4 tsp	salt	4 mL
Pinch	pepper	Pinch

In skillet, melt butter over medium-high heat; cook mushrooms, stirring occasionally, for 3 to 5 minutes or until tender.

❧ In bowl, whisk together eggs and sour cream; stir in mushrooms, cheese, bread crumbs, onions, parsley, salt and pepper.

❧ Pour into buttered 10-inch (25 cm) pie plate or flan pan. Bake in 350°F (180°C) oven for 30 to 35 minutes or until golden and set. Makes 8 servings.

RICH RAISIN BREAD

Use this recipe, rich with eggs and butter, as the basis for a delicious assortment of sweet baked goods
(see Fruit and Nut Variations, next page).

1/2 cup	milk	125 mL
1/4 cup	granulated sugar	50 mL
1/4 cup	butter	50 mL
1 tsp	salt	5 mL
1 tsp	granulated sugar	5 mL
1/2 cup	warm water	125 mL
1	pkg active dry yeast (or 1 tbsp/15 mL)	1
2	eggs, beaten	2
3-1/2 cups	(approx) all-purpose flour	875 mL
1 cup	raisins	250 mL
	EGG GLAZE:	
1	egg yolk	1
2 tbsp	milk	25 mL

In small saucepan, heat together milk, 1/4 cup (50 mL) sugar, butter and salt until butter has melted. Let cool to lukewarm.

❧ Dissolve 1 tsp (5 mL) sugar in warm water; sprinkle in yeast and let stand for 10 minutes or until frothy.

❧ In large mixing bowl, combine yeast mixture, milk mixture and eggs. Using electric mixer, gradually beat in 1-1/2 cups (375 mL) of the flour; beat until smooth, about 2 minutes. With wooden spoon, gradually stir in enough of the remaining flour to make soft, slightly sticky dough.

❧ Turn out dough onto lightly floured surface and knead until smooth and elastic, 5 to 10 minutes. Place in lightly greased bowl, turning to grease all over. Cover with plastic wrap (or greased waxed paper and tea towel); let rise for 1 to 1-1/2 hours or until doubled in bulk.

❧ Punch down dough; knead in raisins and shape into smooth ball. Using side of hand, press to form crease halfway through ball. Fold dough over, roll into oval and fit into greased 9-× 5-inch (2 L) loaf pan. Cover and let rise for about 1 hour or until doubled in bulk.

❧ EGG GLAZE: Stir egg yolk with milk; brush over loaf.

❧ Bake in 375°F (190°C) oven for 35 to 40 minutes or until crust is golden brown and bottom of loaf sounds hollow when tapped. Remove from pan and let cool on rack. Makes 1 loaf.

FRUIT AND NUT VARIATIONS

When adding dried fruit and nuts, knead in after the dough has risen once because they tend to weigh it down.

KUGELHOF

Decrease raisins to 1/2 cup (125 mL). After dough has risen once, knead in raisins and shape into smooth ball. Flatten into 8-inch (20 cm) round. Poke hole in center to create doughnut shape. Arrange whole blanched almonds in hollows of greased 9-inch (3 L) kugelhof mould. Fit dough into mould, pressing evenly into bottom. Cover, let rise and bake as directed, omitting egg glaze. Invert onto rack and let cool. Dust with icing sugar.

CROWN LOAF

Substitute 1/2 cup (125 mL) mixed candied fruit, 1/4 cup (50 mL) raisins and 1/4 cup (50 mL) pecans for the 1 cup (250 mL) raisins. After dough has risen once, knead in fruit and nuts. Divide dough into 7 equal portions; knead each piece into smooth ball. Place 1 ball in center of greased 9-inch (2.5 L) springform pan; arrange remaining balls around circumference of pan. Cover, let rise, brush with egg glaze and bake as directed.

SPIRAL LOAF

Substitute 1/2 cup (125 mL) mixed candied fruit, 1/4 cup (50 mL) raisins and 1/4 cup (50 mL) chopped pecans for the 1 cup (250 mL) raisins. After dough has risen once, knead in fruit and nuts. Roll into 30-inch (76-cm) long rope. Place one end of rope in center of greased 9-inch (2.5 L) springform pan; coil remaining rope around, tucking outside end firmly underneath. Cover, let rise, brush with egg glaze and bake as directed.

EASTER EGG RING

Stir 1 tbsp (15 mL) grated orange rind and 4 tsp (20 mL) crushed aniseed into flour before combining with yeast mixture. Substitute 1/2 cup (125 mL) chopped mixed candied fruit, 1/4 cup (50 mL) raisins and 1/4 cup (50 mL) chopped almonds for the 1 cup (250 mL) raisins. After dough has risen once, knead in fruit and nuts. Divide dough in half. Roll each piece into 26-inch (66 cm) long rope and twist together. Transfer to greased baking sheet. Bring ends together to form into ring, pinching ends to seal. Gently pull twisted ropes apart and tuck 6 whole uncooked eggs (colored if desired) into openings, placing eggs evenly around ring. (Eggs will become hard-cooked during baking.) Cover, let rise, brush with egg glaze and bake as directed.

HOT CROSS BUNS

Stir 1-1/2 tsp (7 mL) cinnamon, 1 tsp (5 mL) grated lemon rind, 1/2 tsp (2 mL) nutmeg and 1/2 tsp (2 mL) allspice into flour before combining with yeast mixture. Substitute 1/2 cup (125 mL) chopped mixed candied fruit, 1/4 cup (50 mL) raisins and 1/4 cup (50 mL) chopped pecans for the 1 cup (250 mL) raisins. After dough has risen once, knead in fruit and nuts. Divide dough into 12 equal portions; knead each piece into smooth ball. Place balls 2 inches (5 cm) apart on greased baking sheet; flatten slightly. Cover, let rise and brush with egg glaze as directed. Using serrated knife or razor, slash cross on tops of buns. Bake for 20 to 25 minutes or until crusts are golden and bottoms of buns sound hollow when tapped. (Combine 1 cup/250 mL icing sugar with 2 tbsp/25 mL milk and drizzle into crosses of cooled buns, if desired.)

ON THE VERANDA

Picture yourself in paradise, the veranda version. . . . A tall frosty glass of lemonade at your elbow, the pitcher close by for a refill. A plate of ginger thins or almond butterfingers to nibble on, maybe a few slices of strawberry tea bread, too. Listen to the faint buzz of bumblebees nosediving into the lupins and delphiniums. . . . How perfectly summer!

ALMOND BUTTERFINGERS

Shortbread-type cookies taste every bit as delicious in the summertime as they do at Christmas.

1 cup	butter, softened	250 mL
1/2 cup	instant dissolving (fruit/berry) sugar	125 mL
1/4 tsp	almond extract	1 mL
1-3/4 cups	all-purpose flour	425 mL
1/2 cup	ground almonds	125 mL

In bowl, cream together butter and sugar; blend in almond extract. Gradually blend in flour and almonds; press into ball. Turn out onto lightly floured surface and knead very lightly until smooth.

🍎 Roll out dough to 1/2-inch (1 cm) thick rectangle. With sharp knife, cut into fingers about 3 inches (8 cm) long and 1/2 inch (1 cm) wide; place on ungreased baking sheet. Prick each cookie several times with fork. Bake in 300°F (150°C) oven for 20 to 25 minutes or until very lightly browned. Let cool for a few minutes on baking sheet; remove to racks to cool completely. Makes about 2-1/2 dozen.

LEMON CRISPS

Crisp, light and very lemony, these are the ultimate in summer cookies.

1/2 cup	butter, softened	125 mL
1 cup	granulated sugar	250 mL
1	egg	1
1 tbsp	grated lemon rind	15 mL
2 tbsp	lemon juice	25 mL
1-3/4 cups	all-purpose flour	425 mL
1/2 tsp	salt	2 mL
1/2 tsp	baking soda	2 mL
1/2 tsp	ginger	2 mL
	TOPPING (OPTIONAL):	
	Granulated sugar	
	Grated lemon rind	

In bowl, cream together butter and sugar; beat in egg, lemon rind and juice. Combine flour, salt, baking soda and ginger; gradually blend into creamed mixture. Cover and refrigerate until firm. Shape dough into cylinder 1-3/4 inches (4 cm) in diameter. Wrap in plastic and chill until very firm (or freeze).

🍎 With sharp knife, cut dough into very thin slices (1/8 inch/3 mm or less); place on greased baking sheets about 2 inches (5 cm) apart.

🍎 TOPPING: If desired, sprinkle cookies lightly with sugar and lemon rind.

🍎 Bake in 375°F (190°C) oven for 6 to 8 minutes or until very lightly browned. Let cool for about 2 minutes on baking sheets; remove to racks to cool completely. Makes about 5 dozen.

Lemon Crisps (left) and Ginger Thins (recipe, p. 130)

124

MATRIMONIAL CAKE

Every new generation discovers how delicious these buttery date squares are. For an extra treat,
serve warm with vanilla ice cream.

1 lb	pitted dates, chopped (about 3 cups/750 mL)	500 g
1-1/2 cups	water	375 mL
1/3 cup	lemon juice	75 mL
1 tbsp	grated lemon rind	15 mL
2 cups	all-purpose flour	500 mL
2 cups	rolled oats	500 mL
1 cup	packed brown sugar	250 mL
1 tsp	baking powder	5 mL
1-1/2 cups	butter	375 mL

In heavy saucepan, combine dates, water, lemon juice and rind; bring to boil. Reduce heat to low and cook, stirring often, for about 10-15 minutes or until smooth and thickened.

❦ In large bowl, combine flour, rolled oats, sugar and baking powder. Using pastry blender, cut in butter until mixture resembles coarse crumbs.

❦ Press half of the crumb mixture into 9-inch (2.5 L) square cake pan; spread with date mixture. Top evenly with remaining crumb mixture. Bake in 350°F (180°C) oven for 35 minutes or until golden brown. Cut into squares to serve. Makes 20 squares.

GARDEN LOAF

Enjoy this moist, lightly spiced loaf with a refreshing cup of tea.

3	eggs	3
1 cup	packed brown sugar	250 mL
1/2 cup	liquid honey	125 mL
1 cup	vegetable oil	250 mL
2 tsp	vanilla	10 mL
1 cup	finely shredded carrots	250 mL
1 cup	finely shredded (unpeeled) zucchini	250 mL
1-1/2 cups	all-purpose flour	375 mL
1-1/2 cups	whole wheat flour	375 mL
1-1/2 tsp	cinnamon	7 mL
1 tsp	baking powder	5 mL
1 tsp	baking soda	5 mL
1 tsp	salt	5 mL
1/2 tsp	nutmeg	2 mL
1/4 cup	coarsely chopped walnuts	50 mL
1/4 cup	raisins	50 mL

In mixing bowl, beat eggs well; gradually beat in sugar and honey. Beat in oil and vanilla; stir in carrots and zucchini. *(Use food processor for superfast shredding of carrots and zucchini.)*

❦ In separate bowl, mix together all-purpose and whole wheat flours, cinnamon, baking powder, baking soda, salt and nutmeg; stir into vegetable mixture. Stir in walnuts and raisins.

❦ Pour into 2 greased 8- × 4-inch (1.5 L) loaf pans; bake in 350°F (180°C) oven for 45 to 55 minutes or until tester inserted in centers comes out clean. Let cool in pans for 10 minutes; turn out onto racks to cool completely. Makes 2 loaves.

THE PERFECT CUP OF TEA

Use fresh cold water brought to a galloping boil. Add a little to the teapot to warm it, then pour the water off. Add tea to the pot (1 tsp/5 mL for each cup and one for the pot — or one teabag for two cups); add boiling water (6 oz/170 mL for each cup served) and let the tea steep for 5 minutes. For a less strong cup of tea, more water may be added after, not before, steeping.

STRAWBERRY TEA BREAD

Fresh berries in season are wonderful for this recipe, but thawed frozen unsweetened berries let you enjoy this delicious loaf year-round. Serve with Strawberry Butter (see sidebar, this page) for even more strawberry flavor.

2 cups	all-purpose flour	500 mL
1-1/2 cups	rolled oats (not instant)	375 mL
1 tsp	cinnamon	5 mL
1 tsp	salt	5 mL
1 tsp	baking soda	5 mL
1/2 tsp	baking powder	2 mL
3	eggs	3
1 cup	granulated sugar	250 mL
1 cup	vegetable oil	250 mL
1 tsp	vanilla	5 mL
2 cups	crushed strawberries (about 4 cups/1 L whole berries)	500 mL

Mix together flour, oats, cinnamon, salt, baking soda and baking powder; set aside.

❧ In large bowl, beat together eggs, sugar, oil and vanilla; stir in dry ingredients just until mixed. Add strawberries and stir to combine completely.

❧ Pour batter into two greased and floured 8- × 4-inch (1.5 L) loaf pans. Bake in 375°F (190°C) oven for 45 to 50 minutes or until tops are browned and firm to the touch, and cake tester inserted in centers comes out clean. Run knife around edges of loaf pans; let cool in pans on rack for 10 minutes. Turn out onto rack; let cool completely. Makes 2 loaves.

STRAWBERRY BUTTER

Flavored butters are tasty on simple tea breads, hot biscuits or scones.

❧ In small bowl, beat 1/2 cup (125 mL) softened butter until light and creamy; beat in 2 tbsp (25 mL) icing sugar. Beat in 1/4 cup (50 mL) crushed strawberries (about 1/2 cup/125 mL whole berries). Spoon into serving dish. Makes about 3/4 cup (175 mL).

SCONES WITH CURRANTS

Hot from the oven, scones are the quintessential partner for a cup of tea. Serve with Strawberry Jam (recipe, p. 177).

2-1/4 cups	all-purpose flour	550 mL
2 tbsp	granulated sugar	25 mL
2-1/2 tsp	baking powder	12 mL
1/2 tsp	baking soda	2 mL
1/2 tsp	salt	2 mL
1/2 cup	cold butter, cubed	125 mL
1/2 cup	currants	125 mL
1 cup	buttermilk	250 mL
1	egg, lightly beaten	1

In large bowl, stir together flour, sugar, baking powder, baking soda and salt. Using pastry blender or two knives, cut in butter until mixture resembles coarse crumbs. Stir in currants.

❦ Add buttermilk all at once, stirring with fork to make soft, slightly sticky dough.

❦ With lightly floured hands, press dough into ball. On lightly floured surface, knead gently 10 times.

❦ Pat out dough into 3/4-inch (2 cm) thick round.

❦ Using 2-1/2-inch (6 cm) floured cutter, cut out rounds. Place on ungreased baking sheet. Gather up scraps and repat dough once; cut out more rounds.

❦ Brush tops of scones with egg. Bake in 425°F (220°C) oven for 12 to 15 minutes or until golden. Makes about 12 scones.

VARIATIONS

DRIED FRUIT AND LEMON SCONES: Substitute 1/2 cup (125 mL) raisins, dried blueberries, dried cranberries, chopped dried cherries (not glacé), apricots or prunes for currants. Add 2 tsp (10 mL) grated lemon rind to dry mixture.

CHEESE SCONES: Omit sugar and currants. Add 1/4 tsp (1 mL) cayenne pepper to flour mixture. Add 1 cup (250 mL) shredded old Cheddar cheese after butter has been cut in.

> When mixing ingredients for scones, stir in liquid only until combined to prevent overworking of dough. Knead dough gently and pat out scraps only once in order to yield flaky results.

BUTTER TART SQUARES

This is the fast and easy way to get a butter tart taste without all the fuss of pastry.

1 cup	all-purpose flour	250 mL
1/4 cup	granulated sugar	50 mL
1/2 cup	butter	125 mL
	TOPPING:	
2 tbsp	butter, melted	25 mL
2	eggs, lightly beaten	2
1 cup	packed brown sugar	250 mL
2 tbsp	all-purpose flour	25 mL
1/2 tsp	baking powder	2 mL
1/2 tsp	vanilla	2 mL
Pinch	salt	Pinch
1 cup	raisins	250 mL
1/2 cup	coarsely chopped pecans	125 mL

In bowl, combine flour with sugar; with pastry blender, cut in butter until crumbly. Press into 9-inch (2.5 L) square cake pan; bake in 350°F (180°C) oven for 15 minutes.

❦ TOPPING: In bowl, mix together butter and eggs; blend in sugar, flour, baking powder, vanilla and salt. Stir in raisins and pecans; pour over base. Bake in 350°F (180°C) oven for 20 to 25 minutes or until top springs back when lightly touched. Let cool on rack before cutting into small squares. Makes 16 squares.

VARIATION

LEMON SQUARES: Substitute white for brown sugar and add 1 tsp (5 mL) grated lemon rind and 3 tbsp (50 mL) lemon juice. Omit raisins and pecans.

Scones with Currants

BACHELOR BUTTONS

Many old-time recipes for bachelor buttons are a variation on thimble cookies, which have a jam-filled depression in the center. For Brown-Eyed Susans, fill centers of just-baked cookies with two or three chocolate chips—they'll melt from the warmth of the cookie.

1 cup	butter, softened	250 mL
1/2 cup	granulated sugar	125 mL
2	egg yolks	2
2 tsp	vanilla	10 mL
2 cups	all-purpose flour	500 mL
2	egg whites, lightly beaten	2
	Coconut or finely chopped nuts	
	Jelly or jam	

In bowl, cream together butter and sugar; beat in egg yolks and vanilla. Gradually blend in flour. Shape dough into 1-inch (2.5 cm) balls; dip into egg whites and roll in coconut.

❦ Place balls on lightly greased baking sheets. With end of wooden spoon handle, make depression in center of each cookie. Bake in 325°F (160°C) oven for 10 to 12 minutes or just until firm. Remove from oven and fill depressions with jelly. Let cool for a few minutes on baking sheet; remove to racks to cool completely. Makes about 4 dozen.

ICEBOX COOKIES

Icebox cookies are a favorite standby in the summertime. Store this slice-and-bake roll of cookie dough in your fridge or freezer — to make freshly baked cookies that are ready in 10 minutes.

1/2 cup	butter, softened	125 mL
1 cup	packed light brown sugar	250 mL
1	egg	1
1 tsp	vanilla	5 mL
1-1/2 cups	all-purpose flour	375 mL
1/2 tsp	baking soda	2 mL
1/2 tsp	salt	2 mL

In bowl, cream together butter and sugar; beat in egg and vanilla. Combine flour, baking soda and salt; gradually blend into creamed mixture. Shape dough into cylinder about 2 inches (5 cm) in diameter. Wrap in plastic wrap and chill thoroughly until very firm (or freeze).

❦ With sharp knife, cut dough into 1/8-inch (3 mm) thick slices; place on greased baking sheets. Bake in 375°F (190°C) oven for 7 to 9 minutes or until very lightly browned. Let cool for a few minutes on baking sheet; remove to racks to cool completely. Makes about 4 dozen.

VARIATIONS

ORANGE-ALMOND COOKIES: Add 1 tbsp (15 mL) grated orange rind, 1/4 tsp (1 mL) almond extract and 1/2 cup (125 mL) finely chopped blanched almonds.

GINGER THINS: Add 2 tbsp (25 mL) molasses to the creamed mixture and 1 tbsp (15 mL) ginger to the flour mixture. If desired, dough can be chilled, then rolled out very thin on lightly floured surface and cut into rounds rather than shaped into cylinder and sliced.

LAZY DAY LEMONADE

With a jar of this lemon syrup in the fridge, it's easy to stir up a glassful or a pitcher for company.

❦ In small saucepan, stir together 1-1/2 cups (375 mL) granulated sugar, 1-1/2 cups (375 mL) water and 2 tbsp (25 mL) lemon rind (yellow part only); bring to boil, stirring constantly. Boil for 5 minutes, stirring occasionally. Remove from heat and let cool. Stir in 1-3/4 cups (425 mL) lemon juice (about 12 lemons). Transfer to jar, cover and refrigerate for up to 3 weeks.

❦ To serve, place 2 ice cubes in each tall glass. Add 1/4 cup (50 mL) lemon syrup and 3/4 cup (175 mL) cold water; stir well. Garnish with lemon slice. Makes 3-1/4 cups (800 mL), enough for 12 servings.

HAZELNUT CHOCOLATE CHIP BARS

These chewy chocolaty bars with hazelnuts can be stored in the refrigerator for up to one week.

1/2 cup	butter, softened	125 mL
1/2 cup	shortening	125 mL
1 cup	granulated sugar	250 mL
1/2 cup	packed brown sugar	125 mL
2	eggs	2
2 tsp	vanilla	10 mL
2 cups	all-purpose flour	500 mL
1 tsp	baking soda	5 mL
1/2 tsp	salt	2 mL
1-1/2 cups	hazelnuts, toasted and coarsely chopped*	375 mL
1-1/2 cups	jumbo chocolate chips	375 mL

In large bowl, cream together butter and shortening; beat in granulated and brown sugars, eggs (one at a time) and vanilla.

❧ Combine flour, baking soda and salt; blend into creamed mixture. Stir in nuts and chocolate chips. Chill dough for 15 minutes.

❧ Using fingertips, spread dough evenly into greased 15- × 10-inch (40 × 25 cm) jelly roll pan. Bake in 375°F (190°C) oven for 18 to 20 minutes or until golden brown and still slightly underbaked in center.

❧ Let cool slightly in pan on rack; cut into bars while still warm. Let cool completely before removing from pan. Makes about 50 bars.

*To toast hazelnuts: Spread on baking sheet and bake in 350°F (180°C) oven for 8 to 10 minutes or until golden and fragrant. Transfer to tea towel; fold over and rub vigorously to remove skins. Let cool; chop.

PECAN-BUTTERSCOTCH COOKIES

These fork-pressed drops combine a pleasant nutty crunch with a butterscotch flavor.

3/4 cup	butter, softened	175 mL
1 cup	packed light brown sugar	250 mL
1	egg	1
1 tsp	vanilla	5 mL
1-1/2 cups	all-purpose flour	375 mL
1/2 tsp	baking powder	2 mL
1/2 tsp	salt	2 mL
1/4 tsp	baking soda	1 mL
3/4 cup	finely chopped pecans	175 mL
	Pecan halves or pieces	

In bowl, cream together butter and sugar; beat in egg and vanilla. Combine flour, baking powder, salt and baking soda; gradually blend into creamed mixture. Stir in chopped pecans.

Shape dough into 1-inch (2.5 cm) balls; place on greased baking sheets. With floured fork, flatten balls in crisscross pattern. Press pecan half into center of each. Bake in 350°F (180°C) oven for 8 to 10 minutes or until lightly browned. Let cool for a few minutes on baking sheet; remove to racks to cool completely. Makes about 4 dozen.

OLD-TIME OATMEAL RAISIN COOKIES

Crunch into one of these crisp raisin-studded cookies for a real old-fashioned treat. If you don't want to bake all the cookies immediately, store any unused batter in the refrigerator for up to 5 days.

3/4 cup	unsalted butter, softened	175 mL
1 cup	firmly packed brown sugar	250 mL
1/2 cup	granulated sugar	125 mL
1	egg	1
2 tbsp	water	25 mL
2/3 cup	all-purpose flour	150 mL
1/2 tsp	cinnamon	2 mL
1/2 tsp	baking soda	2 mL
1/4 tsp	salt	1 mL
3 cups	rolled oats	750 mL
1 cup	raisins	250 mL
1/2 cup	chopped walnuts (optional)	125 mL

In large bowl with electric mixer, cream butter with brown and granulated sugars until fluffy; beat in egg and water.

In separate bowl, combine flour, cinnamon, baking soda and salt; with wooden spoon, blend into creamed mixture. Stir in oats, raisins, and nuts (if using).

Roll heaping teaspoonfuls (5 mL) of batter into small balls; place on greased baking sheets 2 inches (5 cm) apart. With moistened hands, gently flatten cookie to about 1/2-inch (1 cm) thickness. Bake in 350°F (180°C) oven for 10 to 12 minutes or until lightly golden and still soft in center. Transfer immediately to racks and let cool. Makes about 6 dozen.

FOR THE BEST COOKIES

Measure carefully. Don't substitute ingredients unless specified in the recipe—or unless you're willing to experiment. If you want to substitute margarine for butter, use regular (not soft) margarine. When a buttery flavor is important, as in shortbread, do not substitute.

Accurate oven temperatures are crucial. Check your oven periodically with a good oven thermometer and adjust the dial accordingly.

Most cookies bake best (without browning too much on the bottoms) when baking sheets are placed above the center of the oven. Bake one sheet at a time.

Cookies continue baking on hot pans for a few minutes after removal from oven; therefore, it's better to underbake slightly than to overbake.

For greasing pans, shortening is best; butter tends to brown too quickly.

Good-quality aluminum or stainless steel baking sheets distribute heat evenly to produce the best cookies.

MARBLE BROWNIES

*A double dose of chocolate in these moist cakelike brownies will appeal to the eye as well as the taste
of every chocolate lover.*

2 oz	semisweet chocolate	60 g
2 oz	white chocolate	60 g
1/2 cup	butter, softened	125 mL
2/3 cup	granulated sugar	150 mL
2	eggs	2
1/2 tsp	vanilla	2 mL
1/2 cup	all-purpose flour	125 mL

In small bowls over hot (not boiling) water, melt semisweet and white chocolates separately. Let cool slightly.

❦ Meanwhile, in bowl, cream butter with sugar until fluffy. Add eggs one at a time, beating well after each addition. Blend in vanilla; stir in flour. Transfer half of the batter to another bowl; stir in dark chocolate. Stir white chocolate into remaining batter.

❦ Spread half of the dark chocolate batter in greased 8-inch (2 L) square cake pan. Spoon white chocolate batter over top and spread evenly. Drop remaining dark chocolate batter by spoonfuls onto top. Swirl knife through layers to marble. Bake in 350°F (180°C) oven for 20 to 25 minutes or until sides start to pull away from pan; a tester inserted in center should still have a little moist crumb adhering to it. Let cool on rack before cutting into squares. Makes 16 squares.

BLUEBERRY YOGURT POUND CAKE

This moist and buttery blueberry cake is easy to make. The tantalizing fragrance of blueberries and butter coming from the oven will let you know when the cake is almost ready. Serve with afternoon tea, morning coffee or for a special brunch dessert.

1 cup	butter, softened	250 mL
1-1/3 cups	granulated sugar	325 mL
3	eggs	3
3 cups	all-purpose flour	750 mL
1-1/2 tsp	baking soda	7 mL
1/2 tsp	salt	2 mL
2 cups	blueberries	500 mL
1 cup	plain yogurt	250 mL
3/4 cup	orange juice	175 mL
1 tbsp	coarsely grated orange rind	15 mL
	Icing sugar	

In large bowl, cream butter until fluffy; beat in sugar until light and fluffy, 5 to 8 minutes. Beat in eggs, one at a time.

❦ In separate bowl, stir together flour, baking soda and salt; mix in berries. Stir together yogurt, orange juice and rind. Alternately add dry and wet mixtures to creamed mixture, making 3 additions of dry and 2 of wet.

❦ Pour batter into well-greased and floured deep 9- or 10-inch (3 L) tube or Bundt pan; smooth top and tap pan lightly on work surface to release air bubbles. Bake in 350°F (180°C) oven for 60 to 70 minutes or until tester inserted in center comes out clean. Let cool for 15 minutes in pan. Turn out onto rack to cool completely. To serve, set on doily-lined plate and sieve icing sugar over. Makes about 12 servings.

MINI RHUBARB-OATMEAL MUFFINS

These crunchy-topped little muffins go well with afternoon tea and are best when fresh.

1 cup	all-purpose flour	250 mL
3/4 cup	rolled oats	175 mL
1/2 cup	packed brown sugar	125 mL
2 tsp	baking powder	10 mL
1/2 tsp	baking soda	2 mL
1/4 tsp	each salt and nutmeg	1 mL
1 cup	diced rhubarb	250 mL
1 tsp	grated orange rind	5 mL
1/3 cup	vegetable oil	75 mL
1/3 cup	orange juice	75 mL
1	egg	1

STREUSEL TOPPING:

1/4 cup	quick-cooking rolled oats	50 mL
1/4 cup	packed brown sugar	50 mL
2 tbsp	chopped nuts	25 mL
2 tbsp	butter	25 mL
Pinch	each cinnamon and ginger	Pinch

In bowl, stir together flour, oats, sugar, baking powder, baking soda, salt and nutmeg. Mix in rhubarb and orange rind. Whisk together oil, orange juice and egg; add to flour mixture, stirring just until moistened. Spoon batter into 2-inch (5 cm) greased or paper-lined tart tins, filling to top of liners.

❧ STREUSEL TOPPING: In small bowl, mix together oats, sugar, nuts, butter, cinnamon and ginger. Sprinkle evenly over batter. Bake in 400°F (200°C) oven for 18 minutes or until firm to the touch. Let cool on rack. Makes 18 to 20 muffins.

BLUEBERRY-LEMON STREUSEL COFFEE CAKE

Warm from the oven, this luscious layered coffee cake is the ultimate come-over-for-coffee treat.

1/2 cup	butter, softened	125 mL
1 cup	granulated sugar	250 mL
2	eggs	2
1 tsp	vanilla	5 mL
2 cups	all-purpose flour	500 mL
1 tsp	baking powder	5 mL
1/2 tsp	baking soda	2 mL
1/2 tsp	salt	2 mL
1 cup	sour cream	250 mL
1 tbsp	grated lemon rind	15 mL
2 cups	blueberries	500 mL

STREUSEL:

3/4 cup	packed brown sugar	175 mL
1/2 cup	all-purpose flour	125 mL
1 tsp	cinnamon	5 mL
1/4 cup	butter	50 mL

STREUSEL: In bowl, stir together sugar, flour and cinnamon; cut in butter until crumbly. Set aside.

❧ In large mixing bowl, cream butter; add sugar and beat until light and fluffy. Beat in eggs, one at a time. Blend in vanilla.

❧ Stir together flour, baking powder, baking soda and salt; using wooden spoon, stir into creamed mixture alternately with sour cream. Stir in lemon rind.

❧ Spread half of the batter in greased and floured 9-inch (2.5 L) springform pan. Sprinkle with half of the streusel and half of the blueberries. Spread remaining batter over top. Sprinkle with remaining blueberries, then remaining streusel.

❧ Bake in 350°F (180°C) oven for about 1 hour and 15 minutes or until tester inserted in center comes out clean. Let cool in pan for 10 minutes. Remove side of pan and serve warm. Makes 8 to 10 servings.

SWEET ENDINGS

Whether it's the tangy taste of spring rhubarb baked into a lattice pie or a warming apple crisp on a cold winter's day, these delicious desserts celebrate the sweet endings that every season brings us.

❦

LAYERED BERRY CHEESECAKE

This fresh-tasting cheesecake is equally wonderful with raspberries, blackberries or wild blueberries.

1	sponge cake (see sidebar, this page)	1
1/4 cup	frozen concentrated raspberry juice	50 mL
	FILLING:	
1/2 cup	milk	125 mL
2/3 cup	granulated sugar	150 mL
4	egg yolks	4
2	pkg unflavored gelatin	2
1/3 cup	cold water	75 mL
1 lb	cream cheese (at room temperature)	500 g
3 tbsp	raspberry eau de vie (framboise) or 1 tsp (5 mL) vanilla	50 mL
1 cup	whipping cream	250 mL
1-1/2 cups	raspberries	375 mL

Cut strips of waxed paper to fit sides and extend 1 inch (2.5 cm) above sides of 10-inch (3 L) springform pan. Cut cake horizontally in half; place top layer, cut side up, in pan. Drizzle cut side of each cake layer with concentrated raspberry juice. Cover cake and set aside.

❦ FILLING: In saucepan, heat milk and 1/3 cup (75 mL) of the sugar over medium-low heat until bubbles form around edges of pan. Beat egg yolks; whisk one-quarter of the hot milk into yolks. Return to pan and cook, stirring constantly, for about 3 minutes or until thickened.

❦ In small saucepan, sprinkle gelatin over water; let stand for 1 minute to soften. Heat over low heat until gelatin dissolves; stir into custard. Place plastic wrap directly on surface and let cool.

❦ In large bowl, beat cream cheese with remaining sugar until fluffy. Beat in custard and raspberry eau de vie until smooth.

❦ In separate bowl, whip cream; whisk one-quarter into cream cheese mixture; fold in remaining whipped cream. Spread half of the filling over cake in pan. Set aside 1/2 cup (125 mL) of the raspberries for garnish. Spoon remaining berries over filling right to edge of pan. Spoon remaining filling over berries. Top with remaining cake layer, cut side down. Cover and refrigerate for at least 8 hours or overnight.

❦ Remove side of pan; transfer cheesecake to serving plate. Dust with 1 tbsp (15 mL) icing sugar; garnish with mint leaves and reserved raspberries. Makes 10 to 12 servings.

SPONGE CAKE

Grease and flour 10-inch (25 cm) springform pan. Line bottom with waxed paper; set aside.

❦ In warmed bowl, beat 6 eggs until foamy. Gradually beat in 1 cup (250 mL) granulated sugar; beat at high speed for 8 to 10 minutes or until pale yellow and batter falls in ribbons when beaters are lifted. Beat in 1 tsp (5 mL) vanilla.

❦ Sift together 1 cup (250 mL) all-purpose flour, 1/2 tsp (2 mL) baking powder and pinch salt; sift one-third over egg mixture and fold in. Repeat twice. Fold in 1/3 cup (75 mL) melted butter. Pour into prepared pan; bake in 325°F (160°C) oven for about 45 minutes or until cake springs back when lightly touched in center. Let cool in pan for 10 minutes. Turn out onto rack and let cool completely.

(clockwise from center) Layered Berry Cheesecake; French Vanilla Frozen Yogurt with Cherry Sauce (recipe, p. 171); Red Currant and Berry Pudding Loaf (recipe, p. 153)

RHUBARB AND STRAWBERRY TRIFLE

Rhubarb and strawberries are a blissful spring combination, especially in a silky, creamy custard trifle.
Ladyfingers can be used instead of the sponge cake.

3 cups	milk	750 mL
5	egg yolks	5
1/2 cup	granulated sugar	125 mL
1/4 cup	cornstarch	50 mL
1 tsp	vanilla	5 mL
1/2 cup	whipping cream	125 mL
7 cups	cubed angel food cake or sponge cake (one 10 oz/300 g cake)	1.75 L
2 cups	stewed rhubarb	500 mL
2 cups	sliced strawberries	500 mL
	Toasted whole almonds	
	Strawberries	

In saucepan, heat milk until bubbles form around edge. Meanwhile, in separate heavy saucepan, beat egg yolks, sugar and cornstarch until smooth. Gradually whisk in milk; cook over medium heat, stirring, for 3 to 5 minutes or until thickened. Reduce heat to low and simmer, stirring, for 1 minute. Remove from heat and stir in vanilla; let cool. *(Custard can be covered with waxed paper or plastic wrap directly on surface and refrigerated for up to 1 day.)*
❧ Whip cream and whisk one-quarter into custard. Fold in remaining whipped cream. Spread half of the cake in 12- or 14-cup (3 or 3.5 L) glass serving bowl. Spread half of the rhubarb over cake, then half of the strawberries. Spread half of the custard over top. Repeat layers. Chill for at least 1 hour or for up to 8 hours. Garnish with almonds and strawberries. Makes 10 to 12 servings.

BLUEBERRY AND RASPBERRY GRUNT

Grunts and slumps hail from the Maritimes where generations of cooks have turned a bounty of wild blueberries into summer-sweet desserts.

1-1/2 cups	fresh bread crumbs	375 mL
3/4 cup	all-purpose flour	175 mL
3 tbsp	granulated sugar	50 mL
1 tbsp	baking powder	15 mL
1/2 tsp	grated lemon rind	2 mL
1/4 tsp	salt	1 mL
Pinch	nutmeg	Pinch
1/2 cup	milk	125 mL
1	egg	1
1/3 cup	butter, melted	75 mL
	SAUCE:	
1	pkg (300 g) frozen unsweetened raspberries, thawed	1
3 tbsp	granulated sugar	50 mL
1	pkg (300 g) frozen unsweetened blueberries, thawed	1
1 tsp	cornstarch	5 mL

SAUCE: Spread 1 cup (250 mL) of the raspberries on plate; sprinkle with 1 tbsp (15 mL) of the sugar and set aside.

❧ In large saucepan, combine remaining raspberries and sugar, blueberries and cornstarch. Bring to boil and cook, stirring constantly, until thickened, about 4 minutes. Cover and keep warm.

❧ In bowl, stir together bread crumbs, flour, sugar, baking powder, lemon rind, salt and nutmeg. Beat together milk, egg and butter; stir into dry ingredients just until moistened. With floured hands, shape into 8 dumplings.

❧ Bring sauce to gentle simmer; scatter reserved raspberries and any accumulated juice on top. Add dumplings; cover and cook over medium-low heat for 20 minutes. Makes about 8 servings.

MAPLE MOUSSE WITH STRAWBERRY PURÉE

There's nothing more Canadian than a silky smooth maple mousse. A spoonful or two of puréed strawberries is a refreshing contrast to the richness of the cream and sweetness of the maple. For an attractive presentation, garnish each mousse with a whole strawberry. Any leftover purée can be spooned over ice cream.

	STRAWBERRY PURÉE:	
2 cups	sliced strawberries	500 mL
4 tsp	granulated sugar	20 mL
	MAPLE MOUSSE:	
2/3 cup	maple syrup	150 mL
5	egg yolks, beaten	5
1-1/2 tsp	unflavored gelatin	7 mL
2 tbsp	cold water	25 mL
1 cup	whipping cream	250 mL

STRAWBERRY PURÉE: In food processor or blender, purée strawberries until smooth. Strain through fine sieve into bowl; stir in sugar until dissolved. Spoon 1 tbsp (15 mL) purée into each of six 1-cup (250 mL) wine glasses. Refrigerate remainder for topping.

❧ MAPLE MOUSSE: In heavy saucepan, cook maple syrup and egg yolks over low heat, stirring constantly, for 7 to 10 minutes or until thickened.

❧ Meanwhile, in small saucepan, sprinkle gelatin over water; let stand for 1 minute to soften. Heat over low heat until gelatin dissolves; stir into maple mixture. Transfer to large bowl; refrigerate for 15 minutes, stirring occasionally, or until consistency of raw egg whites.

❧ Whip cream; whisk one-quarter into maple mixture. Fold in remaining whipped cream. Divide evenly among glasses. Refrigerate for at least 2 hours or until firm. Spoon 1 tbsp (15 mL) strawberry purée over each mousse. Makes 6 servings.

CLASSIC CRÈME BRÛLÉE

This sinfully pleasing, exquisite combination of rich, smooth custard under a crunchy caramel topping is a tiny perfect dessert for special dinners.

3 cups	whipping cream	750 mL
8	egg yolks	8
1/3 cup	granulated sugar	75 mL
1-1/2 tsp	vanilla	7 mL
1/2 cup	packed brown sugar, sifted	125 mL

In saucepan, heat cream over medium-high heat until steaming hot. In bowl, whisk egg yolks with granulated sugar; very gradually whisk in cream. Whisk in vanilla.

❦ Skim off foam. Divide mixture among eight 3/4-cup (175 mL) ramekins or custard cups.

❦ Place ramekins in 2 large shallow pans. Gently pour boiling water into pans to come halfway up sides of ramekins.

❦ Bake in 350°F (180°C) oven for 30 to 35 minutes or until edges are set but centers still quiver and small knife inserted into centers comes out creamy. Remove from water; let cool on racks. Cover and refrigerate for at least 2 hours or until chilled and set, or for up to 2 days.

❦ Fill two shallow pans with enough ice cubes to surround ramekins; nestle chilled custards among cubes. Pat surface of each custard dry; sprinkle evenly with brown sugar.

❦ Broil 6 inches (15 cm) from heat for 2 to 6 minutes or until sugar bubbles and turns dark brown, rearranging pans and removing each ramekin when ready. Chill, uncovered, for at least 10 minutes before serving, or for up to 3 hours. Makes 8 servings.

VARIATIONS

GINGER CRÈME BRÛLÉE: Add 2 tbsp (25 mL) finely chopped preserved ginger to uncooked custard mixture.

ORANGE CRÈME BRÛLÉE: Add 2 tbsp (25 mL) grated orange rind to cold cream before heating. Strain hot cream and discard rind. Substitute 2 tbsp (25 mL) orange liqueur or orange juice for vanilla.

> When broiling the Crèmes Brûlées, watch them constantly, because caramel turns from amber to black very quickly. Enjoy the crunch and creaminess of Crème Brûlée within 3 hours of broiling, before the caramel melts.

LIGHT GOOSEBERRY FOOL

Traditionally, this dessert has 2 cups (500 mL) whipping cream, whipped and folded in for a rich and easy summer dessert. Drained yogurt gives all the same creaminess and lightness with fewer calories.

1-1/2 cups	plain yogurt	375 mL
5 cups	gooseberries	1.25 L
2 tbsp	frozen orange juice concentrate	25 mL
3/4 cup	(approx) granulated sugar	175 mL
	Mint leaves (optional)	

Pour yogurt into cheesecloth-lined sieve set over glass serving bowl; refrigerate and let drain for 1 hour.

❦ Meanwhile, reserve a few gooseberries for garnish. In saucepan, combine remaining berries with orange juice concentrate; cover and cook over low heat, stirring occasionally, for 25 to 30 minutes or until very tender.

❦ Using potato masher, mash berries. Pass through food mill or purée in food processor; press through sieve to remove skins and seeds. Return to saucepan.

❦ Stir in sugar; simmer for 3 to 4 minutes or until sugar is dissolved. Taste and add more sugar if desired. Refrigerate until chilled.

❦ Stir drained yogurt into purée, leaving attractive swirls. Top and tail reserved gooseberries; arrange on top along with mint leaves (if using) for garnish. Makes 4 servings.

Classic Crème Brûlée

WHISKY APPLES

Hours of labor in the kitchen on some complicated dessert won't get more oohs and satisfied aahs than these warm, slightly boozy apples served beside a big scoop of ice cream.

1/4 cup	lemon juice	50 mL
4	large tart apples, peeled and quartered	4
1/4 cup	butter	50 mL
1/4 cup	packed brown sugar	50 mL
1/4 cup	whisky or applejack	50 mL

Place lemon juice in bowl. Cut apple quarters lengthwise into 1/4-inch (5 mm) thick slices; toss gently in lemon juice.

❧ In heavy skillet, melt butter over medium-high heat until foaming; cook apples, stirring, for 5 minutes or until tender. Stir in sugar. Pour whisky over top; warm through. Makes 6 to 8 servings.

APPLE DUMPLINGS

This wonderful tummy-warming, pastry-wrapped baked apple is a perfect wintertime dessert.

3 cups	all-purpose flour	750 mL
2 tsp	baking powder	10 mL
1 tsp	salt	5 mL
1/2 cup	butter	125 mL
1/2 cup	lard	125 mL
1/2 cup	(approx) ice water	125 mL
	FILLING:	
1/3 cup	packed brown sugar	75 mL
Pinch	ground cloves	Pinch
1 tbsp	butter	15 mL

1/4 cup	raisins	50 mL
6	large apples (about 2 lb/1 kg total)	6
1	egg yolk	1
1 tbsp	milk	15 mL
1 tbsp	granulated sugar	15 mL
6	whole cloves	6

In large bowl, combine flour, baking powder and salt; cut in butter and lard until crumbly. Stirring briskly with fork, gradually add just enough water, 1 tbsp (15 mL) at a time, to make dough hold together. Knead gently several times. Divide dough into 6 parts; press into discs. Wrap and refrigerate for 30 minutes.

❧ FILLING: In small bowl, combine brown sugar with ground cloves; blend in butter until crumbly. Mix in raisins; set aside. Peel and core apples.

❧ On lightly floured surface, roll out each portion of dough into 6-inch (15 cm) circle. Place 1 apple in center of each; sprinkle with sugar mixture. Wrap pastry around each apple, pressing dough over top to enclose. Place on baking sheet.

❧ Beat egg yolk with milk; brush over pastry. With tip of knife, score pastry decoratively around top; sprinkle with granulated sugar. Press 1 whole clove into top of each apple.

❧ Bake in 400°F (200°C) oven for 20 to 25 minutes or until pastry is golden brown and apples are tender when tested with skewer. Let stand for about 5 minutes. Makes 6 servings.

AUTUMN THREE-FRUIT CRISP

This thoroughly modern version of an old-time favorite is a delectable combo of skillet-simmered fall fruit with a crunchy-sweet topping. Follow recipe for Whisky Apples (above), substituting peaches and/or plums for half the apples. Before serving, sprinkle with Hazelnut-Oat Crunch: Combine 3/4 cup (175 mL) each rolled oats and brown sugar, 1/2 cup (125 mL) all-purpose flour, 1/4 cup (50 mL) chopped hazelnuts and 1 tsp (5 mL) cinnamon. Cut in 1/4 cup (50 mL) butter until mixture resembles coarse crumbs. Spread on baking sheet and bake in 375°F (190°C) oven for 10 minutes or until golden brown.

Whisky Apples

FRESH STRAWBERRY BAVARIAN

For a delicious taste of June on a spoon, make this quick and easy dessert with strawberries.
Switch over to raspberries in July.

4 cups	strawberries	1 L
1 cup	granulated sugar	250 mL
1-1/2	pkg unflavored gelatin	1-1/2
1/4 cup	water	50 mL
1 tbsp	lemon juice	15 mL
1 cup	whipping cream	250 mL

In food processor or blender, purée 3 cups (750 mL) of the strawberries until smooth; whirl in sugar. Transfer to large bowl and let stand for about 15 minutes or until dissolved.

 In small saucepan, combine gelatin, water and lemon juice; let stand for 5 minutes to soften. Warm over low heat until gelatin dissolves. Stir into strawberry mixture; cover and refrigerate for about 20 minutes or until almost set.

 Whip cream; gently fold into strawberry mixture. Rinse 6-cup (1.5 L) glass, plastic or stainless steel mould; shake out excess water. Pour in strawberry mixture; cover and refrigerate for about 4 hours or until firm, or for up to 3 days.

 Unmould onto serving platter. Slice remaining strawberries and arrange around Bavarian. Makes about 12 servings.

BLACK AND RED FRUIT SALAD

Full of wonderful summer-fresh flavor, this salad is delicious served with berry sherbet, vanilla ice cream or frozen yogurt. If you can't find some of these fruits, increase the remaining varieties accordingly.

1/3 cup	granulated sugar	75 mL
1/3 cup	water	75 mL
1/3 cup	orange juice	75 mL
1 tbsp	coarsely grated orange rind	15 mL
1/2 cup	black currants, topped and tailed	125 mL
1-1/2 cups	blackberries or black raspberries	375 mL
1-1/2 cups	blueberries	375 mL
1-1/2 cups	sweet cherries, pitted	375 mL
1/2 cup	stemmed red currants	125 mL

In saucepan, combine sugar, water, orange juice and rind; bring to boil over medium-high heat, stirring to dissolve sugar. Reduce heat to medium and simmer for 3 minutes.

 Add black currants to pan; poach for 2 minutes or until softened. Using slotted spoon, remove black currants to large serving bowl. Let syrup cool slightly.

 Add blackberries, blueberries, cherries and red currants to bowl. Pour in syrup and toss gently to mix. Cover and refrigerate until chilled or overnight. Makes 6 servings.

ORANGE SABAYON

Spoon this warm silky-smooth sauce over fresh peaches, raspberries or any seasonal fruit.

1/2 cup	granulated sugar	125 mL
3	egg yolks	3
1/4 tsp	grated orange rind	1 mL
1/2 cup	orange juice	125 mL

In heavy saucepan over low heat or in top of double boiler over barely simmering water, beat sugar, yolks and orange rind with electric mixer until sugar has dissolved and mixture is creamy, about 3 minutes.

 Gradually pour in orange juice, beating constantly. Continue beating until mixture thickens, becomes fluffy and doubles in volume, about 8 minutes. Makes about 3 cups (750 mL) sauce, enough for 6 to 8 servings.

CRANBERRY CRUMBLE CAKE

Serve squares of this cake warm like a pudding, with sour cream, ice cream or whipped cream. For a delicious variation, substitute partridgeberries or wild blueberries.

1/2 cup	butter, softened	125 mL
1 cup	granulated sugar	250 mL
2	eggs	2
2 cups	all-purpose flour	500 mL
1 tsp	baking powder	5 mL
1 tsp	baking soda	5 mL
1/2 tsp	salt	2 mL
1 cup	sour cream	250 mL
1 tsp	grated lemon rind	5 mL
1 tbsp	lemon juice	15 mL
	TOPPING:	
3/4 cup	packed brown sugar	175 mL
1/2 cup	rolled oats	125 mL
1/3 cup	all-purpose flour	75 mL
1 tsp	cinnamon	5 mL

1/4 cup	butter	50 mL
4 cups	cranberries	1 L
1/3 cup	granulated sugar	75 mL

TOPPING: In bowl, combine brown sugar, oats, flour and cinnamon; cut in butter until crumbly and set aside. Toss cranberries with granulated sugar; set aside.

❦ In large bowl, beat butter with sugar until fluffy. Beat in eggs, one at a time. Combine flour, baking powder, baking soda and salt. Stir together sour cream, lemon rind and juice. Alternately add flour mixture and sour cream mixture to butter mixture, making 3 additions of dry and 2 of wet.

❦ Spoon into greased 13- × 9-inch (3.5 L) cake pan. Spoon berry mixture over top. Sprinkle with oatmeal mixture. Bake in 350°F (180°C) oven for 45 to 50 minutes or until topping is crisp, berries begin to bubble and tester inserted into center of cake comes out clean. Set pan on rack to cool slightly before cutting into squares. Makes about 12 servings.

CHERRY CRUMBLE CAKE

This pie-like cake is equally delicious served warm with ice cream, or at room temperature. You can substitute canned or frozen cherries in wintertime but drain them well.

1-1/2 cups	rolled oats	375 mL
1/2 cup	packed brown sugar	125 mL
1/3 cup	all-purpose flour	75 mL
1 tsp	cinnamon	5 mL
1/2 cup	butter, softened	125 mL
	FILLING:	
3/4 cup	ground almonds	175 mL
2/3 cup	granulated sugar	150 mL
2 tbsp	butter	25 mL
2	eggs	2
1/4 cup	all-purpose flour	50 mL
1/2 tsp	baking powder	2 mL
1/4 tsp	salt	1 mL
2 cups	pitted sour cherries	500 mL
1/4 tsp	almond extract	1 mL

In bowl, combine rolled oats, sugar, flour and cinnamon; cut in butter until crumbly. Press firmly into 11-inch (27 cm) flan pan with removable bottom or 10-inch (25 cm) pie plate. Bake in 375°F (190°C) oven for 10 to 12 minutes or until lightly browned.

❦ FILLING: Meanwhile, in bowl, combine 1/2 cup (125 mL) of the almonds and 2 tbsp (25 mL) of the sugar; cut in butter until crumbly. Set aside.

❦ Using electric mixer, beat eggs with remaining sugar for 3 to 5 minutes or until pale yellow and thickened. Combine remaining almonds, flour, baking powder and salt; stir into egg mixture. Stir in cherries and almond extract.

❦ Pour batter into baked shell. Sprinkle with reserved almond mixture. Shield edges of crust with foil to prevent overbrowning. Bake in 375°F (190°C) oven for 35 to 45 minutes or until top is golden and tester inserted into center comes out clean. Let cool on rack before removing side of pan. Makes 8 servings.

FROZEN LEMON CHEESECAKE SQUARES

Tangy lemon squares that you can make ahead and freeze are most suited to fun summer occasions. But then, why keep all the easy desserts for the easy-living season—these are great any time of the year!

2 cups	crushed vanilla wafers (about 50)	500 mL
1/2 cup	chopped toasted almonds*	125 mL
1/2 cup	butter, melted	125 mL
3	egg yolks	3
1 cup	granulated sugar	250 mL
1 lb	cream cheese (at room temperature)	500 g
1/4 cup	lemon juice	50 mL
4 tsp	grated lemon rind	20 mL
1/2 tsp	vanilla	2 mL
1 cup	whipping cream	250 mL

In bowl, combine crushed wafers, almonds and butter. Line 13 × 9-inch (3.5 L) baking dish with foil or parchment paper; grease. Press crumb mixture into bottom of pan. Set aside.

❦ In large heatproof bowl set over saucepan of gently simmering water, and using electric mixer, beat egg yolks with 1/2 cup (125 mL) of the sugar until pale, creamy and thickened, about 5 minutes. Remove bowl from heat and let cool slightly.

❦ In large bowl, beat cream cheese and remaining sugar until fluffy. Beat in egg yolk mixture, lemon juice and rind, and vanilla until smooth. In separate bowl, whip cream; whisk one-quarter into cream cheese mixture. Fold in remaining whipped cream. Spread over crust. Cover and freeze until firm, at least 8 hours or up to 1 week. Cut into squares. Makes 12 servings.

*Toast almonds on baking sheet in 350°F (180°C) oven for 6 to 8 minutes or just until golden brown.

BLACKBERRY CHEESECAKE

British Columbia is famous for its blackberries. They give a lusciously creamy cheesecake a heady taste of summer.
If you can't find blackberries, raspberries are just as wonderful.

2-1/2 lb	cream cheese, softened	1.25 kg
3/4 cup	granulated sugar	175 mL
1 tsp	cornstarch	5 mL
2	eggs	2
2 cups	strained puréed blackberries (about 2-1/4 cups/550 mL whole berries)	500 mL
	CRUST:	
2 cups	graham cracker crumbs	500 mL
1/2 cup	granulated sugar	125 mL
1 tsp	cinnamon	5 mL
1/2 cup	butter, melted	125 mL
	GARNISH:	
1 cup	blackberries	250 mL
1/2 cup	whipped cream	125 mL

CRUST: In bowl, combine graham cracker crumbs, sugar and cinnamon; stir in butter. Press evenly onto bottom and halfway up sides of 10-inch (3 L) springform pan.

In bowl, beat cream cheese, sugar and cornstarch until fluffy. Beat in eggs, one at a time. Fold in blackberry purée; pour into crust. Bake in 325°F (160°C) oven for about 50 minutes or until set around edge and still slightly wobbly in center. Remove to rack. Immediately run knife around inside of pan. Let cool completely to room temperature. Cover and refrigerate until chilled.

GARNISH: Remove side of pan; place cake on serving plate. Garnish with blackberries and whipped cream. Makes about 16 servings.

BERRY CREAM RUFFLES

This summer berry shortcake is surprisingly easy to make with lacy brandy snaps.

4 cups	strawberries	1 L
1/2 cup	blueberries	125 mL
1-1/2 cups	whipping cream	375 mL
	Icing sugar	
	WAFERS:	
1/4 cup	packed brown sugar	50 mL
1/4 cup	butter	50 mL
1/4 cup	corn syrup	50 mL
1/3 cup	all-purpose flour	75 mL
3 tbsp	finely chopped almonds	50 mL
1/2 tsp	brandy or vanilla	2 mL

WAFERS: In heavy saucepan, combine sugar, butter and corn syrup; bring to boil over medium heat, stirring constantly. Remove from heat.

❧ Combine flour with nuts; add to sugar mixture along with brandy and mix well. Drop batter, 1 rounded tsp (5 mL) for each wafer, to form three rounds about 3 inches (8 cm) apart on greased (not nonstick) baking sheet. Bake, 1 sheet at a time, in 350°F (180°C) oven for 6 to 8 minutes or until golden brown and bubbles break but don't fill in. Let cool for about 1 minute or until easily lifted with wide spatula.

❧ Remove 1 wafer at a time to rack; using both hands, quickly pinch edges to create ruffled appearance. (If wafer becomes too brittle, return to oven briefly until pliable.) Repeat with remaining batter to make 12 wafers. Let cool. *(Wafers can be stored for up to 2 days in an airtight container.)*

❧ Set aside 2 strawberries (halved) and 8 blueberries for garnish. Slice remaining strawberries. Whip cream.

❧ To assemble: For each serving, spread 2 tbsp (25 mL) cream over 1 wafer on serving plate. Top with some of the strawberries and a few blueberries, then 2 tbsp (25 mL) cream. Top with second wafer and repeat layers. Top with third wafer. Garnish each serving with whipped cream, icing sugar, halved strawberry and 2 blueberries. Makes 4 servings.

PEACH STREUSEL PICNIC CAKE

Make this big cake and take it right in the pan to your potluck barbecue, reunion picnic or cottage weekend.

3/4 cup	chopped walnuts or pecans	175 mL
1/2 cup	rolled oats	125 mL
1/2 cup	packed brown sugar	125 mL
1/4 cup	butter, melted	50 mL
3	large peaches	3
1 tbsp	lemon juice	15 mL
1 cup	butter, softened	250 mL
1 cup	granulated sugar	250 mL
3	eggs	3
1 tsp	grated lemon rind	5 mL
1-1/3 cups	all-purpose flour	325 mL
1-1/2 tsp	baking powder	7 mL
1/4 tsp	salt	1 mL
1/4 tsp	mace or nutmeg	1 mL
1/4 cup	milk	50 mL

Combine nuts, rolled oats, brown sugar and butter; set aside. Peel and pit peaches. Cut into thin slices and toss with lemon juice; set aside.

In bowl, beat butter; gradually beat in granulated sugar until light and fluffy. Beat in eggs, one at a time. Stir in lemon rind. Combine flour, baking powder, salt and mace; stir into batter alternately with milk, making two additions of each (batter will be stiff).

Spread in greased and floured 13- × 9-inch (3.5 L) cake pan. Arrange peaches in neat rows over batter; sprinkle evenly with nut mixture. Bake in 375°F (190°C) oven for 35 to 40 minutes or until cake tester inserted into center comes out clean. Let cool in pan on rack. Makes 15 servings.

PECAN-WHISKY CAKE

A pecan topping and a glaze laced with rye whisky make this a very special Adults Only cake.
It's wonderful with tea in front of the fire.

1 cup	chopped pecans	250 mL
1-1/2 cups	butter, softened	375 mL
1 cup	granulated sugar	250 mL
6	eggs	6
1/4 cup	rye whisky	50 mL
1-1/2 tsp	vanilla	7 mL
2-1/4 cups	all-purpose flour	550 mL
1-1/2 tsp	baking powder	7 mL
1/4 tsp	salt	1 mL
	GLAZE:	
1/4 cup	butter	50 mL
1 cup	granulated sugar	250 mL
1/4 cup	water	50 mL
1/2 cup	rye whisky	125 mL
	Whipped cream	

Lightly butter and flour 9- or 10-inch (3 or 4 L) tube or Bundt pan. Sprinkle nuts over bottom. Set aside.

In large bowl, cream butter thoroughly; gradually beat in sugar until light and fluffy. Add eggs, one at a time, beating well after each addition. Stir in rye and vanilla. Stir together flour, baking powder and salt; add to butter mixture, stirring just until combined.

Spoon batter over pecans. Bake in 325°F (160°C) oven for about 1 hour or until tester inserted in center comes out clean. Let cool in pan for 5 minutes; invert on rack set over baking sheet.

GLAZE: Meanwhile, in small saucepan, melt butter; stir in sugar and water. Bring to boil, stirring constantly. Reduce heat to low and simmer for 5 minutes, without stirring. Remove from heat; stir in rye.

Using long skewer, make several holes through top of cake, almost to bottom. Drizzle some of the warm glaze over hot cake and brush over sides. Let cake absorb glaze; repeat drizzling until all glaze is used. Let cool. Garnish top with rosettes of whipped cream. Makes 10 to 12 servings.

CHOCOLATE ANGEL FOOD CAKE

Chocolate adds a new twist to this light-as-a-feather angel food cake. Served with fresh fruit or Orange Yogurt Sauce, it's a dessert special enough for any occasion.

3/4 cup	sifted cake-and-pastry flour	175 mL
1-1/2 cups	granulated sugar	375 mL
1/4 cup	unsweetened cocoa powder	50 mL
1-1/2 cups	egg whites (about 11 eggs), at room temperature	375 mL
1 tbsp	lemon juice	15 mL
1 tsp	cream of tartar	5 mL
1/2 tsp	salt	2 mL
1 tsp	vanilla	5 mL
1/2 tsp	almond extract	2 mL

ORANGE YOGURT SAUCE:

4 cups	plain yogurt	1 L
1 cup	orange juice	250 mL
2 tbsp	granulated sugar	25 mL
2 tbsp	grated orange rind	25 mL
2 tbsp	orange juice concentrate	25 mL

GARNISH:

Orange segments

Into bowl, sift together flour, 3/4 cup (175 mL) of the sugar and cocoa; sift again. Set aside. In large mixing bowl (not plastic), beat egg whites until foamy. Add lemon juice, cream of tartar and salt; beat until soft peaks form.

❧ Gradually add remaining sugar, 2 tbsp (25 mL) at a time, beating until mixture is glossy and stiff peaks form.

❧ A quarter at a time, sift flour mixture over egg whites, gently folding in each addition until well blended. Gently fold in vanilla and almond extract. Pour into ungreased 10-inch (4 L) tube pan.

❧ Run spatula through batter to eliminate any large air pockets. Smooth top with spatula. Bake in 350°F (180°C) oven for 40 to 45 minutes or until cake springs back when lightly touched.

❧ Turn pan upside down and let hang on legs attached to pan or on inverted funnel, or bottle, until completely cool. Remove from pan. *(Cake can be stored in airtight container for up to 2 days or frozen for up to 1 month.)*

❧ ORANGE YOGURT SAUCE: Line plastic sieve with cheesecloth; set over bowl. Spoon in yogurt; cover and let drain in refrigerator for at least 12 hours or until thick. Discard liquid. Whisk together drained yogurt, orange juice, sugar, orange rind and juice concentrate. Pour sauce over each serving. Garnish with orange segments. Makes 10 to 12 servings.

VARIATIONS

CLASSIC ANGEL FOOD CAKE: Increase sifted cake-and-pastry flour to 1 cup (250 mL). Omit cocoa powder.

CITRUS ANGEL FOOD CAKE: Prepare Classic Angel Food Cake. Fold in 1 tbsp (15 mL) each grated lemon and lime rind with vanilla. Omit almond extract.

To get the most volume when beating egg whites, it's important that they're free of even a trace of yolk and that they're at room temperature. If using eggs straight out of the refrigerator, cover them with warm water just until warmed to room temperature. You'll recognize the right stage when beating egg whites because soft peaks will flop when the beater is raised slowly and stiff peaks will stand up and remain standing.

LEMON JELLY ROLL

This is a real jelly roll, with a light and moist foolproof cake rolled with a glossy lip-puckering lemon curd.

4	eggs, separated	4
1 cup	granulated sugar	250 mL
3 tbsp	hot water	50 mL
1 tsp	vanilla	5 mL
1 cup	sifted cake-and-pastry flour	250 mL
3/4 tsp	baking powder	4 mL
Pinch	salt	Pinch
1/4 tsp	cream of tartar	1 mL
	Icing sugar	
	Lemon Curd (recipe follows)	
	Grated lemon rind (optional)	

Line 15- × 10-inch (2 L) jelly roll pan with parchment or waxed paper; set aside.

❦ In small bowl and using electric mixer, lightly beat egg yolks. Gradually beat in 1/2 cup (125 mL) of the sugar; continue beating at high speed until thick and very pale in color, about 5 minutes. Beat in water and vanilla. Sift together flour, baking powder and salt. Add to yolk mixture and beat at low speed until smooth, about 1 minute; set aside. Wash beaters thoroughly.

❦ In large bowl, beat egg whites with cream of tartar until soft peaks form; gradually beat in remaining sugar until stiff shiny peaks form. Pour yolk mixture over whites; fold in thoroughly with rubber spatula. Turn into prepared pan; smooth surface. Bake in 325°F (160°C) oven for 25 minutes or until top springs back when lightly touched.

❦ Sprinkle icing sugar over tea towel; invert cake on top. Remove parchment paper and gently roll cake in tea towel from long side. Let cool on rack. Unroll cake and spread with Lemon Curd. Roll up and dust with icing sugar; sprinkle with lemon rind (if using). Makes 12 servings.

	LEMON CURD:	
3	eggs, beaten	3
1 cup	granulated sugar	250 mL
1/2 cup	lemon juice	125 mL
1/4 cup	butter	50 mL
1 tbsp	grated lemon rind	15 mL

In small very heavy saucepan, combine eggs, sugar, lemon juice, butter and lemon rind. Cook over medium heat, whisking constantly, for 5 to 6 minutes or until mixture boils and thickens. Let cool. Makes about 1-1/2 cups (375 mL).

> If recipe calls for sifted flour, sift before measuring. Then spoon flour lightly into a dry measure and level off top with knife. Don't tap or pack down.

RED CURRANT AND BERRY PUDDING LOAF

Put red currants and other berries to elegant use in this marvelous make-ahead summer dessert.

2 cups	blueberries	500 mL
1 cup	stemmed red currants	250 mL
1 cup	granulated sugar	250 mL
2 cups	raspberries	500 mL
1 cup	sliced strawberries	250 mL
1	pound cake (about 1 lb/500 g)	1
1 cup	whipping cream	250 mL
	Red currants with stems	

In heavy saucepan, combine blueberries, red currants and sugar; cook over low heat for about 5 minutes or until juicy and fruit is slightly tender. Remove from heat; add raspberries and strawberries. Let cool.

❦ Meanwhile, line 8- × 4-inch (1.5 L) loaf pan with plastic wrap, leaving enough overhang to cover loaf. Cut cake into 1/2-inch (1 cm) thick slices. Line bottom and sides of pan with slices, trimming to fit; brush with 2 tbsp (25 mL) of the juice from fruit mixture. Fill with fruit mixture and juice; cover with remaining cake. Pour any remaining juice over cake.

❦ Set pan on large plate; fold overhang over cake. Cover cake with plastic-wrapped firm cardboard cut to fit; weigh down with heavy can, reserving any juice that overflows. Refrigerate for at least 6 hours or up to 2 days.

❦ To serve, fold back plastic wrap and turn loaf out onto rectangular plate; drizzle with any reserved juice. Whip cream and spread or pipe onto loaf. Garnish loaf with red currants. Makes 8 servings.

APPLECAKE WITH HOT BUTTERSCOTCH SAUCE

The recipe for this simply superlative apple cake originated at The Spike & Spoon restaurant in Collingwood, Ontario.

1-1/4 cups	chopped dates	300 mL
1/2 cup	Calvados or apple cider	125 mL
3/4 cup	unsalted butter	175 mL
1-1/2 cups	packed brown sugar	375 mL
2	eggs	2
2-1/2 cups	grated peeled apples	625 mL
3 cups	all-purpose flour	750 mL
4 tsp	cinnamon	20 mL
1 tbsp	baking soda	15 mL
1 tsp	nutmeg	5 mL
1/2 tsp	ground cloves	2 mL
	Hot Butterscotch Sauce (recipe follows)	

In saucepan, combine dates and Calvados; cover and heat until bubbly; simmer for 1 minute. Let cool.

❦ In large bowl, cream butter with sugar until fluffy. Beat in eggs, one at a time; stir in apples and date mixture.

❦ Stir together flour, cinnamon, baking soda, nutmeg and cloves; gently stir into batter just until mixed. Spread in greased 13- × 9-inch (3.5 L) cake pan; bake in 350°F (180°C) oven for 40 to 45 minutes or until cake springs back when lightly touched in center. Let cool slightly on rack. Serve warm with Hot Butterscotch Sauce. Makes 12 servings.

HOT BUTTERSCOTCH SAUCE:		
1 cup	granulated sugar	250 mL
3/4 cup	corn syrup	175 mL
1/3 cup	butter	75 mL
1-1/3 cups	light cream	325 mL
1-1/2 tsp	vanilla	7 mL

In saucepan, bring sugar, syrup and butter to boil, stirring; boil for 3 minutes. Stir in cream and return to boil. Remove from heat; add vanilla. Makes 2-1/2 cups (625 mL).

ONE-BOWL BANANA CAKE

There's an old-fashioned flavor of banana in this failure-proof cake. A quicky chocolate and peanut butter icing adds a touch that's sure to please kids.

2 cups	sifted cake-and-pastry flour	500 mL
1-1/4 cups	granulated sugar	300 mL
2 tsp	baking powder	10 mL
1/2 tsp	baking soda	2 mL
1/2 tsp	salt	2 mL
1 cup	mashed very ripe bananas	250 mL
1/2 cup	shortening	125 mL
1/2 cup	buttermilk	125 mL
2	eggs	2
1/2 tsp	vanilla	2 mL
	Chocolate Peanut Butter Icing (recipe follows)	
	Chopped peanuts (optional)	

In large bowl, mix together flour, sugar, baking powder, baking soda and salt. Add bananas, shortening, buttermilk, eggs and vanilla. Using electric mixer, beat at medium speed for 2 minutes. ❦ Pour into greased 9-inch (2.5 L) square cake pan; bake in 350°F (180°C) oven for 40 to 45 minutes or until top springs back when lightly touched. Let cool in pan on rack. Spread with Chocolate Peanut Butter Icing. Sprinkle with chopped peanuts (if using). Makes 12 servings.

CHOCOLATE PEANUT BUTTER ICING:		
1 cup	semisweet chocolate chips	250 mL
2 tbsp	peanut butter	25 mL
1/2 cup	sour cream	125 mL

In small bowl over barely simmering water, melt chocolate and peanut butter. Remove from heat and stir in sour cream. Chill until spreading consistency if necessary. Makes about 1-1/4 cups (300 mL).

> For easiest blending of one-bowl cakes, it's important to use shortening rather than butter or margarine.

CREAMY RICE PUDDING

This is a dream of a rice pudding. It owes its velvety creaminess to short, not long, grain rice. It's one of those easy-to-vary puddings—make it thinner with more milk if you like, or cook raisins, currants, coconut or pistachios with the rice, or top with a sprinkle of cinnamon or nutmeg.

2 tbsp	chopped almonds	25 mL
2 tbsp	butter	25 mL
1/2 cup	short grain rice	125 mL
2 tbsp	granulated sugar	25 mL
2-1/2 cups	milk	625 mL
1 tbsp	chopped candied ginger (or 2 tsp/10 mL grated lemon rind)	15 mL

In small skillet, toast almonds over medium heat for 2 minutes or until golden; set aside.
❦ In large saucepan, melt butter over medium heat; stir in rice to coat. Stir in sugar and milk; cover and bring to boil. Reduce heat to medium-low and simmer for 25 to 30 minutes or until most of the milk is absorbed and rice is tender, stirring frequently. Stir in ginger.
❦ Sprinkle with almonds just before serving warm or chilled. Makes 4 servings.

BAKED LEMON PUDDING

Often called lemon sponge or lemon pudding cake, this old-time favorite is still a pleaser. During baking, it separates into a cake-like topping with lemon sauce underneath.

1 cup	granulated sugar	250 mL
1/4 cup	all-purpose flour	50 mL
1/4 tsp	salt	1 mL
1/4 cup	lemon juice	50 mL
1 tbsp	grated lemon rind	15 mL
2	eggs, separated	2
1 tbsp	butter, melted	15 mL
1 cup	milk	250 mL

In bowl, combine sugar, flour and salt. Stir in lemon juice and rind, beaten egg yolks, butter and milk. In separate bowl, beat egg whites until stiff peaks form; fold into lemon mixture.

❦ Pour into buttered 6-cup (1.5 L) casserole. Place in larger pan; pour in enough hot water to come 1 inch (2.5 cm) up sides of pan. Bake in 350°F (180°C) oven for about 40 minutes or until topping is set and golden brown. Serve warm. Makes about 4 servings.

RHUBARB PUDDING CAKE

Bring back all the tastes of an old-fashioned self-saucing pudding with this crispy rhubarb-flavored cake.

3 cups	coarsely sliced rhubarb	750 mL
3 tbsp	butter, softened	50 mL
1-1/4 cups	granulated sugar	300 mL
3/4 cup	all-purpose flour	175 mL
1 tsp	baking powder	5 mL
1/2 tsp	cinnamon	2 mL
1/4 tsp	nutmeg	1 mL
Pinch	salt	Pinch
1/2 cup	milk	125 mL
1 tbsp	cornstarch	15 mL
1 tsp	grated orange rind	5 mL
1/2 cup	boiling orange juice	125 mL
	Whipped cream (optional)	

Spread rhubarb in greased 8-inch (2 L) square glass baking dish; set aside.

❦ In bowl, cream butter with 3/4 cup (175 mL) of the granulated sugar. Combine flour, baking powder, cinnamon, nutmeg and salt; stir into butter mixture alternately with milk, beginning and ending with flour mixture. Spread over rhubarb.

❦ In small bowl, combine remaining 1/2 cup (125 mL) sugar, cornstarch and orange rind; mix in boiling orange juice. Pour over batter. Bake in 350°F (180°C) oven for 45 to 60 minutes or until top is golden and crusty and rhubarb is bubbly. Let stand for 20 minutes. Cut into squares and serve with dollop of whipped cream (if using). Makes about 8 servings.

KNOW YOUR FLOURS

ALL-PURPOSE FLOUR is milled from 100 per cent Canadian hard wheat, which has a high protein content. When mixed with liquid, this protein forms the strong gluten that is necessary for bread because it has the elasticity to stretch and hold the gases produced by rising yeast. All white flours are enriched with B vitamins and iron to make them nutritionally similar to whole wheat (except for fiber).

CAKE-AND-PASTRY FLOUR is 100 per cent soft wheat flour with low protein content and very fine granulation. It is best for light cakes and pastries where a tender, fine texture is desired. It can be used for all baking except yeast breads. Although results will not be identical, all-purpose flour can be substituted for cake-and-pastry flour by using 2 tbsp (25 mL) less per cup (250 mL).

RHUBARB UPSIDE-DOWN CAKE

Use tender pink rhubarb for this delicious spring cake. Top with Rhubarb Sauce (recipe, p. 157) if desired.

3 tbsp	butter, melted	50 mL
2/3 cup	granulated sugar	150 mL
1 lb	trimmed rhubarb (about 10 stalks)	500 g
1-1/2 tsp	grated orange rind	7 mL
	CAKE:	
1/2 cup	butter, softened	125 mL
3/4 cup	granulated sugar	175 mL
2	eggs	2
1 tsp	vanilla	5 mL
1-1/2 cups	all-purpose flour	375 mL
1-1/2 tsp	baking powder	7 mL
1 tsp	baking soda	5 mL

1 tsp	grated orange rind	5 mL
1/4 tsp	salt	1 mL
1 cup	plain yogurt	250 mL

Grease sides of 9-inch (2.5 L) springform pan; pour in butter and sprinkle with sugar. Cut rhubarb into 2-inch (5 cm) pieces. Arrange in tight rows in bottom of pan, starting with middle 3 rows and trimming to fit. Chop remaining pieces coarsely; sprinkle on top along with orange rind. Set aside.

❧ CAKE: In large bowl, cream butter with sugar until fluffy. Beat in eggs, one at a time, and vanilla. Stir together flour, baking powder, baking soda, orange rind and salt. Stir half of flour mixture into creamed mixture; stir in yogurt and remaining flour mixture. Spread carefully over rhubarb, mounding higher at edges. Wrap foil around bottom of pan and set on baking sheet. Bake in 350°F (180°C) oven for about 1 hour or until cake springs back when lightly touched. Let cool on rack for 15 minutes.

❧ Invert cake onto serving platter. Serve warm. Makes 8 to 10 servings.

RHUBARB CRISP

Granola and chopped pecans make this warming dessert extra-crisp.

4 cups	coarsely chopped rhubarb	1 L
1-1/4 cups	all-purpose flour	300 mL
1/4 cup	granulated sugar	50 mL
1/2 cup	strawberry jam	125 mL
1-1/2 cups	granola	375 mL
1/2 tsp	cinnamon	2 mL
1/2 tsp	ginger	2 mL
1/2 cup	packed brown sugar	125 mL
1/2 cup	chopped pecans	125 mL
1/2 cup	butter, softened	125 mL

In bowl, combine rhubarb, 1/4 cup (50 mL) of the flour and granulated sugar. Stir in jam; set aside.

In separate bowl, combine remaining flour, granola, cinnamon and ginger. Stir in brown sugar and pecans; work in butter until crumbly. Press 2 cups (500 mL) of the mixture into 8-inch (2 L) square baking dish. Spoon rhubarb mixture over top; cover evenly with remaining granola mixture. Bake in 375°F (190°C) oven for 40 to 50 minutes or until deep golden brown and rhubarb is tender. Makes about 8 servings.

APPLE CRISP

Yellow Delicious, Spy, or any juicy cooking apple works in this recipe. This crisp is doubly delicious served with whipped cream or ice cream.

6 cups	sliced apples	1.5 L
1 tbsp	lemon juice	15 mL
2/3 cup	packed brown sugar	150 mL
2/3 cup	all-purpose flour	150 mL
2/3 cup	rolled oats	150 mL
1 tsp	cinnamon	5 mL
Pinch	nutmeg	Pinch
1/3 cup	butter, softened	75 mL

In buttered 8-inch (2 L) square baking dish, arrange apple slices; sprinkle with lemon juice.

Stir together brown sugar, flour, rolled oats, cinnamon and nutmeg; using fingertips, blend in butter. Sprinkle evenly over apples.

Bake in 375°F (190°C) oven for 30 minutes or until apples are fork-tender and topping browned. Makes 6 servings.

VARIATIONS

6 cups (1.5 L) sliced fresh peeled peaches, peeled pears or pitted, quartered prune plums can be used in place of apples.

1/2 cup (125 mL) raisins or fresh or frozen cranberries can be mixed with apple slices.

RHUBARB SAUCE

Spoon this tangy-sweet sauce over Rhubarb Upside-Down Cake or vanilla ice cream.

In saucepan over medium heat, bring 5 cups (1.25 L) chopped rhubarb, 1/2 cup (125 mL) granulated sugar and 1/3 cup (75 mL) water to boil, stirring; simmer for 5 minutes or until tender. Set aside 2 tbsp (25 mL) rhubarb pieces; press remaining rhubarb in sieve to extract 1 cup (250 mL) juice; discard pressed rhubarb. Dissolve 1 tbsp (15 mL) cornstarch in 1 tbsp (15 mL) of the juice. Bring cornstarch mixture to boil in saucepan. Cook over medium heat, whisking constantly, for 3 minutes or until slightly thickened. Stir in reserved rhubarb. Cover and refrigerate until serving. *(Sauce can be refrigerated for up to 1 week.)* Makes 1 cup (250 mL).

Easy Apple Strudel

A classic apple strudel—with layers of flaky buttery pastry—makes an impressive dessert. This easy-to-make version tastes as delectable as it looks. For a taste difference, try the cheese, mincemeat and rhubarb variations.

4	apples, peeled and quartered	4
1/2 cup	granulated sugar	125 mL
1/4 cup	chopped walnuts, pecans or almonds	50 mL
1/4 cup	raisins	50 mL
1 tsp	grated lemon rind	5 mL
1/2 tsp	cinnamon	2 mL
6	sheets phyllo pastry	6
1/2 cup	(approx) butter, melted	125 mL
1/3 cup	fine dry bread crumbs	75 mL
	Icing sugar	

Finely slice apple quarters crosswise. Place in bowl and toss with sugar, nuts, raisins, lemon rind and cinnamon; set aside.

❦ Place 1 sheet of phyllo on damp tea towel. Cover remaining phyllo with damp cloth. Brush sheet with some of the butter; sprinkle with 1 tbsp (15 mL) bread crumbs.

❦ Layer remaining phyllo, brushing each sheet with butter and sprinkling with remaining bread crumbs.

❦ About 2 inches (5 cm) from one long edge of pastry, spoon apple mixture lengthwise down pastry in 3-inch (8 cm) wide strip, leaving 2-inch (5 cm) border of pastry at each short end.

❦ Starting at long edge nearest filling, carefully begin to roll phyllo over filling.

❦ Roll up strudel jelly roll-style, folding in edges as you roll.

❦ Roll up firmly but allow a little slack for expansion. Carefully place strudel seam side down on greased baking sheet. Brush with butter.

❦ Cut 7 slits in top. Bake in 400°F (200°C) oven for 30 to 35 minutes or until crisp and golden. Transfer to rack or serving platter. Just before serving warm or at room temperature, dust with icing sugar. Makes 8 servings.

Variations

Cheese Strudel: For fruit mixture, substitute cottage cheese mixture: In large bowl, beat together 1/4 cup (50 mL) butter, 1/4 cup (50 mL) granulated sugar, 1 egg yolk, 1 tsp (5 mL) vanilla, 2 tbsp (25 mL) sour cream and 1 cup (250 mL) pressed cottage cheese.* Stir in 1/3 cup (75 mL) raisins and 1 tsp (5 mL) grated lemon rind. Fold in 2 stiffly beaten egg whites.

*To make 1 cup (250 mL) pressed cottage cheese, drain 1-1/4 cups (300 mL) cottage cheese in fine sieve to remove excess liquid.

Mincemeat Strudel: Substitute 2 cups (500 mL) mincemeat and 2 chopped peeled pears for apples. Omit sugar, walnuts, raisins and cinnamon.

Rhubarb Strudel: Substitute 4 cups (1 L) of 1/2-inch (1 cm) pieces of rhubarb for apples. Increase sugar to 1 cup (250 mL); toss with rhubarb along with 2 tbsp (25 mL) quick-cooking tapioca (or 3 tbsp/50 mL if using frozen rhubarb). Omit walnuts, raisins and cinnamon.

For release of steam and easy slicing, make vents in the strudel before baking. Using a serrated knife, cut 7 slits in top through thickness of phyllo.

BUTTER TART PIE

Much easier to make than individual tarts, this extra-rich pie is just as addictive. Serve in minuscule wedges, and for
a truly excessive dessert experience, top with ice cream or whipped cream.

3	eggs	3
3/4 cup	packed brown sugar	175 mL
3/4 cup	corn syrup	175 mL
3 tbsp	butter, melted	50 mL
4 tsp	all-purpose flour	20 mL
1-1/2 tsp	vanilla	7 mL
1/4 tsp	salt	1 mL
2-1/4 cups	currants	550 mL
1	9-inch (23 cm) unbaked pie shell	1

In bowl, beat eggs lightly. Stir in brown sugar, corn syrup, butter, flour, vanilla and salt until blended. Stir in currants. Pour into pie shell.

❦ Bake in 400°F (200°C) oven for 5 minutes. Reduce heat to 350°F (180°C). Bake for about 35 minutes longer or until center is just firm to the touch, covering edges of pastry with foil if browning too much. Let cool completely before cutting. Makes 10 servings.

APPLE ALMOND STREUSEL TART

This is definitely a special-occasion apple pie. Slices of apple bake in a cake-like ground-almond filling, and crunchy sliced almonds stud the topping.

1-1/2 cups	all-purpose flour	375 mL
2 tbsp	granulated sugar	25 mL
1/2 cup	cold butter	125 mL
1	egg yolk	1
2 tbsp	(approx) cold water	25 mL
	FILLING:	
1/2 cup	butter	125 mL
1/2 cup	granulated sugar	125 mL
2	eggs	2
1 tbsp	brandy or rum	15 mL
1/2 cup	ground almonds	125 mL
1/4 cup	all-purpose flour	50 mL
3	apples (preferably Golden Delicious)	3
	STREUSEL:	
1/2 cup	all-purpose flour	125 mL
1/4 cup	packed brown sugar	50 mL
1/4 tsp	each cinnamon and nutmeg	1 mL
1/4 cup	cold butter	50 mL
1/2 cup	sliced almonds	125 mL

In bowl, combine flour with sugar; with pastry blender, cut in butter until mixture resembles coarse crumbs. Beat together egg yolk and water; gradually add to flour mixture, stirring with fork and adding more water if necessary to make dough hold together. Press into ball. On lightly floured surface, roll out pastry and fit into 10-inch (25 cm) flan pan. Chill while making filling.

☙ FILLING: In bowl, cream together butter and sugar; beat in eggs one at a time. Beat in brandy; stir in almonds and flour. Spread in pastry shell. Peel and thinly slice apples; arrange over filling.

☙ STREUSEL: Combine flour, sugar, cinnamon and nutmeg; cut in butter until crumbly. Stir in almonds; sprinkle over apples. Bake in 425°F (220°C) oven for 10 minutes; reduce heat to 350°F (180°C) and bake for 25 minutes longer or until tester inserted in center comes out clean. Let cool to room temperature. Makes 8 to 10 servings.

ACADIAN SUGAR PIE

This sugar pie is rich and sweet and is best served in very small wedges topped with whipped cream.

	Pastry for 9-inch (23 cm) single-crust pie	
2 cups	packed brown sugar	500 mL
2 tbsp	all-purpose flour	25 mL
Pinch	salt	Pinch
2	eggs	2
1	egg yolk	1
1 cup	milk	250 mL
1 tsp	vanilla	5 mL

On lightly floured surface, roll out pastry and fit into 9-inch (23 cm) pie plate; trim and flute edge.

☙ In bowl, blend sugar, flour and salt. In separate bowl, beat eggs and yolk until frothy; beat in milk and vanilla. Stir into sugar mixture until smooth.

☙ Pour into pie shell. Bake in 400°F (200°C) oven for 10 minutes; reduce heat to 350°F (180°C) and bake for about 35 minutes longer or until crust is golden brown and filling is set. Makes 6 to 8 servings.

Apple Almond Streusel Tart

PLUM TART

Ground walnuts, flour and sugar sprinkled on the crust help absorb juices and prevent the crust from becoming soggy. Use red or purple plums.

2 cups	all-purpose flour	500 mL
1/2 tsp	salt	2 mL
1/2 cup	unsalted butter, cubed	125 mL
2 tbsp	shortening, cubed	25 mL
1/2 cup	(approx) ice water	125 mL
	FILLING:	
1/4 cup	ground walnuts	50 mL
1/4 cup	granulated sugar	50 mL
2 tbsp	all-purpose flour	25 mL
1 lb	plums, quartered	500 g
	CUSTARD:	
1	egg	1
1/4 cup	granulated sugar	50 mL
1/3 cup	hot light cream	75 mL
1/4 tsp	vanilla	1 mL

In large bowl, combine flour and salt. Using pastry blender or 2 knives, cut in butter and shortening until mixture resembles fine crumbs with a few larger pieces. With fork, stir in enough water to make dough hold together. Press into ball and flatten into disc; wrap and refrigerate for 30 minutes.

❦ On lightly floured surface, roll out dough to 1/4-inch (5 mm) thickness. Fit into 9-inch (23 cm) flan pan with removable bottom, building up sides about 1/4 inch (5 mm) above rim of pan. Cover and freeze for 30 minutes.

❦ FILLING: Stir together walnuts, 2 tbsp (25 mL) of the sugar and flour; sprinkle over tart shell. Arrange plums on top; sprinkle with remaining sugar. Bake in 400°F (200°C) oven for 20 to 30 minutes or until pastry is lightly browned.

❦ CUSTARD: In bowl, beat together egg and sugar. Stir in hot cream and vanilla; pour over plums. If necessary, shield edges of pastry with foil to prevent browning. Return to oven and bake for 20 to 25 minutes or until custard is set. Let cool on rack for 5 minutes. Remove side of pan and let cool slightly. Serve warm or chilled. Makes 6 to 8 servings.

PERFECT PASTRY EVERY TIME

Even experienced pie makers use this never-fail recipe. When measuring the flour, spoon it into a dry measure and level with a knife.

6 cups	cake-and-pastry flour (or 5-1/4 cups/1.3 L all-purpose flour)	1.5 L
1-1/2 tsp	salt	7 mL
2-1/3 cups	lard or shortening (1 lb/454 g)	575 mL
1	egg	1
1 tbsp	white vinegar	15 mL
	Ice water	

In large bowl, combine flour with salt. Using pastry blender or 2 knives, cut in lard until mixture resembles fine crumbs with a few larger pieces.

❧ In measuring cup and using fork, beat together egg and vinegar until blended. Add enough ice water to make 1 cup (250 mL).

❧ Stirring briskly with fork, gradually add just enough egg mixture, 1 tbsp (15 mL) at a time, to flour mixture to make dough hold together. Divide into 6 portions and press each into ball. Wrap in plastic wrap and refrigerate for 30 minutes. *(Dough can be refrigerated for up to 1 week, or frozen for up to 3 months.)* Let cold pastry stand for 15 minutes at room temperature before rolling out. Makes enough for three 9-inch (23 cm) double-crust pies.

STRAWBERRY PIE

It's simply the best!
Whole strawberries and cooked, strained berry filling in a nutty, buttery shell—this scrumptious pie is a must at least once every strawberry season.

PECAN PASTRY:

1 cup	all-purpose flour	250 mL
1/4 cup	packed brown sugar	50 mL
1/2 tsp	salt	2 mL
1/2 cup	butter	125 mL
1/2 cup	ground pecans	125 mL
2 tbsp	cold water	25 mL
1	egg yolk	1

FILLING:

8 cups	strawberries	2 L
1 cup	granulated sugar	250 mL
1/4 cup	cornstarch	50 mL
1/2 cup	water	125 mL
1 tbsp	butter	15 mL

GARNISH:

1 cup	whipping cream	250 mL
2 tbsp	icing sugar	25 mL

PECAN PASTRY: In bowl, combine flour, sugar and salt; cut in butter until mixture resembles coarse crumbs. Stir in pecans. Beat together water and egg yolk; using fork, stir into flour mixture until crumbly and moist. Press into 10-inch (25 cm) pie plate. Flute edges, cover and refrigerate for 30 minutes.

❧ Using fork, prick pastry all over. Line with foil; fill with dried beans or pie weights. Bake in 375°F (190°C) oven for 10 minutes. Remove weights and foil. Bake for 10 to 12 minutes or until golden brown. Let cool completely on rack.

❧ FILLING: In food processor or blender, purée 4 cups (1 L) of the strawberries until smooth. In saucepan, combine sugar with cornstarch; blend in water. Add puréed berries; bring to boil over medium-high heat, stirring constantly. Reduce heat to low; cook for 1 to 2 minutes or until translucent and slightly thickened, stirring constantly. Remove from heat; blend in butter. Press mixture through sieve. Let cool until lukewarm.

❧ Arrange whole berries, tips up, in pastry shell. Pour in filling; refrigerate for at least 2 hours or until set. Just before serving, whip cream with icing sugar; spread or pipe around edge of pie. Makes 8 to 10 servings.

SUMMER IN A PIE

To make a fruit pie well, with the berries and fruit just the right juiciness, the bottom crust flaky and the top crust
a golden crisp brown, is an art. But, not an impossible art. Success starts with the chart below
for five of the summer's favorite fruit pies.

Double-Crust Fruit Pies

Type of Pie	Prepared Fruit	Granulated Sugar	All-purpose Flour	Flavorings
Blueberry	4 cups (1 L)	2/3 cup (150 mL)	3 tbsp (45 mL)	1 tsp (5 mL) grated lemon rind
Peach	5 cups (1.25 L), peeled and sliced	3/4 cup (175 mL)	1/4 cup (50 mL)	2 tbsp (25 mL) chopped candied ginger
Plum	5 cups (1.25 L), quartered if large, halved if small	1 cup (250 mL)	1/4 cup (50 mL)	1/2 tsp (2 mL) cinnamon
Raspberry	4 cups (1 L)	1 cup (250 mL)	3 tbsp (45 mL)	none needed
Sour Cherry	4 cups (1 L), pitted	1 cup (250 mL)	1/4 cup (50 mL)	1/2 tsp (2 mL) almond extract

TO MAKE A PERFECT FRUIT PIE:

Line 9-inch (23 cm) pie plate with pastry.

❧ In large bowl, combine prepared fruit, sugar, flour, 1 tbsp (15 mL) lemon juice and flavoring (see chart above for amounts).

❧ Fill pastry shell with fruit mixture; dot filling with 1 tbsp (15 mL) butter.

❧ Moisten edges of bottom crust. Cover with top crust. Trim and flute edges. Cut steam vents. Brush top with milk or cream; sprinkle lightly with granulated sugar.

❧ Bake in 425°F (220°C) oven for 15 minutes; reduce heat to 350°F (180°C) and bake for 45 to 60 minutes longer or until fruit is tender, filling thickened and crust golden.

❧ You can also freeze well-wrapped unbaked fruit pies for up to 4 months, with the following changes: increase the amount of flour in each pie by 1 tbsp (15 mL) and don't cut steam vents until just before baking. Bake still-frozen pies in 450°F (230°C) oven for 15 minutes; reduce heat to 375°F (190°C) and bake for up to 60 minutes longer or until filling is thickened and crust golden brown.

MAKING PASTRY IS EASY AS PIE:

❧ Use a stockinette covering for your rolling pin and roll out the dough on a heavy pastry cloth. A good rolling pin that is at least 12 inches (30 cm) long is a must, preferably one with handles that roll easily on bearings.

❧ Use chilled shortening, lard or butter. The fat particles will stay separate and your pastry will be flakier as a result.

❧ Use ice water. Let the cubes melt in water as you're cutting the fat. Sprinkle water over the dough by the tablespoonful (15 mL), always sprinkling on the driest ingredients and tossing the mixture with a fork at the same time. As soon as the pastry can be gathered into a ball, gather it, pressing lightly.

❧ Use a good pie plate. Glass, enamel or pottery pie plates work well and are widely available. Avoid foil plates — the shiny surface reflects heat, preventing the pastry from setting and browning, and their flimsy structure allows the pie filling to seep under the bottom crust, making your pie soggy.

❧ Allow pastry to chill for at least 30 minutes before rolling it out. The stretchiness (gluten) in the flour relaxes to produce a more tender crust.

RHUBARB LATTICE PIE

Just thinking about the flaky crust, the juicy tangy-sweet filling and the heavenly aroma of this Canadian classic sets your mouth watering. You can substitute 1/4 cup (50 mL) whole or 2% milk and 1/4 cup (50 mL) water for 1/2 cup (125 mL) skim milk.

3 cups	sifted cake-and-pastry flour	750 mL
1/2 tsp	salt	2 mL
1 cup	lard	250 mL
1/2 cup	(approx) skim milk	125 mL
	FILLING:	
5 cups	chopped rhubarb (1-inch/2.5 cm pieces)	1.25 L
2 tsp	grated orange rind	10 mL
1 cup	granulated sugar	250 mL
1/3 cup	all-purpose flour	75 mL

In bowl, combine flour with salt. Using pastry blender, cut in lard until mixture resembles coarse crumbs with a few larger pieces. Stirring briskly with fork, gradually add just enough milk, 1 tbsp (15 mL) at a time, to make dough hold together. Form into ball and divide in half; flatten into discs, wrap and refrigerate.

❦ FILLING: In large bowl, combine rhubarb with orange rind. Stir together sugar and flour; sprinkle over rhubarb. Toss well and set aside.

❦ On lightly floured surface, roll out half of the pastry into 1/8-inch (3 mm) thickness; line 10-inch (25 cm) pie plate, letting edges of pastry overhang. Roll out remaining pastry to same thickness; cut into 1/2-inch (1 cm) wide strips.

❦ Spoon filling into prepared shell; weave pastry strips about 1/2 inch (1 cm) apart to form lattice over filling. Trim excess pastry from edges. Fold edges of bottom crust over latticed edges; crimp to seal. Bake in 450°F (230°C) oven for 15 minutes. Reduce heat to 375°F (190°C); bake for 35 to 40 minutes longer or until pastry is golden brown, filling is bubbly and rhubarb is tender. Makes 8 servings.

DUTCH APPLE PIE

This Southwestern Ontario favorite is best made with big wedges of Spy, Empire, Cortland or Idared apples.

	Pastry for deep 10-inch (25 cm) single-crust pie	
5	large apples (about 2 lb/1 kg total)	5
1/4 cup	whipping cream	50 mL
3/4 cup	packed brown sugar	175 mL
2 tbsp	all-purpose flour	25 mL
3 tbsp	cold butter	50 mL
1/2 tsp	cinnamon	2 mL

On lightly floured surface, roll out pastry and fit into 10-inch (25 cm) pie plate; trim and flute edges. Peel and core apples; cut each into 6 wedges. Arrange wedges snugly in single layer in pie shell; drizzle with half of the cream.

❧ In small bowl, combine sugar and flour; cut in butter until crumbly. Sprinkle over apples; dust with cinnamon. Drizzle with remaining cream.

❧ Bake in 450°F (230°C) oven for 15 minutes; reduce heat to 350°F (180°C) and bake for 30 to 35 minutes longer or until apples are tender, shielding edges of pastry with foil if browning too much. Let cool. Makes 8 servings.

VARIATION

DUTCH PEAR PIE: Substitute firm, just-ripe Bosc pears for the apples. Increase flour to 1/3 cup (75 mL), sprinkling 2 tbsp (25 mL) over pears and adding remainder to brown sugar.

MILE-HIGH APPLE PIE

Use Spy or Empire apples for this golden-domed apple pie.

	Pastry for deep 9-inch (23 cm) double-crust pie	
1 tbsp	light cream	15 mL
1 tsp	granulated sugar	5 mL
	FILLING:	
8 cups	sliced peeled apples	2 L
3/4 cup	granulated sugar	175 mL
3 tbsp	all-purpose flour	50 mL
2 tsp	coarsely grated orange rind	10 mL
1/4 tsp	nutmeg	1 mL
1-1/2 tsp	butter	7 mL
1-1/2 tsp	orange juice	7 mL

On lightly floured surface, roll out half of the pastry and fit into deep 9-inch (23 cm) pie plate.

❦ FILLING: In large bowl, toss together apples, sugar, flour, orange rind and nutmeg; spoon into prepared pie shell. Dot with butter; sprinkle with orange juice.

❦ Roll out top pastry. Moisten rim of shell and cover with top pastry. Trim and flute edge. Brush lightly with cream and sprinkle with sugar. Cut steam vents in top. Bake in 425°F (220°C) oven for 20 minutes; reduce heat to 375°F (190°C) and bake for 35 to 40 minutes longer or until apples are tender and pastry is golden. Makes 8 servings.

CRANBERRY AND PEAR CRUMBLE PIE

This pie's ruby tones make it an ideal Christmas dessert. It's delicious on its own, but fantastic with ice cream and frankly, why not?

	Pastry for deep 9-inch (23 cm) single-crust pie	
4 cups	chopped peeled ripe pears	1 L
2 cups	cranberries	500 mL
2 tsp	coarsely grated orange rind	10 mL
3/4 cup	granulated sugar	175 mL
1 tbsp	quick-cooking tapioca	15 mL
1/2 tsp	cinnamon	2 mL
1/4 tsp	ground coriander	1 mL
3/4 cup	sliced almonds	175 mL
	TOPPING:	
1/2 cup	all-purpose flour	125 mL
1/3 cup	packed brown sugar	75 mL
1/4 cup	butter	50 mL

On lightly floured surface, roll out pastry to 1/8-inch (3 mm) thickness; fit into deep 9-inch (23 cm) pie plate. Trim and flute edges. Refrigerate while preparing filling.

❦ In large bowl, combine pears, cranberries and orange rind. Mix together sugar, tapioca, cinnamon and coriander; sprinkle over fruit and toss to mix. Spoon into pie shell; sprinkle with almonds.

❦ TOPPING: In bowl, combine flour with brown sugar; with pastry blender, cut in butter until crumbly. Sprinkle over filling. With knife, make attractive pattern in topping.

❦ Bake in 425°F (220°C) oven for 15 minutes. Reduce heat to 350°F (180°C); bake for 35 to 45 minutes longer or until crust is golden and juices bubble around edge. Let cool on rack. Makes about 8 servings.

SPICE UP A PIE

Cinnamon is traditional in apple pie, while the other fruits are usually used without spicing. But for a change, enhance any fruit with a generous pinch of cinnamon, nutmeg or mace. Peach is delicious with a little chopped preserved ginger; cherry with a few drops of almond extract. Grated orange rind perks up plum, apple or cranberry. For extra flavor, add a spoonful of rum or fruit liqueur. Raisins, toasted almonds or chopped pecans can also make interesting additions to fruit pie fillings.

PRIZE-WINNING PUMPKIN PIE

This delectable cinnamony filling is every pumpkin-pie-lover's dream.

	Pastry for 9-inch (23 cm) single-crust pie	
	FILLING:	
2	eggs	2
1-1/2 cups	cooked pumpkin	375 mL
1-1/4 cups	light cream	300 mL
1 cup	packed brown sugar	250 mL
1 tsp	cinnamon	5 mL
1/2 tsp	ginger	2 mL
1/2 tsp	salt	2 mL

On lightly floured surface, roll out pastry and fit into 9-inch (23 cm) pie plate; trim and flute edge.

🌿 FILLING: In large bowl, beat eggs lightly; blend in pumpkin, cream, sugar, cinnamon, ginger and salt. Pour into pie shell. Bake in 425°F (220°C) oven for 15 minutes; reduce heat to 350°F (180°C) and bake for about 35 minutes longer or until tip of pointed knife inserted in center comes out clean. Let cool on rack. Makes 6 servings.

APPLE BLACKBERRY PIE

This English-style fruit pie has a top crust only and the flavorful juices are not thickened. Serve with custard sauce.

3 tbsp	butter	50 mL
8	apples, peeled and quartered	8
3 tbsp	packed brown sugar	50 mL
1/2 tsp	cinnamon	2 mL
	Grated rind of half a lemon	
1 cup	blackberries	250 mL
Half	pkg (411 g) frozen puff pastry, thawed	Half
1 tbsp	granulated sugar	15 mL
	SPICED CIDER:	
1/3 cup	unsweetened apple cider	75 mL
2 tbsp	packed brown sugar	25 mL
1/4 tsp	nutmeg	1 mL
Pinch	ginger	Pinch
1	stick (1-inch/2.5 cm) cinnamon	1
	Pared rind of half a lemon	

SPICED CIDER: In saucepan, combine cider, sugar, nutmeg, ginger, cinnamon and lemon rind; heat over medium heat until sugar has dissolved. Let cool.

🌿 In large skillet, melt butter over medium heat; cook apples and brown sugar, stirring occasionally, for 10 to 15 minutes or just until tender. Stir in cinnamon and lemon rind.

🌿 In 8-inch (1.25 L) deep-dish pie plate, arrange half of the apple mixture; top with blackberries, then remaining apple mixture. Discard cinnamon stick and lemon rind from cider; pour over apple mixture and let cool.

🌿 Roll out puff pastry to 1/8-inch (3 mm) thick circle. Drape over fruit; flute edges and cut steam vents in top. Sprinkle with granulated sugar. Bake in 400°F (200°C) oven for 25 to 30 minutes or until crust is golden brown and apples are tender. Let cool. Makes 6 servings.

PITCHER-POURING CUSTARD

This is simply heaven over a bowl of berries, peaches or juicy fruit pies.

🌿 In heavy saucepan over low heat, heat 2 cups (500 mL) milk until bubbles form around edge of pan. In bowl, whisk 6 egg yolks with 1/3 cup (75 mL) granulated sugar and pinch of salt; whisk in about 1/2 cup (125 mL) of the milk. Stir back into pan and cook, stirring constantly with wooden spoon, until thick enough to coat spoon. Remove from heat; stir in generous dash of vanilla. Strain through fine sieve into pitcher; let cool, stirring often to prevent skin forming on surface. Cover surface with waxed paper or plastic wrap and refrigerate for up to 2 days. Makes about 2-1/2 cups (625 mL).

LEMON MERINGUE PIE

This is the perfect recipe for those who love an old-fashioned classic lemon meringue pie — the filling is generous,
very full-flavored and lemony. For best results, be sure to measure cornstarch accurately.

1	**9-inch (23 cm)** **baked pie shell**	1
	FILLING:	
1-1/4 cups	granulated sugar	300 mL
6 tbsp	cornstarch	100 mL
1/2 tsp	salt	2 mL
2 cups	water	500 mL
3	egg yolks, lightly beaten	3
3 tbsp	butter	50 mL
1/2 cup	lemon juice	125 mL
1 tbsp	grated lemon rind	15 mL
	MERINGUE:	
3	egg whites	3
1/4 tsp	cream of tartar	1 mL
6 tbsp	granulated sugar	100 mL

FILLING: In heavy-bottomed saucepan, combine sugar, cornstarch and salt; gradually stir in water. Bring to boil over medium-high heat, stirring constantly. Reduce heat to medium-low; boil gently for 3 minutes, stirring almost constantly.

Remove from heat. Whisk a little hot mixture into egg yolks; whisk back into saucepan. Cook over medium heat, stirring constantly, for 2 minutes (there should be no raw taste of starch or yolk). Remove from heat; stir in butter, lemon juice and rind. Let cool slightly, about 3 minutes. Pour into baked pie shell. Let cool slightly while making meringue.

MERINGUE: In bowl, beat egg whites with cream of tartar until soft peaks form. Gradually beat in sugar, about 1 tbsp (15 mL) at a time, until stiff peaks form. Spread over hot filling, sealing to crust to prevent shrinking. With spatula, knife or back of spoon, swirl meringue into attractive peaks. Bake in 350°F (180°C) oven for 12 to 15 minutes or until lightly browned. Let cool thoroughly (at least 2 hours); do not refrigerate. Makes 6 servings.

FRENCH VANILLA FROZEN YOGURT WITH CHERRY SAUCE

In the summertime, nothing's more delectable with fresh berries or cherry sauce than this refreshing vanilla-scented frozen yogurt.

1 cup	milk	250 mL
1/2 cup	granulated sugar	125 mL
4	egg yolks	4
1 cup	plain yogurt	250 mL
1-1/2 tsp	vanilla	7 mL
	Cherry Sauce (recipe follows)	

In small heavy saucepan, stir milk with sugar; heat just until bubbles appear around edge of pan. Gradually whisk into egg yolks; return egg yolk mixture to saucepan. Cook over medium heat, stirring constantly, for 3 to 5 minutes or just until steaming and thickened enough to coat spoon. Do not boil.

❦ Immediately remove from heat; strain through fine sieve into clean bowl. Stir in yogurt and vanilla. Chill thoroughly. Freeze in ice-cream maker following manufacturer's instructions. Spoon into serving dishes and top with warm Cherry Sauce. Makes about 4 servings.

CHERRY SAUCE:

1/2 cup	granulated sugar	125 mL
1/2 cup	water	125 mL
3 tbsp	orange juice	50 mL
1 tbsp	grated orange rind	15 mL
1 tbsp	lemon juice	15 mL

4 tsp	cornstarch	20 mL
2 cups	sweet black cherries, pitted	500 mL

In stainless steel or enamelled saucepan, combine sugar, water, orange juice and rind, and lemon juice; bring to boil, stirring to dissolve sugar. Blend cornstarch with 1 tbsp (15 mL) water; stir into sugar mixture along with cherries. Cook, stirring, over medium heat for 2 minutes or until thickened. Serve warm or chilled. *(Sauce can be covered and refrigerated for up to 3 days.)* Makes 2 cups (500 mL).

STRAWBERRY FROZEN YOGURT

In food processor, purée 2 cups (500 mL) whole strawberries with 1/3 cup (75 mL) instant dissolving (fruit/berry) sugar. Blend in 1/2 cup (125 mL) plain yogurt and 1 tbsp (15 mL) orange juice.

❦ Freeze in ice-cream maker following manufacturer's instructions. (Or, transfer to shallow metal cake pan; freeze until almost solid. Break into chunks and process in food processor until smooth. Freeze in chilled airtight container for 30 to 60 minutes or until firm.) *(The frozen yogurt can be stored in the freezer for up to 4 days.)* Let soften in the refrigerator for 30 minutes before serving. Makes 4 servings.

CHOCOLATY CHOCOLATE ICE CREAM

This wonderful chocolate ice cream tastes like the classic Fudgsicle.

6 oz	semisweet chocolate, coarsely chopped	175 g
3 cups	whipping cream	750 mL
1/2 cup	granulated sugar	125 mL
4	eggs	4
1 tsp	vanilla	5 mL

In saucepan, melt chocolate with cream over low heat, stirring occasionally. Whisk in sugar until dissolved.

❦ In small bowl, beat eggs; gradually stir in 1/2 cup (125 mL) of the hot cream mixture. Return egg mixture to saucepan; cook, without boiling, over medium-low heat, stirring constantly, for 10 to 15 minutes or until thick enough to coat spoon. Strain through fine sieve into bowl. Let cool to room temperature. Stir in vanilla. Cover and chill for about 4 hours.

❦ Freeze in ice-cream maker following manufacturer's instructions. Store in freezer for up to 4 days. Let soften in refrigerator for 20 minutes before serving. Makes 6 servings.

PRESERVING SUMMER

Putting food by is an old-fashioned art worth keeping. Even though we no longer need to fill our basements with jars, crocks and barrels to supply us over the winter, the pleasures of preserving are just as satisfying today — the enticing colors of golden bread-and-butter relishes standing alongside jars red with chunky chili sauce, and the sweet hit of summer as you open a jar of berry jam on a snow-filled January morning. That's worth preserving!

GOLDEN BREAD-AND-BUTTER MEDLEY

The very best pickle to serve on sandwiches. Use small field cucumbers in this new golden twist on an old favorite.

12 cups	thinly sliced (unpeeled) cucumbers	3 L
2 cups	thinly sliced white onions	500 mL
1 cup	strips sweet red pepper	250 mL
1 cup	strips sweet yellow pepper	250 mL
1/4 cup	pickling salt	50 mL
3 cups	cider vinegar	750 mL
2 cups	granulated sugar	500 mL
4 tsp	mustard seeds	20 mL
2 tsp	celery seeds	10 mL
1 tsp	turmeric	5 mL

In large bowl, combine cucumbers, onions, red and yellow peppers and salt; cover with 3-inch (8 cm) layer of ice cubes and let stand for 4 hours. Drain and rinse under cold water; drain well.

❦ In large heavy nonaluminum saucepan, combine vinegar, sugar, mustard seeds, celery seeds and turmeric; bring to boil. Add cucumber mixture and return just to boil. Fill and seal canning jars; process in boiling water bath for 10 minutes (see Preserving Basics, p. 180). Makes about 11 cups (2.75 L).

DILLED PEARL ONIONS

It takes a little time to peel pearl onions, but these excellent pickles are worth it.

8 cups	pearl onions, peeled (about 1-3/4 lb/875 g)	2 L
1/4 cup	pickling salt	50 mL
2 cups	white vinegar	500 mL
2 cups	water	500 mL
2 tbsp	granulated sugar	25 mL
2 tsp	mixed pickling spice	10 mL
6	heads dill or sprigs tarragon	6
6	whole peppercorns	6

In large glass, plastic or stainless steel bowl, combine onions with salt; pour in enough cold water to cover. Let stand in cool spot in kitchen for 2 hours; drain. Rinse under cold water and drain well.

❦ In large nonaluminum saucepan, combine vinegar, water, sugar and pickling spice; bring to boil.

❦ Meanwhile, place 2 dill heads and 2 peppercorns in each of 3 sterilized 2-cup (500 mL) canning jars. Pack jars with onions, leaving 1/2-inch (1 cm) headspace. Pour in vinegar mixture, leaving 1/4-inch (5 mm) headspace. Seal and process in boiling water bath for 10 minutes (see Preserving Basics, p. 180). Makes about 6 cups (1.5 L).

(on windowsill at right) Hamburger Relish (p. 176) (on counter, clockwise from bottom) plum sauce; Tomato-Pepper Salsa (p. 176); Pearl Onions; Golden Bread-and-Butter Medley; Tomato-Apple Chutney (p. 175)

RED PEPPER JELLY

Pepper jelly—really a jellied pepper relish—is a true golden oldie of the preserving world. If you like it hot, either substitute hot red peppers for up to one-quarter of the sweet ones, or add 1-1/2 tsp (7 mL) hot pepper sauce to the jelly at the end of cooking. For a colorful ''confetti'' effect, use a combination of red, green and golden bell peppers. Serve with chicken, especially cold leftovers, and lamb. Or, heat until softened and brush over ham, pork loin or chops as an easy glaze.

6	small sweet red peppers (1-1/4 lb/625 g total)	6
1 cup	white or cider vinegar	250 mL
1/2 tsp	salt	2 mL
5 cups	granulated sugar	1.25 L
1	bottle (170 mL) liquid pectin	1

Seed and core red peppers; cut into chunks. In food processor or food grinder fitted with medium blade, process peppers until finely chopped. Measure out 2 cups (500 mL) peppers and juice.

❧ In large heavy nonaluminum saucepan, combine peppers, vinegar and salt; bring to boil. Reduce heat and simmer, covered, for 10 minutes or until peppers are tender. Stir in sugar. Return to rolling boil; boil hard, uncovered and stirring constantly, for 1 minute.

❧ Remove from heat and immediately stir in pectin. Stir for 5 minutes or until peppers remain evenly distributed throughout jelly.

❧ Pour into hot sterilized jars and seal (see Preserving Basics, p. 180). Store in cool, dark, dry place. Makes 5 cups (1.25 L).

CLASSIC CHILI SAUCE

This spicy fall relish is a must on burgers or meat loaves. Make it during harvesttime or freeze bags of measured chopped tomatoes and simmer up a batch later in the year when you crave the aromas of summer.

8 cups	chopped peeled tomatoes (about 4-1/2 lb/2 kg)	2 L
1-1/2 cups	chopped onions	375 mL
1-1/2 cups	chopped sweet red pepper	375 mL
1 cup	chopped sweet green pepper	250 mL
1-1/2 cups	white vinegar	375 mL
1 cup	chopped celery	250 mL
3/4 cup	(approx) granulated sugar	175 mL
1 tbsp	finely chopped hot pepper	15 mL
1	clove garlic, minced	1
1 tsp	salt	5 mL
1 tsp	mustard seeds	5 mL
1/2 tsp	each celery seeds, ground cloves and cinnamon	2 mL
1/4 tsp	each ginger and black pepper	1 mL
Pinch	(approx) cayenne pepper	Pinch

In large heavy nonaluminum saucepan, combine tomatoes, onions, red and green peppers, vinegar, celery, sugar, hot pepper, garlic, salt, mustard seeds, celery seeds, cloves, cinnamon, ginger, black and cayenne peppers.

❧ Bring to boil, stirring frequently; reduce heat and simmer briskly, stirring frequently, for about 1 hour or until thickened. Taste and add up to 1/4 cup (50 mL) more sugar and a little more cayenne if desired.

❧ Fill and seal canning jars; process in boiling water bath for 10 minutes (see Preserving Basics, p. 180). Makes about 6 cups (1.5 L).

MICRO-DRYING HERBS

Use your microwave to dry leafy herbs such as tarragon, parsley, mint, marjoram and oregano. Micro-drying helps keep the herbs green and retains much of their original flavor.

❧ Wash herbs and dry thoroughly. Pluck leaves from stems; measure 2 cups (500 mL) of leaves. Spread on paper towel; cover with second paper towel and microwave at High, turning over halfway through, for 2 to 3 minutes or until no longer moist. Let cool on racks; crumble and store in jars in cool, dark place.

SMALL-BATCH ZUCCHINI MUSTARD RELISH

Mustard pickle is a barbecue must. This tangy bright yellow pickle adds that addictive sweet and sour tang to burgers, pork chops and sausages.

4 cups	chopped zucchini	1 L
2	onions, chopped	2
1/2 cup	each chopped sweet red and green pepper	125 mL
1 tbsp	pickling salt	15 mL
1-1/3 cups	cold water	325 mL
1 cup	granulated sugar	250 mL
3 tbsp	all-purpose flour	50 mL
1 tbsp	dry mustard	15 mL
1/2 tsp	turmeric	2 mL
1/2 tsp	each mustard seeds and celery seeds	2 mL
1 cup	white vinegar	250 mL

In bowl, combine zucchini, onions and red and green peppers; sprinkle with salt. Pour in 1 cup (250 mL) of the water; stir well. Let stand for 1 hour, stirring occasionally. Drain and rinse under cold water; drain and press out excess moisture.

In heavy saucepan, combine sugar, flour, mustard, turmeric, mustard seeds, celery seeds, vinegar and remaining water; bring to boil. Add drained vegetables and return to boil, stirring frequently. Reduce heat to medium-low and simmer, uncovered and stirring occasionally, for 20 to 25 minutes or until thickened but vegetables are still crunchy. (Alternatively, in 8-cup/2 L glass measure, mix together sugar, flour, dry mustard, turmeric, mustard seeds and celery seeds; gradually stir in vinegar and remaining water. Add drained vegetables and microwave, uncovered, at High for 17 to 20 minutes or until thickened but vegetables are still crunchy, stirring three times.)

Fill jars and process in boiling water bath for 10 minutes (see Preserving Basics, p. 180). Makes about 5 cups (1.25 L).

TOMATO-APPLE CHUTNEY

Wonderfully chunky and rich in flavor, this chutney is delicious with meats or bread and cheese. Try it with Meat Loaf Muffins (recipe, p. 54), Beef and Kidney Pie (recipe, p. 56) or Quick and Comfy Macaroni and Cheese (recipe, p. 62).

12 cups	chopped peeled tomatoes	3 L
8 cups	chopped peeled apples	2 L
4 cups	packed brown sugar	1 L
3 cups	chopped onions	750 mL
2 cups	cider vinegar	500 mL
1 cup	currants	250 mL
2 tbsp	minced gingerroot	25 mL
2	large cloves garlic, minced	2
2 tsp	salt	10 mL
1 tsp	each dry mustard and mustard seeds	5 mL
1 tsp	hot pepper flakes	5 mL
1/2 tsp	each cinnamon and allspice	2 mL

In large heavy nonaluminum saucepan, combine tomatoes, apples, sugar, onions, vinegar, currants, ginger, garlic, salt, mustard, mustard seeds, hot pepper flakes, cinnamon and allspice; bring to boil over medium-high heat. Reduce heat to medium; simmer, stirring often, for about 2 hours or until thickened. Fill and seal canning jars; process in boiling water bath for 10 minutes (see Preserving Basics, p. 180). Makes about 12 cups (3 L).

HAMBURGER RELISH

Like most relishes, this one tastes better after it's mellowed for 3 weeks. Serve with burgers, of course, or any leftover roast beef or pork.

2 cups	chopped (unpeeled) cucumbers	500 mL
1 cup	each chopped sweet red, yellow and green peppers	250 mL
1 cup	chopped celery	250 mL
1 cup	chopped onion	250 mL
1/4 cup	pickling salt	50 mL
4 cups	chopped seeded peeled tomatoes	1 L
3 cups	white vinegar	750 mL
1 tbsp	mustard seeds	15 mL
1 tsp	turmeric	5 mL
1/2 tsp	cinnamon	2 mL
1/2 tsp	allspice	2 mL
1/4 tsp	cayenne pepper	1 mL
2 cups	granulated sugar	500 mL
1/4 cup	tomato paste	50 mL

In large bowl, combine cucumbers, sweet peppers, celery, onion and salt; cover with boiling water and let stand for 1 hour. Drain and rinse under cold water; drain well and set aside.

❧ In large heavy nonaluminum saucepan, combine tomatoes, vinegar, mustard seeds, turmeric, cinnamon, allspice and cayenne pepper; bring to boil, stirring often. Reduce heat to medium and simmer for 30 minutes or until tomatoes are softened.

❧ Stir in sugar and drained vegetables; bring to boil, stirring often. Reduce heat to medium and boil gently, stirring often, for 15 minutes. Stir in tomato paste; cook, stirring often, for 5 minutes or until thickened.

❧ Fill and seal canning jars; process in boiling water bath for 10 minutes (see Preserving Basics, p. 180). Makes about 7 cups (1.75 L).

TOMATO-PEPPER SALSA

You can serve this versatile salsa with burgers or grilled cheese sandwiches — or mix it with cream cheese for a spicy dip that's great with corn chips. It is also delicious spooned over popular Tex-Mex dishes such as burritos.
Wear rubber gloves when chopping the hot peppers to avoid burns.

8 cups	chopped peeled tomatoes	2 L
4 cups	chopped cubanelle, Anaheim or sweet banana peppers	1 L
2 cups	chopped onions	500 mL
2 cups	cider vinegar	500 mL
1 cup	chopped sweet red peppers	250 mL
1 cup	chopped seeded jalapeño peppers	250 mL
4	cloves garlic, minced	4
1	can (5-1/2 oz/156 mL) tomato paste	1
2 tbsp	granulated sugar	25 mL
1 tbsp	salt	15 mL
2 tsp	paprika	10 mL
1 tsp	dried oregano	5 mL
1/4 cup	chopped fresh coriander (optional)	50 mL

In large heavy nonaluminum saucepan, combine tomatoes, cubanelle peppers, onions, vinegar, red peppers, jalapeño peppers, garlic, tomato paste, sugar, salt, paprika and oregano; bring to boil, stirring often.

❧ Reduce heat to medium-low; simmer for about 1 hour or until thick enough to coat spoon. Stir in coriander (if using); simmer for 5 minutes longer. Fill and seal canning jars; process in boiling water bath for 20 minutes (see Preserving Basics, p. 180). Makes about 9 cups (2.25 L).

STRAWBERRY JAM

Few jams are as beloved as strawberry. Its gorgeous red color is a year-round reminder of a June day
and a strawberry-perfumed patch.

8 cups	strawberries, hulled (about 2 lb/1 kg)	2 L
4 cups	granulated sugar	1 L
1/4 cup	lemon juice	50 mL

In wide bowl, lightly crush about 1 cup (250 mL) berries at a time with potato masher; measure fruit to make 4 cups (1 L). Place 2 small plates in freezer for testing setting point of jam later.

❧ In large heavy-bottomed stainless steel or enamel saucepan, combine crushed strawberries, sugar and lemon juice; stir over low heat until sugar is dissolved. Increase heat to high and bring to a full rolling boil, stirring often. Boil hard, uncovered, for 10 minutes, stirring often.

❧ Meanwhile, wash jars, measuring cup and wide-mouth metal funnel in hot soapy water; rinse but do not dry. Set on rimmed baking sheet and place in 225°F (110°C) oven for 15 minutes. Turn off heat and leave in oven until needed.

❧ Remove jam from heat. Drop 1/2 tsp (2 mL) onto one chilled plate; freeze for 2 minutes. Run finger through jam on plate; if surface wrinkles, setting point has been reached. If sample doesn't wrinkle, return jam to heat. Using clean chilled plate, repeat test every few minutes until jam reaches setting point. Let jam cool for 5 minutes, skimming off foam and stirring often.

❧ Using funnel and measuring cup, fill jars to within 1/2 inch (1 cm) of top. Let cool slightly for 2 minutes.

❧ Meanwhile, place a few blocks of paraffin in clean metal can; squeeze edge to form spout. Set in pan of water and heat over low heat until melted. To seal jars, pour thin layer of paraffin over jam, tilting and rotating jar to extend seal to rim. Prick any air bubbles. Let cool completely. Repeat with second thin layer of paraffin. Cover jars with clean lids; store in cool, dry, dark place. Makes about 5 cups (1.25 L).

To freeze fresh strawberries for making jam later, hull specified amount and freeze on tray. Then package in freezer bag, making sure you remove air. Or, crush fresh berries and freeze in 4-cup (1 L) quantities.

❧ You can use jars with self-sealing lids instead of sealing with paraffin. Always use new discs that have been boiled for 5 minutes immediately before sealing.

PURE AND SIMPLE RASPBERRY JAM

Raspberry jam is an all-time favorite that is simple and very quick to make in small quantities. If you don't have time in the summer, freeze your berries and make the jam when the weather is cooler.

3 cups	granulated sugar	750 mL
2 cups	crushed raspberries	500 mL
1/4 cup	lemon juice	50 mL

In large nonaluminum saucepan, combine sugar, raspberries and lemon juice. Let stand for about 1-1/2 hours or until sugar has dissolved.

❦ Bring to full rolling boil over high heat, stirring constantly; boil hard for 4 to 5 minutes or until setting point is reached (see p. 180). Remove from heat; skim off foam with metal spoon. Ladle into hot sterilized jars and seal (see Preserving Basics, p. 180). Makes about 3 cups (750 mL).

PEACH AND PEAR CONSERVE WITH LEMON

Here's an easy conserve that will help you remember the fragrance of freshly picked fruit every time you open a jar.

	One and a half lemons	
6	peaches (1-1/2 lb/750 g total)	6
3	pears (1 lb/500 g total)	3
3-1/2 cups	granulated sugar	875 mL
1/4 cup	golden raisins	50 mL
1/3 cup	halved maraschino cherries	75 mL

Squeeze juice from half a lemon; reserve juice and discard peel. Cut remaining lemon into chunks; remove seeds and stem end. In food processor or food grinder fitted with medium blade, process until finely chopped.

❦ In small nonaluminum saucepan, combine reserved lemon juice, chopped lemon and juices, and 1/4 cup (50 mL) water; cover and simmer over very low heat until peel is translucent and very tender, about 45 minutes. Add more water to keep mixture moist if necessary.

❦ Meanwhile, peel peaches and pears. Pit and core, then chop into 1/2-inch (1 cm) chunks. In heavy saucepan, combine peaches, pears and 1/4 cup (50 mL) water; cover and simmer, stirring often, until slightly softened, about 10 minutes.

❦ Add lemon mixture. Stir in sugar and raisins. Bring to rolling boil, uncovered and stirring frequently; boil, stirring, for 10 to 15 minutes or until conserve has reached setting point (see p. 180). Remove from heat and stir in cherries.

❦ Pour into hot sterilized jars and seal (see Preserving Basics, p. 180). Store in cool, dark, dry place. Makes about 4 cups (1 L).

CRANBERRY-ORANGE RELISH

This tart and chunky relish is perfect with turkey, whether it's hot on the big day or cold in sandwiches.

1-1/2 cups	cranberries	375 mL
1	tart apple, peeled and cored	1
2/3 cup	granulated sugar	150 mL
1/2 cup	chopped pecans, toasted*	125 mL
1/4 cup	raisins	50 mL
1/4 cup	orange marmalade	50 mL
1 tbsp	coarsely grated lemon rind	15 mL
1 tbsp	lemon juice	15 mL
Pinch	cinnamon (optional)	Pinch

In food processor or grinder, chop cranberries and apple. In bowl, combine cranberry mixture, sugar, pecans, raisins, marmalade, lemon rind, lemon juice, and cinnamon (if using). Transfer to jar; cover and refrigerate for at least 8 hours or up to 1 week. Makes about 2 cups (500 mL).

*To toast pecans, spread on baking sheet and bake in 350°F (180°C) oven for about 5 minutes or until golden.

PLUM-ORANGE CONSERVE

To be sure of a good set, use firm just-ripe plums—you'll need about 2 lb (1 kg).

1	seedless orange (unpeeled), sliced	1
6 cups	coarsely chopped plums	1.5 L
1/2 cup	water	125 mL
4 cups	granulated sugar	1 L

In food processor or grinder, mince orange finely. In large wide saucepan, combine orange, plums and water; cover and bring to boil over medium-low heat, stirring often. Cook, covered, until skins are very tender, 20 to 25 minutes.

❧ Stir in sugar and bring to boil, stirring constantly. Reduce heat to medium and cook, stirring often for about 15 minutes or until thickened and setting point is reached (see p. 180). Ladle into hot sterilized jars and seal (see Preserving Basics, p. 180). Store in cool, dark, dry place. Makes about 6 cups (1.5 L).

WINTER SUNSHINE MARMALADE

Seville oranges, rich in pectin, make the clearest, most fabulously tangy marmalade.

5	Seville oranges (about 2 lb/1 kg)	5
1	lemon	1
6 cups	water	1.5 L
8 cups	(approx) granulated sugar	2 L

Using sharp knife, trim stem end from oranges and lemon; cut into quarters. Remove seeds; set aside.

❧ Cut fruit into slices about 1/8 inch (3 mm) wide; place in large nonaluminum Dutch oven or wide heavy saucepan; pour in water. Tie seeds in spice bag or square of cheesecloth; add to fruit mixture. Bring to boil; reduce heat to low and gently simmer, covered, for 2 hours to make about 8 cups (2 L). Remove and discard seeds.

❧ Add equal volume of sugar; stir until dissolved. Bring to boil over high heat and boil briskly, stirring often, for about 20 minutes or until setting point is reached (see sidebar). Remove from heat; stir for 5 minutes, skimming off any foam with metal spoon. Ladle into hot sterilized jars and seal (see Preserving Basics, p. 180). Store in cool, dark, dry place. Makes about 9 cups (2.25 L).

> To test for setting point: Place 2 small plates into freezer to chill. Drop 1/2 tsp (2 mL) hot preserve onto one chilled plate and refrigerate for 2 minutes. Run finger through preserve; if surface wrinkles, it has reached setting point. If sample remains syrupy, return preserve to heat. Using clean chilled plate, repeat test every few minutes until preserve reaches setting point.

PRESERVING BASICS

THE RIGHT EQUIPMENT

The right equipment will make preserving a lot easier and safer. Tongs, heatproof measuring cups, wide-mouthed funnels, jar lifter, clean dishcloths, large heavy-bottomed saucepan or Dutch oven, large boiling water bath canner and canning (mason) jars with two-piece lids are enough to start with. Use only perfect canning jars free from nicks or scratches, and rust-free and unbent screw bands. Always use new discs to ensure a good and safe seal.

PREPARING JARS, LIDS AND CANNER

Wash jars and bands in hot sudsy water, rinse and air-dry. For jars processed in boiling water bath less than 10 minutes, extra sterilization is required. Place jars, upright, on sturdy pizza pan or rimmed baking sheet, along with metal 1/2-cup (125 mL) measure for pouring, stainless steel kitchen knife and metal funnel. Heat in 225°F (110°C) oven for 15 minutes; leave in oven until needed. Set a small pot of water on stove, ready to boil discs for 5 minutes before filling jars.

❦ Fill boiling water bath canner about two-thirds full of water; as preserve nears end of cooking time, heat water to just under boil and keep hot. Boil a kettle of water and keep handy.

FILLING JARS

Fill jars, using prepared funnel and measure to avoid slopping preserve onto rims of jars. Always leave recommended headspace, generally 1/4 inch (5 mm) for jams, jellies, marmalades and conserves, 1/2 inch (1.25 cm) for pickles, relishes and chutneys. Using sterilized knife, press out any air bubbles; add more preserve if necessary to reestablish headspace. Center prepared disc on jar and apply screw band until fingertip tight.

PROCESSING IN BOILING WATER BATH CANNER

Place jars in rack set on edge of canner; lower into hot water and pour in enough of the extra heated water to cover

jars at least 1 inch (2.5 cm). Cover with lid; bring to boil and time processing time from time water boils.

❦ Using jar lifter, transfer jars from canner to rack or

folded towel. Check for seal: if the disc has snapped down, curving downward, satisfactory seal has occurred. Any improperly sealed jars should be refrigerated and used as soon as possible.

STORING
All preserves, jams, jellies, pickles and relishes should be kept in a cool, dark and dry place. Once a jar is opened, store it in the refrigerator.

THE CONTRIBUTORS

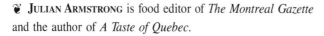

❧ **ELIZABETH BAIRD** is food director of *Canadian Living* magazine and one of Canada's best-known food writers. The author of several bestselling cookbooks, including *Classic Canadian Cooking, Summer Berries* and *Elizabeth Baird's Favourites*, her name is synonymous with Canadian cooking and with the contemporary flair she brings to comforting homestyle food. She reviewed over 500 recipes from Canada's leading food writers to choose only the very best for this special cookbook, and has also included many of her own favorites.

❧ **JULIAN ARMSTRONG** is food editor of *The Montreal Gazette* and the author of *A Taste of Quebec*.

❧ **DICK BROWN** is remembered for his many magazine articles on the pleasures of food and his wonderful suggestions for enjoying it with family and friends.

❧ **VICKI BURNS** is a member of the *Canadian Living* Test Kitchen staff and is also a contributor to the magazine.

❧ **JAMES CHATTO** writes about food, wine and travel for several Canadian magazines.

❧ **JUDITH COMFORT** is a food writer based in Port Medway, Nova Scotia. She is the author of several cookbooks, including *Judith Comfort's Christmas Cookbook*.

❧ **EILEEN DWILLIES** is a west coast food writer, consultant and food stylist. She also teaches cooking and hosts a television program on creative cooking.

❧ **NANCY ENRIGHT** is a food writer, consultant and the author of *Nancy Enright's Canadian Herb Cookbook*.

❧ **CAROL FERGUSON** was *Canadian Living*'s first food editor and is also the editor of *The Canadian Living Entertaining Cookbook* and the first *Canadian Living Cookbook*. She is now a food writer and consultant.

❧ **MARGARET FRASER** is a former associate food editor of *Canadian Living*. She has played a prominent role as editor of

several *Canadian Living* cookbooks, including the *Light and Healthy Cookbook* published earlier this year.

❧ **HELEN PHEBE HATTON** and her husband, Ron Morris, travel extensively and enjoy researching and writing about food.

❧ **LAURA HUGHES** and her husband own Springridge Farm in Milton, Ontario, where you can pick the very best of the summer's strawberries, cherries and berry baked goods.

❧ **PATRICIA JAMIESON** was manager of *Canadian Living*'s Test Kitchen for 4 years until her move last year to *Eating Well* magazine, a publication of Telemedia (U.S.) in Vermont.

❧ **ALICE JENNER** is a Saskatchewan home economist and the author of *The Amazing Legume*.

❧ **ANNE LINDSAY** is a food writer, consultant and author of several bestselling cookbooks, including *Lighthearted Everyday Cooking* which was published earlier this year.

❧ **NAN MACKINTOSH-SMITH** restored the charming Ontario schoolhouse which is featured in the photo on page 31 of this cookbook.

❧ **MARY MCGRATH** is a food writer with *The Toronto Star*.

❧ **NANCY MILLAR** is a Calgary-based food writer and broadcaster. She also writes and publishes cookbooks.

❧ **BETH MOFFATT** is a freelance home economist, food stylist and food writer.

❧ **DEAN MOLLON** is chef at the Woodstock Country Inn on Galiano Island in British Columbia. The island is famous for its blackberries, and for the Blackberry Cheesecake recipe we've included in this book.

❧ **ROSE MURRAY** is a food writer, consultant, broadcaster and the author of several cookbooks. Her most recent is *Rose Murray's Comfortable Kitchen Cookbook*, published this fall.

❧ **ERIC PETERSON** is owner and part-time chef at April Point Lodge on Quadra Island, one of the beautiful Gulf Islands off the coast of British Columbia.

❦ **Iris Raven** is a freelance food writer and frequent contributor to *Canadian Living* magazine.

❦ **Susan Restino** lives in Baddeck, Nova Scotia and is the author of several natural food cookbooks, including *Mrs. Restino's Country Kitchen.*

❦ **Gerry Shikatani** is a print and broadcast journalist with a special interest in food. His mother, Mitsuko Shikatani, was the inspiration for the Really Good Beef Stew recipe which appears in this book.

❦ **Bonnie Stern** is proprietor of The Bonnie Stern Cooking School in Toronto. She is also a food writer, broadcaster, columnist and the author of several popular cookbooks, most recently *Appetizers by Bonnie Stern.*

❦ **Anne Wanstall**, a former food editor with *The Toronto Star*, now lives in Granville Ferry, Nova Scotia and grows garden-fresh produce for her kitchen and her cooking.

❦ **Lucy Waverman** is a food writer, consultant, teacher and the author of several cookbooks, including *Lucy Waverman's fast and fresh cookbook*, published earlier this year.

❦ **Cynny Willet** is a food writer at *The Calgary Herald* and has a special interest in comforting, old-fashioned cooking.

❦ *Canadian Living's* **Test Kitchen** developed many of the delicious recipes in this cookbook and updated traditional favorites for today's tastes and kitchens.

Photography Credits

Fred Bird: front and back covers; title page; contents page; Introduction; back flap; pages 11, 13, 14, 17, 21, 24, 32, 33, 34, 35, 38, 39, 41, 43, 44, 47, 49, 51, 53, 55, 57, 58, 61, 62, 65, 66, 69, 71, 72, 75, 77, 78, 81, 83, 85, 86, 87, 89, 91, 93, 94, 98, 100, 103, 105, 109, 112, 114, 117, 119, 122, 123, 125, 127, 128, 131, 133, 134, 137, 138, 141, 145, 147, 148, 151, 152, 156, 158, 159, 165, 166, 169, 170, 173, 177, 180.

Christopher Campbell: pages 175, 179, 192.

Frank Grant: photo of Elizabeth Baird (inside back flap); pages 19, 31, 108.

Claude Noel: page 99.

John Stephens: pages 23, 90, 95, 96, 97, 110, 121, 143, 162.

Clive Webster: page 27.

Robert Wigington: page 36.

Stanley Wong: pages 107, 161.

Food Styling/Front Cover: **Sue Bailey**

Props Coordinator/Front Cover: **Debby Boyden**

Special Thanks

❦ Cookbooks are never a solo effort. This is especially true when the cookbook comes from *Canadian Living*. Our creative writers, whose names and accomplishments are listed above, are major contributors. Our talented Test Kitchen staff — Vicki Burns, Janet Cornish, Heather Howe and Ruth Phelan — work with manager Daphna Rabinovitch to make sure every recipe tastes as delicious as possible and will succeed in our readers' kitchens, while our super-careful editorial team, Beverley Renahan and Susan Lawrence, polish the words. To them all, heartfelt thanks for their part in making this a cookbook to enjoy over and over again.

❦ Special thanks to Madison Press project editor Wanda Nowakowska for her unflagging efforts, good judgment and spirits.

To Patricia Jamieson, former Test Kitchen manager, whose taste buds and strong arms are behind many of our bread recipes. To the many fine cooks across Canada who have shared their recipes with us, including Shannon Ferrier, originator of the wonderful patties on page 54; the great bakers, Ora Campbell and Rose Winter, whose perfect pies have won them many a prize at the Warkworth, Ontario Perfect Pie Contest; Annie Van Haren, who created her cucumber salad for the St. Anne's of the Lake annual chicken barbecue; and to Newfoundlander Barbara Mercer, chowder maker supreme and warm welcomer at Galecliff Bed and Breakfast.

E.B.

INDEX

❦

A

B

Design and Art Direction:	Gordon Sibley Design Inc.
Editorial Director:	Hugh Brewster
Project Editor:	Wanda Nowakowska
Editorial Assistance:	Beverley Renahan Catherine Fraccaro Shirley Knight Morris
Production Director:	Susan Barrable
Production Assistance:	Donna Chong
Typography:	On-line Graphics
Color Separation:	Colour Technologies
Printing and Binding:	Friesen Printers
Canadian Living Advisory Board:	Robert A. Murray Bonnie Baker Cowan Elizabeth Baird Anna Hobbs

Canadian Living's Country Cooking
*was produced by Madison Press Books
under the direction of Albert E. Cummings.*